The
Stamp King

The Stamp King

by

G. DE BEAUREGARD

and

H. DE GORSSE

Translated from the French by

EDITH C. PHILLIPS

STANLEY GIBBONS
London and Ringwood

By Appointment to Her Majesty The Queen
Stanley Gibbons Ltd, London
Philatelists

Published by Stanley Gibbons Ltd
Editorial, Publications Sales Offices
and Distribution Centre:
7 Parkside, Christchurch Road, Ringwood,
Hants BH24 3SH

© Stanley Gibbons Ltd 2010

British Library Cataloguing in
Publication Data.
A catalogue record for this book is available from the British Library.

Errors and omissions excepted.

ISBN-10: 0-85259-746-0
ISBN-13: 978-0-85259-746-0

Item No. R2803-09

Printed by Latimer Trend

Preface

'*The Stamp King*' was published in instalments in *Gibbons Stamp Weekly* between February 1904 and December 1905.

Although the writing style harks back to years gone by, the story of the search for a rare and valuable stamp and the competition between two philatelists to acquire it is one that will be appreciated by all true stamp collectors.

We have decided to publish the story exactly as it appeared in *Gibbons Stamp Weekly*, leaving in the odd notes which may appear above or below each week's instalment, as these also offer a fascinating insight into the philatelic issues of the day.

The opportunity to publish 'The Stamp King' in its present form has been made possible by a project being carried out at the moment to capture the entire archive of articles published in *Gibbons Stamp Monthly*, *Gibbons Stamp Weekly* and the *Stanley Gibbons Monthly Journal*, right back to issue 1 in July 1890. The archive will, naturally, be packed with invaluable information, fully searchable, so users will be able to call up long out-of-print information in their researches. It is expected that the *Gibbons Stamp Monthly* archive will be available in time for the International exhibition in London in May 2010 and further details will appear in GSM nearer the date.

The 'Brahmapootra stamp' of the story will never be the subject of serious philatelic research, but we hope that 21st century readers will enjoy following the adventures of William, Betty, John, Victoria and a host of other characters as they become involved in what Victoria describes as 'this insane craze' - now, I wonder what that could be?

HUGH JEFFERIES,
Editor, Gibbons Stamp Monthly
November 2009

THE STAMP KING

By G. DE BEAUREGARD AND H. DE GORSSE

Translated from the French by EDITH C. PHILLIPS

WILLIAM KENISS LEANT AGAINST THE CHIMNEY-PIECE

CHAPTER I

In which one sees to what lengths the Love of Postage Stamps is carried by true Philatelists

"I TELL you," said William Keniss with decision, "I believe her to be quite capable of doing it."

"It is ridiculous !" said stout Dr. Buxon, emphasising the remark with a shrug of his shoulders.

"Well, well," said little Mrs. Evans-Bradford, "who knows ! Nothing is impossible to a true American. Now Miss Betty is one of the real sort, I can answer for it."

"Pooh !" replied Buxon, his fat cheeks quivering. "Such a pretension is much less the act of an amateur in stamps than of a professional."

At these words, spoken with an unpleasant laugh, William Keniss rose.

"Doctor," cried he, "you are not very polite ; and you will have plenty of time to make fun of Miss Betty when she is shown to be defeated."

"There, there !" said the doctor, startled by the unexpected outburst. "Be calm. I was only joking. Really, you fire up so suddenly——"

"But," said Mr. Hartlepool, "you might explain to me just what happened. I have heard a rumour with regard to this new feat of Miss Betty Scott, but I come here less often than I could wish, and——"

"Zounds !" said old Pearding. "You don't call yourself a collector ? You scarcely deserve the name of an amateur ; and besides——"

"It is true ! it is true ! Mr. Hartlepool is a false brother !" clamoured the assembly, laughing at the protesting gestures made by the unfortunate man.

"But I solemnly declare," cried he as soon as he was able to put in a word, "that I really do collect the finest stamps, and plenty of them."

"To save the little Chinese," said Mrs. Evans-Bradford.

There was a burst of laughter so catching that even the immovable Tilmarnock permitted the shadow of a smile to escape him.

"I wager," hazarded Buxon, "that Mr. Hartlepool does not even know where he is this evening, and that he has only come here by mistake."

"Pardon me, Doctor ; on the contrary, I know perfectly that I am at the New York Philatelic Club, that I am a titular member of the same, and have every qualification for being so."

"I doubt if you even know what the qualifications are."

"What a libel ! One must, in order to belong to the Club, prove one's self to be at least twenty times a millionaire ; I am one thirty-three times over. One must promise never to discuss politics or religion ; I have a horror of such controversies. Finally, one must be interested in postage stamps and prove that one possesses a collection ; I am interested in them, and I have a collection."

"A fine collection, on my faith," returned the voluminous doctor, who was much given to contradiction. "Scarcely twenty-five thousand stamps——'

"Oh, you expect too much ; I have only been collecting for seven years ; one must have time. And then, how many of us here have a complete collection ? Probably not one."

"Pardon me," observed old Mr. Pearding, "that of Mr. William Keniss is absolutely up to date."

"That is a fact," said the collector simply.

"But with all this," returned Mr. Hartlepool, not without some impatience, "no one has told me the story of Miss Betty Scott."

"A lot more forward you'll be when you do know it," grumbled the malevolent Doctor Buxon.

MISS BETTY SCOTT ENTERED THE ROOM

"Doctor," returned William Keniss sharply, "all which concerns our charming fellow-philatelist interests us, Mr. Hartlepool among the rest, and you must either be much better informed than we, or much less courteous, to speak of her as you do."

"You are not engaged to defend her," objected Buxon, his fat cheeks colouring.

"I am not engaged for that purpose, but I take the engagement upon myself, and I will not permit anyone to speak ill of Miss Betty, especially in her absence. I do no more, in defending her, than all these gentlemen are ready to do. Is it not so, gentlemen?"

William, glancing round the group of auditors, read universal approbation.

"Mr. Keniss is right," declared Mr. Hartlepool; "Miss Betty Scott is a most charming young lady."

"With an exquisite reserve and modesty," said Mrs. Evans-Bradford.

"Of a discretion that her twenty-two years and her orphan state have never given opportunity of question," added Mrs. Tilmarnock.

"And with intrepid courage," supported a certain Mr. Whitby.

"In short, an American," pronounced the Honourable Buxon.

A snorted "Pooh! Pooh!" was Buxon's only reply.

"But for goodness' sake," supplicated Mr. Hartlepool, "tell me the story someone. Do have pity on my ignorance."

"Listen, then," said William Keniss, supporting himself against the chimney-piece.

He was a young man twenty-five years of age, with a slim and elegant figure, attired in the latest fashion, and of a most prepossessing aspect. He was a favourite among his fellow-philatelists for his courtesy and his unfailing good-humour. His immense fortune, amounting to almost forty million dollars, gave him an opportunity of being at the same time a charitable philanthropist, a generous friend, a magnificent host, and a collector of the first rank.

He, like Miss Betty Scott, was an orphan, but, unlike her, he had been devoted from his cradle, as it were, to the study of philately; in fact, his father, Edward Keniss, had carried his mania for stamps to such an extent, and amassed so much money by the sale of rarities, that he was known through all the United States, as his son William is known to-day, as the "Stamp King." The young "King," along with the dollars, had found in the paternal inheritance a unique collection of every genuine stamp legally issued, without one exception. This he felt bound to keep up to date, which was no small matter; but he disdained the inferior class of collections, in which are to be found errors, reversed watermarks, inexact or altered shades, incomplete perforations, and other minor varieties, which have no real interest but are mere matters of detail.

And the stamp mania was carried to such a pitch in his house that John Cockburn, his confidential valet, a somewhat rubicund fellow, but ready and intelligent, set to work to make a collection, a curiosity of its kind, of the forged stamps found sometimes among those received by his master, and which were immediately handed over to him.

William's wealth was legendary, his rectitude unimpeachable, and even those who envied him availed themselves of his knowledge, and asked his opinion before coming to any decision in matters philatelic.

"Six months ago," he began, "at one of our monthly dinners—oh! but I must tell you, dear Mr. Hartlepool, that we meet one day in every month at a fraternal banquet, in order to celebrate our researches and our finds. As you never come you may perhaps be ignorant of this fact."

Everyone began to laugh, Mr. Hartlepool among the first, while he excused himself for his unfortunate and by no means American tendency to unpunctuality.

"Six months ago," continued William Keniss, "Miss Betty Scott solicited the honour of being admitted to

the Philatelic Club. The new candidate, you may well believe, was a valuable one—beautiful, charming, honourable. You heard what was just said about her, and added to all that one of the largest fortunes in the States—sixty million dollars, I believe. But unfortunately for her candidature Miss Betty was worse than a novice in philately, so much so that she did not even know that the Cape stamps in 1853 were triangular, and that in 1873 labels were issued in Biscay bearing the portrait of Don Carlos. We caused her to be told as gently as possible that she was lacking in the most important qualification, and risked a rebuff if she persisted in the matter. Do you suppose she gave in? Miss Scott, as you have been told, thinks nothing impossible. Hearing that I possessed a complete collection she declared to me that by the date of the April banquet, 1896, that is to say, to-day, she would have an album like mine, engaging, moreover, to put in all the stamps herself, and not to procure it ready filled."

At this point a superior smile might be seen on the face of many of his auditors. Doctor Buxon shrugged his shoulders imperceptibly, but his arm-chair creaked at the movement of so great a weight.

"Naturally," continued William, "we could do no other than register the engagement, and promise that if she succeeded she should be admitted with acclamation. 'Very well,' were her concluding words, 'you will see me arrive at the April meeting, 1896, at the dinner hour, with my collection complete to remind you of your promise. Moreover, as a reception gift I will present the Club with some fine rooms on Broadway, so that it may have a home of its own instead of remaining here a miserable tenant.' There, my dear sir, that is all the story. You now know as much as we."

"It is very curious," said Mr. Hartlepool. "I only regret that the non-fulfilment of her engagement deprives us of so gracious a member."

"Excuse me," corrected William, "we do not dine till seven o'clock, and it is more than twenty minutes to that hour. So we may still expect Miss Betty, her collection, and—the rooms."

"It is most improbable."

As the chances of her coming diminished with every moment the discussion grew more animated; and William, as president of the Club, was just on the point of ordering the place prepared for her at table to be removed when the young lady herself walked into the room.

Miss Betty Scott was indeed charming. Slightly breathless from running up the stairs, her cheeks flushed with emotion, and her dark blue eyes shining beneath a cloud of fair hair with a splendour caused by the joy of triumph.

"Well? well?" sounded on every side.

"Well, here I am," she replied, while her small red lips, half opened in a smile, showed teeth white as pearls.

"And the collection?" asked Mrs. Tilmarnock.

"It is here. I have brought it complete."

"Complete?"

"Absolutely so."

"Let us see it! Let us see it!"

Miss Betty Scott returned to the door, opened it, and called "Victoria."

A tall, thin, insipid-looking young woman of about thirty entered, whose face, which ought to have been fresh and pleasing, had already begun to fade. This was Victoria, the celebrated Victoria Crockett, who was born in the service of the Scott family and was resolved to die therein, that is, supposing her projects with regard to John Cockburn, the jovial confidential valet of Mr. Keniss——. But to continue. She was encumbered with two huge parcels which she carried with great difficulty, one under each arm; and reaching the middle of the room quite out of breath, she deposited her burdens on a round table and walked out again without a word.

THE STAMP KING

By G. DE BEAUREGARD AND H. DE GORSSE

Translated from the French by EDITH C. PHILLIPS

CHAPTER I. (*continued*)

*In which one sees to what lengths the Love of Postage
Stamps is carried by true Philatelists*

"THIS," said Betty, pointing to one of the parcels, "is the album. The other contains all the letters, telegrams, and papers of all sorts, which prove that I have made my collection bit by bit, stamp by stamp."

They all gathered round the table, and William Keniss, as president of the Club, solemnly opened the album.

Everything had been done with extreme care. The stamps were all fixed with gummed hinges on little separate pieces of cardboard. Under each Betty had had the patience to write with her own hand the price,

"SHE WAS ENCUMBERED WITH TWO PARCELS"

date of issue, country, and the collector or dealer from whom she had obtained it ; and there were thirty-four thousand eight hundred and seventy-four stamps.

On the first page was a piece of old yellow-looking paper, frayed along the edges. It was a specimen of the first post-paid letter issued at the Paris Palais de Justice in 1653. Then came the complete sets of postage stamps, newspaper stamps, fiscals of all countries, all colours, all prices, and all dates. Not one, even of the rarest, was missing. The 1d., orange, Mauritius, 1847, occupied a prominent place, as well as the 81 paras, Moldavia, 1858 ; the 30 centimes, 1852, Réunion, black on blue ; the British Guiana 2 cents, rose, 1850 ; the 1870 1 rupee, brown-violet, of Afghanistan, and others of which hardly a copy is to be found were represented there by perfect specimens, without spot or tear or blemish of any kind.

"This is very good, very good indeed," murmured William, gently turning over the leaves, while the other spectators, in the effort to see all they could of such marvels, leaned forward, straining their necks, and devoured with their eyes the well-filled pages.

When the young president of the Philatelic Club came to the end of his examination Betty asked if they would like to see the papers of proof contained in the other parcel, but they all declared with one voice that they trusted implicitly in the new philatelist, and that such proof was entirely unnecessary. Perhaps the pangs of hunger were beginning to assert themselves, for the Hon. Tilmarnock on turning round caught sight of the clock, and remarked gravely, as if pronouncing a death sentence, "It is seventeen minutes past eight."

No one could believe the time had passed so quickly, but the really infatuated, while looking at stamps, forget there is anything else to live for.

"I am quite sure," said Betty, laughing, "that you had given up expecting me."

"Permit me," said William, offering her his arm, "to prove to you the contrary."

They headed the small procession and passed into the dining-room, where Betty could see for herself that opposite the president a place of honour was reserved, before which was a superb arrangement of flowers.

"This," said William Keniss, leading her to it, "is where we instal our new recruits of the fair sex, when they do us the honour of dining with us for the first time."

The guests were just about to seat themselves when William demanded to speak one more word, that all might be done in order, and, in his capacity as president, immediately gave himself the required permission.

"Ladies and gentlemen, you will not, I hope, blame me for carrying out our rules to the letter. Miss Betty Scott has not yet the right to appear at this table. I propose to give her that right by voting that, according to our promise, we admit her unanimously as a titular and permanent member of our Club."

The last words were drowned in deafening cheers, and after this enthusiastic investiture they all sat down to dinner.

For a time nothing was heard but a clatter of spoons. Eloquence was drowned in soup, so famished were the unfortunate members. It was only at the third course that their tongues found time to occupy themselves with any other duty besides that of tasting. Then Betty told them how she had been able, in so short a time, to get together a collection such as many other people had found it impossible to make even in long years.

"Listen to this, Hartlepool," said someone, "and profit by it."

She explained how she had written to all the dealers in the world, detailed her proceedings, her journeys here and there, how she had been taken in, and her continued surprises.

"I have given myself no end of trouble," she concluded, "but I do not regret it, since I am here in the midst of you, possessed of a collection in all respects similar to that of our amiable president, that is to say, as fine and as complete as it is possible to be."

Once again the applause broke out, and as the champagne was poured into the sparkling glasses William rose with his in his hand and, silence being restored, said :

"Miss Betty Scott has just given to Americans a great example of resource and energy. She has accomplished that which appeared impossible, and it is a memorable occasion for us sons of the Union to testify once more the admiration with which such enterprise, devoted to so good a purpose, inspires us."

"Bless me!" muttered Buxon, "will he never finish? I prefer dessert to a homily."

"I beg your pardon, Doctor?" said William, interrupting himself.

"I said—I said—oh, I said that what you said was very well said," faltered the great man.

"Oh, very good. I raise my glass then and cry, 'Hurrah for Miss Betty Scott!'"

There arose a perfect tumult of deafening cheers, some shouting "Hip, hip, hip!" while others cried, "Hurrah!" and others again, "Bravo!" till Betty felt perfectly bewildered.

They had just sat down again, and started gaily on the *bombes glacées*, when a waiter entered and handed William a registered letter.

"Hollo!" said he, examining the address. "This is from Moulineau, the great Paris stamp dealer, with whom I do so much business. This may be some new find. Will you allow me?"

"Certainly, certainly," was murmured on all sides.

He cut the envelope and unfolded a sheet of paper, on which, above the written lines, a stamp was fixed, and having read to the end of the letter cried, "Well, this is extraordinary!"

All eyes were turned on him inquiringly, and the Stamp King, not wishing to further arouse a curiosity already touched to the quick, and being also bound by the rules of the Club to let the other members share in his discoveries, said:

"Listen to this. I repeat it is most extraordinary." And he read aloud: 'Sir,—In accordance with the agreement existing between us, I am bound to procure for you a specimen of every legal issue which comes to my knowledge, where such is possible. I enclose a particularly rare one of a stamp which the Maharajah of Brahmapootra intended to use for the next issue. By a sudden caprice or from some unknown cause this prince has had the block from which they are printed destroyed, keeping absolutely only two specimens—this is an indubitable fact—which had been sent to him as essays.'

"An essay!" interrupted Dr. Buxon. "What is the good of that? You don't collect essays."

"Let him finish," said the Hon. Tilmarnock coldly.

"'I know you do not include essays in your collection,'" continued William, "'and that you only want stamps which have been in legal use. But though this stamp may be called an essay, it has been used, and lawfully used, for the Maharajah of Brahmapootra himself employed it to cover the postage of a letter to the Viceroy of India. Through this curious whim of his I have been able to get hold of it, but at a tremendous sacrifice. You will understand that this stamp, being probably the only one to be had—as the Maharajah himself has kept the other—is of very great value. It is impossible for me to part with it under a hundred thousand francs, or, if you prefer it, twenty thousand dollars.'"

"I will give fifty thousand," cried Betty.

"Pardon me, Miss Scott," said William, smiling, "but the stamp is not for sale. It belongs to me. Listen to the rest. 'As I have a large deposit to your account, and have your instructions to purchase rarities at any price, I take it for granted you will keep the stamp, and have the honour to remain, yours, etc.'"

Everyone was anxious to see this wonderful stamp, and when its new owner passed it round the table they were enthusiastic in its praise.

It was indeed a most effective work of art; both design and framework were of gold, printed on very fine, closely-grained, white paper. In the border, made of garlands of flowers lightly entwined, were mingled innumerable Hindoo characters of such delicate tracery that it was almost impossible for the eye to distinguish them. In the centre was the

Maharajah, seated on his throne with all the insignia of royalty, surrounded by symbolic emblems. The clearness of every detail rendered the stamp a unique work of art, showing at the same time the consummate skill of the engraver.

"It is splendid! splendid!" repeated Mrs. Evans-Bradford, examining it closely, while Mr. Whitby and Mr. Hartlepool corroborated the statement.

"Good!" pronounced the Hon. Tilmarnock. "Very good!"

"Say rather 'Unheard of! fabulous! inimitable!'" cried Mrs. Tilmarnock, overflowing with admiration.

The stamp was now handed to Miss Betty Scott, who examined it closely without a word; and then, passing it to her neighbour, said, "If I understood you aright, there were two of them?"

"Yes, Miss Scott," replied William, "but no doubt the other is destroyed. There are difficulties always in the way of conquest."

Hereupon the company rose and returned to the salon.

"Well, well," said Buxon to Betty, who appeared scarcely to be listening, "here is all your trouble thrown away."

"What do you mean?"

"Why, of course, your collection is no longer complete." And he went off into a laugh as gross as himself, in the consciousness of having made a disagreeable remark.

The others were complimenting William on his unexpected good fortune in annexing so unrivalled a stamp—one, too, which no other collector could ever boast of possessing.

"Who knows!" said Betty, who, coming up quietly, had caught the last words.

"Believe me," said William gallantly, "I am really sorry to possess again an advantage which I should be only too glad to have over any one else; but with regard to you it is quite different."

"One must yield to circumstances," returned Betty evasively; and with these words she retired, though they tried hard to persuade her to remain longer, Buxon not failing to insinuate that she looked furious.

"Not at all," said Mr. Hartlepool. "Just for a stamp that one hasn't got! That would be a fine cause for misery!"

"Ah, you have never loved stamps," said William. "If you had you would go to the end of the world for less than that."

"Perhaps she will go," said the Hon. Tilmarnock as quietly as if he were speaking of an every-day occurrence.

The thought shot like lightning through William's brain—"If she—but no; what folly! And yet, perhaps——"

In vain he tried to join in the conversation. Betty's departure had left him full of anxiety, and unable to conceal it any longer, he walked up and down the room, gradually approaching the door, and then, American though he was, slunk away like an Englishman.

"Wasn't I right?" said Buxon, tenaciously clinging to his first opinion. "Her sudden love of stamps has carried her so far that she has become stamp-mad."

On leaving the salon Betty had found her maid trying hard to keep herself awake, by joining John Cockburn in an interminable game of bezique at one of the tables in the vestibule.

"Two hundred and fifty! You have lost!" cried he, triumphantly throwing down his cards.

Victoria, in a fit of petulance, had just dashed her marker on the floor when she perceived her mistress, and, hastening to settle her comfortably in her carriage, took her seat beside her.

And while the carriage rolled silently and swiftly along on its rubber tyres, drawn by two magnificent horses, Betty remained in deep thought, but Victoria was slumbering comfortably among the cushions.

THE STAMP KING

By G. DE BEAUREGARD AND H. DE GORSSE

Translated from the French by EDITH C. PHILLIPS

CHAPTER I. (*continued*)

In which one sees to what lengths the Love of Postage Stamps is carried by true Philatelists

SUDDENLY the girl seized her maid's arm.
"Why," she said, "you are actually asleep!"
"Oh, what is it? what is it?" cried poor Victoria, waking with a start.
"It is, my good girl, that we have just now many more important things to do than to sleep."
"Miss Betty, you have no pity. It's past midnight, and I'm not used to being up so late. It is unreasonable to go home in the middle of the night——"
"I return home when I please," said Betty in a dry tone which was not usual with her, for she looked upon her good Victoria, who had been with her in her babyhood, more as a companion, or even as a friend and confidante, than as a maid.
Victoria, who was now wide awake, seeing that Miss Betty was gravely preoccupied, began to excuse herself for speaking so freely, although her thirty years spent entirely in the service of the Scott family, and her long devotion to her young mistress, gave her some right to advise, or, if need be, to remonstrate.
Full of confusion she met Betty's outburst with a murmured, "Forgive me, Miss Betty, if I meddle with what is no concern of mine, but I am so greatly attached to you that I cannot help feeling a little vexed when I think of the feverish life you lead since you took up this insane craze."
"All right, Victoria, all right," said Betty, smiling. "There's no need to apologise"; and she relapsed into silence.
As the carriage passed out of Stuyvesant Square into Fourth Avenue, where Betty lived, she asked quietly, as if to efface her hasty words:
"Victoria, what day is it to-day?"
"You are joking, Miss Betty; you know quite well it is Friday, the seventeenth of April, 1896."
"Are you certain?" and Betty murmured to herself, "What an eternity! To have to wait until to-morrow!" But after a few moments' deep thought she cried joyfully, "But it is to-day; it is not yesterday!"
Victoria, who had recovered her good humour, burst out laughing.
"Really, Miss Betty," she said, "you are as good as M. de la Palice."
"You are making fun of me," returned Betty, pinching her ear. "And after all you are the more simple of the two, for it is past midnight, and Friday gave place to Saturday a good half-hour ago."
"Why, so it did, so it did," repeated Victoria, amazed that so simple an explanation had not occurred to her.
"But then—perhaps—however, we shall see," concluded Betty enigmatically.
At this moment the carriage passed through the heavy folding gates and stopped opposite the great glass door of the vestibule. The footman opened the door and the two women alighted.
"Pancrace," said Betty to the coachman, "do not take the horses out, but turn the carriage round and be ready to start off again unless I countermand the order."
"Really this is too much," grumbled the coachman, half asleep and tired out.

"Heavens!" thought Victoria. "What crotchet has she got in her head now?"
The porter and footman, also compelled to remain at their posts, were no better pleased; and as Betty disappeared up the massive staircase they vented their anger on their mistress.
Everywhere—on the landings and in the ante-rooms —the electric light threw a profusion of bluish rays, which were reflected by huge mirrors on the polished marbles. The gilt frames, silk drapery of windows and doors, and precious tapestries shone out in a thousand sparkling lights, while massive arrangements of rare plants in every spare corner threw great trembling shadows on the walls.
Betty ran hastily about giving orders, telling one to be ready to attend her at any moment, another not to put out the lights, and a third to light them in the linen room, everyone wondering what was going to happen, beginning with Victoria, who breathlessly followed her mistress into her room.
It was furnished in a pleasantly severe style. A few rare ornaments of great price in bronze, terra-cotta, and porcelain were arranged on what-nots and tables, but there were none of those useless nothings—those insignificant trifles which generally fill up the rooms of young girls. A large writing-table covered with books and papers occupied one panel of the room between two windows overlooking the avenue. You might have thought yourself in the room of a young student still absorbed in his work if a few little details, only visible to a keen observer, had not spoken of a woman's presence—a faded flower in a vase or a piece of ribbon left by accident on the table.
The electric lights were arranged in the form of a bunch of tulips, which threw over all a flood of variegated rays. On the onyx chimney-piece, ornamented with chased bronze, a bright copper urn, simmering over a lamp for the evening tea, gave out little clouds of steam accompanied by a pleasant monotonous singing.
"Do you wish me to help you to undress?" asked Victoria, a little more hopefully.
"Give me the steamer time-table," was the only response.
Victoria's heart fell as she searched among a heap of pamphlets on the large table, hardly knowing what she was looking for, until Betty, quite out of patience, went and found it herself, and began turning over the leaves with the utmost coolness. The poor maid watched her with growing uneasiness, fearing some new development of the craze; in fact, during the six months that had passed since Betty resolved to gain admission to the Philatelic Club by making a collection as good as that of William Keniss, Victoria had assisted in the most extraordinary and unequalled scene imaginable.
In order to give her whole attention to philately, and to arrive at the longed-for result in the shortest possible time, Betty had at once abandoned all her ordinary occupations and cut herself off from communication with her nearest friends. Forsaking all the usual occupations and pleasures of a young lady— dances, fashions, and what not—she had but one end in view, to succeed in her enterprise; the more so as everyone else believed it to be impossible. To this end she had shrunk from nothing. The most tiring proceedings, the most intricate researches, nothing

appalled her ; not even the innumerable letters it was necessary to write to distant correspondents for the stamps she needed, and which, as soon as received, she hastened to fix in place on the pages which were to form the collection.

And at last, after all the trouble, she had tasted the sweets of victory. The collection had been recognised as complete and well arranged. The young philatelist had been received with an enthusiastic ovation, and Victoria herself, having had the honour of placing the precious portfolio on the Club table, had had her share in the triumph to which, it cannot be denied, she had given valuable assistance. Now at last she had begun to hope she might be allowed to rest. This was the thought in her mind when Betty, suddenly closing the time-table, said :

" What time is it ? "

" Two o'clock, Miss Betty."

" Good ! then we have two hours left ; time for a cup of tea."

With a trembling hand the maid turned the tap of the urn, filled a cup of fine Dresden china, and handed it to her mistress.

" Take care," said Betty, " or you will spill it all. Are you cold that you tremble like that ? "

" No, Miss Betty, I am not cold."

" What is it then ? Are you in pain ? "

" No, Miss Betty. But if you no longer need the carriage——"

" Well ? "

" Well, then, I can tell Pancrace and the others to go to bed."

" Then you may as well confess you are sleepy," concluded Betty, smiling.

" It's so late——"

It was evident Betty had something to say, but though she was, after all, mistress, and could do as she liked, it was no less evident that she hesitated before revealing to Victoria what was in her mind. The poor girl seemed so tired and sleepy that the young American, usually so prompt in action, was filled with scruples. Moreover, Victoria was wont to give her advice and she to listen to it, seeing it was always dictated by the tenderest affection and absolutely disinterested.

However, it must be done, so with a slight blush Betty put down her cup, rose, and in a voice which she tried hard to make firm and peremptory, said :

" We start for France in two hours."

If a thunderbolt had fallen in the middle of the room Victoria could not have been more astounded.

" Start for France in two hours ! " she cried. It was so unlooked-for, so impossible, that for some moments she could not believe she had heard aright. " For France ! In two hours ! " she repeated. " Are you really serious ? "

" As serious as it is possible to be," returned the inflexible Miss Betty. " We go by the *Touraine*, which weighs anchor at six o'clock this morning ; so you see we haven't a minute to lose, not one minute. So be quick and get your luggage packed ; unless, indeed, you prefer to go just as you are. You look very nice so, but it will hardly be comfortable day and night during the week's crossing."

Miss Betty's speech was so much to the point that Victoria saw this was not one of her caprices which a few sensible words spoken at the right moment might have power to dispose of. She began to perceive that her mistress was so determined upon this unforeseen departure that nothing, absolutely nothing, could be done to make her change her mind. So she only said :

" Very well, miss, I will go and get everything ready."

However, as she was going out of the room she hesitated.

" May I at least be allowed to know the reason of this hasty departure, Miss Betty ? "

" It is a very simple matter," replied the girl. " Mr William Keniss has just received from Paris a stamp of which only two specimens exist, the one which he now possesses and the one of which we are going in search."

" So," cried the maid, with a toss of the head meant to show that she thought Miss Betty quite mad this time, " so it is for a *stamp* that we are starting on this senseless journey ! "

" Yes, my good Victoria, it is for a stamp."

" Do you even know where it is, Miss Betty ? "

" No ; all I know about it is that the first one was supplied to William Keniss by a great Paris dealer, M. Moulineau. He therefore ought to know where the second one is, and consequently it is quite natural I should go and ask him. That is why we are setting out for France before undertaking perhaps longer and more perilous journeys."

On hearing Betty speak thus of possible journeys in countries even more remote than France, Victoria, in spite of the blow she had before received, which ought to have prepared her for anything, found it necessary to become faint and fall all her length on the floor. She was, in fact, one of the most phlegmatic women in the States, and her young mistress, especially since she had taken up this stamp craze, inspired her by her adventurous nature with veritable terror. Every morning on rising she asked herself anxiously what new folly it was possible for Miss Betty to commit, so that little by little she had grown into the habit of not being astonished at anything. But this was really beyond anticipation.

" Do I really understand, Miss Betty," she began once more when she had recovered a little, " that you would run after this stamp if it wasn't in Paris—or even in France ? "

" Perfectly. I am determined to get it no matter where I go in search of it. You understand, no matter where. But why all these questions ? Do you hesitate to go with me ? "

" Oh, Miss Betty ! " was Victoria's quick reply, " you know quite well that wherever you go, I go."

" Yes, I do know, and thank you for it. You are a good, kind girl and I am nothing but a fool. But what would you have ? I cannot remake myself."

At this moment the clock struck one shrill little warning note.

" Half-past three ! " cried Betty. " We have only an hour and a half left."

Immediately bells were rung, doors began to slam, and the servants running up received orders to pack the luggage with the least possible delay. And soon there might be seen up and down the stairs, in vestibules, corridors, and bedrooms, a crowd of infatuated domestics rushing to and fro, carrying hastily-made parcels, elbowing and hustling each other, and using all manner of invectives.

" I warn you," said Betty to Victoria, " if you are not ready I shall start without you."

" Don't be afraid, Miss Betty ; I shan't be long."

Victoria, panting and half choked with emotion and surprise, hastened up to her room, and began to stuff into a portmanteau whatever clothes came first to hand.

Soap, shoes, linen, brushes, were piled together in bewildering confusion. She crammed, crushed, stuffed in everything. In another moment, had it not been for its size, the wardrobe itself would have disappeared in the depths of the bag, so distracted was she by the suddenness of this great event, and so anxious lest she should not have finished in time.

In fact, Victoria was in a hurry, in a greater hurry even than her mistress, who really wanted to go. And she was flurried, for a sudden thought had just occurred to her, the thought of her friend, John Cockburn, the valet of William Keniss, and this thought had immediately plunged her into the very depths of despair.

THE STAMP KING

By G. DE BEAUREGARD AND H. DE GORSSE

Translated from the French by EDITH C. PHILLIPS

"AND IS IT INDEED TO MISS BETTY SCOTT THAT I HAVE THE HONOUR OF SPEAKING?"

CHAPTER II

How Miss Betty always went Straight to the Point

JOHN COCKBURN and Victoria Crockett had become acquainted nearly two years ago, at a house where both Betty Scott and William Keniss were visiting. They had talked together, been mutually pleased, and finally decided to unite their destinies. Now if it had depended on Victoria alone the marriage would long ago have been celebrated, but John, who appreciated the charms of liberty at their full value, was less anxious to change his state. But then, he had not been able to save a penny, while Victoria, with prudent foresight, had amassed a pretty little fortune. On the other hand, Victoria was thirty and John only twenty-three, and the idea of having a wife older than himself, who would probably rule the roost, had made him hesitate all this time.

"It's all very well," Victoria had decided—for she was as stubborn as most Americans, and had, besides, a horror of becoming an old maid; "John may hold back as long as he likes, but I shall get my own way in time. What is it the French say? 'What a woman wishes a man does.'"

So she had not let a day pass without going to see her friend John, in the hope of persuading him to make up his mind at last. And now she was heartbroken at having to go so far away from him, and for so long a time; especially when he was just on the eve of solemnly fixing the date of their marriage.

Despairingly she descended the stairs to Betty's room, carrying with difficulty the portmanteaus into which she had crushed her belongings.

On the staircase she encountered the butler.

"Where are you going?" he asked.

"To Paris."

"Impossible!"

"True, all the same. Let me pass, please."

While the news of this unexpected departure was being passed from mouth to mouth, Victoria entered Miss Betty's room.

"Ah, there you are!" said she. "Just in time. Come and fasten my dressing-case."

As she buckled the straps Victoria was helplessly wondering how she could possibly leave New York without first letting John Cockburn know, without reminding him of his promise, which the stupid fellow was sure to forget as soon as she was out of his sight, out of his thoughts, perhaps, in Europe. She could not leave him like this, without seeing him again, without at least one hand-shake. What would the poor man think when the whole day, the next day, other days passed without his receiving his daily visit? It was certainly necessary at any price to have one last interview; but at that hour in the morning what was the use of thinking of it? Besides, she had not time to run to Mr. William Keniss's—all the way to Hudson Street, more than two miles. Oh, the misery of it!

"Now, my good Victoria," said Betty, "you had better go yourself and find a carriage to take the luggage to the station. We will go in our own. Be sure and bring a good horse who will be able to follow us closely. Five o'clock! Only an hour, so go at once."

A sudden inspiration surged through Victoria's brain. Why should she not make use of the carriage she was sent to fetch to go at full speed to Hudson Street to see John? Yes, why not? Could she not explain her prolonged absence to Miss Betty by pleading the difficulty of finding a cab at so late, or rather, at so early an hour? But if they missed the steamer through her fault! The thought made her tremble.

However, she had not reached the street door before the time was reckoned up and her resolution taken. Twelve minutes to go; twelve minutes to return;[*] ten minutes to get the door opened, see John, and jump back into the carriage; total, including one minute to find the carriage, thirty-five minutes; leaving twenty-five minutes to gain the quay and get on board.

"It will be enough," said Victoria, astonished at her own assurance, and she walked unhesitatingly out of the house. A carriage was passing at that very moment, and she hailed the driver—a stout man with a nose almost as red as his lamps.

"Driver," said she, "five dollars if you will take me to Hudson Street and back in half an hour."

"Hudson Street? Half an hour? What number?"

"Number three."

"Number three? All right."

Victoria threw herself into the carriage, and the driver gave the horse one vigorous lash of the whip, at which he first dashed forward and then backed with all his might, to show that the treatment was not at all to his taste. But a few more lashes soon disposed of his feeble resistance, and the good beast, becoming suddenly brisk, threw up his head, neighed, and then started like an arrow on his giddy course, striking out sparks with his hoofs right and left.

It was a mad rush through streets and avenues. The passengers on foot, luckily rare at this hour, had scarcely time to get out of the way of the vehicle, but jumped on to the pavement with cries of alarm.

Thanks to the rapidity of their pace, Victoria arrived at her destination in less than eleven minutes. She ran swiftly up the staircase which led to the apartments of Mr. William Keniss, and rang the bell. John opened the door.

"Victoria!" cried he. "What has happened? What are you doing here at this time of night?"

"I have come to tell you," said Victoria breathlessly, "that Miss Betty and I are starting for Paris this morning."

"For Paris!"

"Yes, for Paris. It seems Miss Betty is going in search of a stamp which your master possesses and which she hasn't got yet."

"A stamp? Do you know which?"

"Oh, they are all the same to me! Only, you see, I couldn't go without wishing you good-bye. That is what I came for. Now I must fly, for I haven't a second to spare. The *Touraine*, the steamer we are going by, weighs anchor in half an hour."

"In half an hour!"

"Promise you will not forget me, John."

"I promise."

"And that you will marry me when I come back."

"I promise that too."

"Then good-bye, John, and may we meet again soon."

"Very soon, Victoria."

The maid ran down again, gave the man the five dollars she had promised, beseeching him to say nothing to her mistress of this escapade, and to drive back at once to Stuyvesant Square; then she got into the carriage again, and they set off at the same breakneck speed as before.

Miss Betty had had her trunk brought down by the servants, and was waiting at the door with feverish impatience for Victoria and her carriage.

"At last!" she cried. "I thought you were never coming."

* The New York cabs are evidently faster than those of London if they go two miles in twelve minutes!

In a few seconds the trunk was hoisted up and the two equipages were on their way.

It was a good distance from Stuyvesant Square to the port, but the horses were fresh enough to do it in the half-hour that remained. The driver with the luggage, who was leading, thought, indeed, that he had time to spare, so slackened pace a little, with the result that they only arrived at the quay just three minutes before the steamer left. The adventurous young American, after liberally paying the driver and handing over the luggage to two porters who were waiting about, ran with Victoria to the gangway, which they had scarcely crossed when the captain ordered all but the passengers on shore. The boat was ready to start, and the anchor weighed just as the surrounding clocks struck six.

While these last incidents were taking place an event of great importance was also happening at William Keniss's. After Victoria's visit John had reflected deeply on the news he had just heard, of Miss Scott's sudden departure in search of a stamp, and had then resolved, in spite of the early hour, to wake his master, knowing he would be forgiven, as the news would interest him in no small degree. As he entered the room William Keniss opened one eye and began to storm at him for disturbing his sleep, but when the honest fellow began his story he immediately opened the other eye.

"Do you mean to say, John, that Miss Betty is starting for France this morning in search of a stamp which I possess and she doesn't?"

"Yes, sir."

"Then it must be that Brahmapootra stamp that I got yesterday."

"No doubt, sir."

William Keniss sat up in bed.

"She shall not have it!" he cried. "Either I will persuade her not to go, by pointing out the perils of such an undertaking on the part of a young lady, or, if that is unavailing, I will go too. My collection is the only complete one in the world, and I do not intend that there shall be another." And leaping out of bed he cried, "My clothes, John—trousers, waistcoat, coat. We will be off at once."

As soon as John, nonplussed at the thought that he was going to meet his dear Victoria once more on the bridge of the *Touraine*, had handed his master's clothes with a very bad grace, the latter said:

"Now get your hat and come."

"But our luggage?" cried the valet.

"Never mind that. We can buy all we need in Paris." And descending to the street they both jumped into a carriage.

Unfortunately, though, William Keniss had not taken the precaution of examining the horse, which had arrived at the very last stage of attenuation. In spite of the blows lavished upon him by the driver, bribed by the promise of an extra fare, he could do no more than trot at a hopelessly slow pace, so that when William Keniss and John arrived at the quay it was already too late. The *Touraine* had left the stage and was steaming away towards the ocean, while Miss Betty's carriage was slowly returning to the town. But what was passing on board the vessel?

At first in the uproar of departure no one noticed that the population thereof had just been augmented by two new arrivals; and Miss Betty and Victoria, entrenched behind their luggage, observed a modest silence, for fear they might be told that all the berths were full and that there was yet time to land them again.

The two great screws cut through the waves of the Hudson, leaving in the wake of the steamer a double train of boiling foam. The water opened to make way for the slender bows, rolling off on either side in great waves, which finally broke against the river banks. In the misty morning atmosphere the siren uttered its occasional wild bellow, warning bells sounded, and the voice of the captain was heard from the bridge shouting brief and contradictory orders to the engineer below; for they were still in the narrow channel, and it was no easy matter to steer this colossal structure—one hundred and sixty metres long by twenty wide—more gigantic than the great nave of Notre Dame.

The monster moved forward with great precaution as if scenting out the way, now darting forward with great turns of the screws, now hesitating, stopping almost, only to start again with a fresh impetus. You could feel that the pressure was at its height as the engines threw out, as from huge lungs, panting jets of vapour, which rose above like two enormous plumes of black smoke issuing from the red funnels. The sides of the vessel shot forth columns of water from the pumps, and the morning as it brightened gave to the movements of the colossus a strange character of life and grandeur.

The *Touraine* now bore forward at full speed in the widening estuary. The houses of New York had disappeared, then those of the suburbs, and finally the river banks themselves were lost in the misty distance. It was a lovely morning as the pale golden sun rose out of the pink mist just over the point of Long Island, which could be dimly seen in the distance.

"And now," said Miss Betty to Victoria, when the vessel was so far on her way, "there is no longer any danger that they will send us back, so we may as well see after a cabin."

"Oh my! Oh my! What a folly this is!" said the maid, overcome by the freshness of the morning air and far from resigned to her fate.

"It will be all right," said Betty encouragingly. "Don't be miserable, but go and find me the steward." But at this moment the steward appeared on his tour of inspection. Just before he reached the two women he was joined by a stylishly dressed gentleman, apparently English, with red hair and a light flowing moustache. He was evidently a person of importance, for the steward saluted him deferentially. The gentleman, conscious of his own dignity, returned the salute with a nod without deigning to remove his gloved hands from the pockets of his travelling-coat.

"Steward," said he, "can you tell me if the young lady standing near us is Miss Scott?"

The steward after glancing at her returned, "Well, sir, it is all the more difficult for me to tell you, as I do not know who Miss Scott is."

"What, you have never heard of Miss Scott, the beautiful New York millionaire, with a fortune of three hundred million francs—sixty million dollars—twelve million pounds sterling! Why, every steamer brings over princes, dukes, counts, come expressly from Europe to solicit her hand. It is only fair to add that they return also by every steamer, disdainfully refused by the intractable young lady."

"I perceive, sir," said the steward, "that you know her well."

"Only as all New York knows her—by reputation, and a little by sight, since I am not at all sure that it is she."

Victoria had by this time come forward.

"Sir," said she to the steward, "my mistress wishes to speak to you."

"Certainly. Excuse me, sir."

"But if that really is Miss Scott," said the gentleman, detaining him a moment, "you will have the kindness to present me to her?"

"Willingly, sir."

The steward approached Miss Betty, thinking the while that even on board she would not escape suitors in quest of a large fortune.

"My companion and I arrived only at the last moment," said she, "and have not booked our passage, but we should like one of the best cabins."

"But, madam, there is not one left!"

"Not even one on the lower deck?"

"No, madam, not one."

"How annoying," cried the disappointed Miss Betty. "I will pay anything necessary. Find me one at any price."

"Alas! madam, I cannot turn anyone out of a cabin booked beforehand. The *Touraine*, you know, on account of its luxury and comfort, is the most in request of all our boats, especially by first-class passengers."

"Whatever shall we do, then?"

"The simplest plan, indeed the only one, is to share one of the second-class cabins with two others. There is room for four, and it is absolutely the only place I have left for you."

Betty's face lengthened considerably, for the idea of being relegated to the second class and having to share a cabin was very distasteful. But at this moment the gentleman, who had drawn near enough to hear the conversation, saw his opportunity and spoke.

"Will you do me the favour of presenting me?" said he, lifting his cap.

"Sir Oscar Tilbury," said the steward to Miss Betty.

"And is it indeed to Miss Betty Scott that I have the honour of speaking?"

"Yes," said the girl, surprised at the unexpected intervention.

Satisfied on this most important point, Sir Oscar continued, with a more profound bow than before: "I must ask you to forgive me, Miss Scott, not for having listened to, but for having overheard, your unsuccessful request. As I saw I might be of use to you I took the liberty of speaking."

"But what can you do——?"

"I can take a place in a second-class cabin instead of you and ask you to accept mine, which is on the promenade deck, and one of the best on the boat."

For a moment Miss Betty's eyes shone with pleasure, but only for a moment.

"I cannot cause you so much inconvenience," she said.

"Not the least inconvenience in the world, Miss Scott," returned Sir Oscar Tilbury. "I merely require a cabin to sleep in at night; the rest of the time I wander about, smoke, or play." In short, the gallant Englishman pleaded his cause so well, mingling respectful reserve with so much kind insistence in his offer, that a quarter of an hour afterwards Miss Betty and Victoria took possession of the superb cabin, while Sir Oscar had his luggage removed to the second class. But it was arranged that the latter, having paid for a luxurious place, should naturally retain the permanent use of the saloons and of the first-class dining-table. He even, by the help of a judicious tip, arranged that his seat at table should be next to that of Miss Betty.

THE STAMP KING

By G. DE BEAUREGARD AND H. DE GORSSE

Translated from the French by EDITH C. PHILLIPS

CHAPTER II (*continued*)

How Miss Betty always went Straight to the Point

DURING all this first day, which was very fine and calm, neither Betty nor Victoria appeared on deck, for they were in great need of rest after their sleepless night and the fatigue of their hasty departure. In the evening, however, having recovered a little, they dressed, and Miss Betty went into the great saloon, while Victoria, not daring to assume the rank of lady-companion, remained in the cabin, where her meals were to be served in order to save her the annoyance of dining with the servants.

As the young lady entered, Sir Oscar, in evening dress, with a flower in his button-hole and his ruddy locks freshly curled, quitted the group to whom he was holding forth and went to meet her.

"I need not ask, Miss Scott," said he earnestly, "how you are since this morning, for the beautiful colour in your cheeks tells me you are in a perfect state of health."

Miss Betty thanked him with a smile, while he continued even more amiably—

"Will you permit me to escort you round the saloon?"

SIR OSCAR OFFERED HER HIS ARM

The girl accepted, and Sir Oscar presented to her a number of people whose acquaintance he had already made on board; then, as the dinner bell had just sounded, he offered his arm and led her into the dining-room.

The meal was a merry one. The accomplished Englishman met every wish of his graceful neighbour and paid her every possible compliment, but always with perfect deference and that entire absence of affectation which is only seen in the acts and words of the most accomplished men of the world.

Betty, though perfectly reserved, was enough of a woman and an American not to be offended by this assiduous flattery. So she conversed with Sir Oscar without restraint, even telling him she was going to Paris, though without confessing the real object of her journey. And Sir Oscar, charmed and enraptured, spoke of France and the delightful times he had had

there, charming all who heard him, and finding opportunity to reply to each with equally good grace.

When they rose from dinner it became evident that the vessel had no longer the same stability as before. Now and then the floor seemed to slide away from under them, and a few of the more convivial spirits could hardly keep on their feet, which caused the rest of the company great amusement. The chart, which indicated their course, showed they had now arrived off Nova Scotia, from which one of the passengers concluded they had begun to feel the full swell of the open sea.

Betty Scott promenaded the deck, still on the arm of Sir Oscar Tilbury. The night was dark and the *Touraine* pitched more and more each moment. Now the bows rose in the air as if making a straight course for the stars and then sank softly as though into the midst of a heap of down ; all of which was not without its effect on the digestion of the greater number of the passengers. Many of the ladies retired in a very unhappy condition. A few men disappeared in their turn, to the amusement of those who had not begun to suffer, and particularly of Miss Betty. Sir Oscar's spirits sank considerably as the sea rose. His words became fewer, his anecdotes shorter, and Betty, in passing under one of the electric lights which lighted the deck, observed that his face was livid, his features drawn, and his appearance by no means valorous ; so not to annoy him by remarking on these symptoms she pleaded her own fatigue, and returning to her cabin set him free.

It was high time, for the unhappy Sir Oscar had barely time to take refuge in his to avoid being seen, by the few passengers still left on deck, in the most miserable condition it is possible to imagine for such an elegant and fastidious gentleman. And so, with its pleasures and its miseries, the night passed and the second day broke.

CHAPTER III

Showing how very Slowly a Fast Steamer can go

A BITTER wind was blowing from the N.N.W., fine rain began to fall, and to the surprise of the passengers the boat remained immovable for two hours. But no one volunteered any information on the subject, and the cause of the stoppage could only be conjectured. At length, when supposition had spent itself and the passengers were giving free vent to their impatience, the captain himself assembled them all in the saloon, and said very coolly—

"Ladies and gentlemen, there is no cause for alarm. A connecting-rod having got out of gear, the engines were stopped somewhat too abruptly; this strained one of the piston-rods, which we have, consequently, to repair. As bad luck would have it, the other engine, which caused the accident, is similarly damaged. We have all the necessary tools for making it right, but you must give us time. Twenty hours will, in my opinion, be sufficient to complete the job, and you will, I am sure, excuse this delay, which, under the circumstances, is quite unavoidable ; and I can assure you that, beyond this little inconvenience, you have nothing to fear."

With these words he slipped out of the saloon and went to overlook the work, leaving his hearers dumbfounded.

But there was not much leisure for criticism, for the boat grew more unsteady than ever, alternately rolling and pitching, this time with a motion which became more violent every minute.

Soon it was scarcely possible to keep one's seat, and Miss Betty thought she would like to see what the weather looked like outside. Clinging tightly to the mahogany rail to avoid being thrown against the partition, she reached the deck and hung on to the side.

The sky was black as ink, the darkness impenetrable. The wind, risen to a tempest, whistled through the stays, sweeping everything before it. The ocean, lashed into enormous billows, black, deep, and unfathomable, overwhelmed everything within its reach. Wave after wave dashed against the vessel and fell heavily on the deck with a thunderous roar. The noise was deafening, but Betty, struck with the fearful grandeur of the scene, scarcely felt the water streaming from her soaked garments or the wind raging around her.

She soon discovered, however, that it would be impossible for her to move, or to relax for a moment her convulsive grip. Moreover, the fury of the elements was increasing, and breathless and exhausted she felt the time would soon come when, loosing her hold, she would be swept overboard.

Now the boat, heeling to larboard, offered one flank to the raging cyclone; now she plunged still farther on the other side, between walls of water, only to rebound again with furious somersaults.

"What are you doing here?" shouted a formidable voice in Betty's ear, and without giving her time to reply a strong arm snatched her from her perilous point of observation and launched her at the risk of her life down the stairs of the saloon, the door of which was immediately locked behind her.

It was just in time, for a huge wave caught up the enormous boat as if it had been a feather, and let it drop into the immense hollow beyond. The bridge and decks were drenched. The water even dashed into the funnels and fell like a waterspout into the furnaces. The captain, lashed to the bridge, tried in vain to pierce the thick darkness, while the boat drifted without the help either of engines or rudder, for the latter had been broken by the tempest. The whistle of the sirens could alone be heard above the tumult.

In the saloons the greatest confusion reigned. The passengers, most of whom were sick and frightened, were thrown from side to side, knocking against each other in a way that would have been laughable had it not been so disastrous. Fearful crashes were heard in every direction; everything movable was thrown on to the floor, where it was caught in the roll of the vessel and tossed this way and that. Haggard mothers hugged their children, whose cries of terror added to the general misery. The men, pale and helpless, could do nothing to help. Ever the same terrible shocks, ever the same sickening fear that the steamer was about to capsize.

At intervals one of the officers would enter, keeping his feet with difficulty, and try to reassure them all.

"It is only a squall," he would say, "and will soon be over. There's nothing to be afraid of." But they could scarcely hear, and still less could they believe him.

In fact, the whole crew—the more worthy of admiration since they themselves had the more cause for fear, knowing the gravity of the situation—seemed to be everywhere, caring for one, encouraging another, exerting themselves to comfort everyone, while at the

SHE CLUNG TIGHTLY TO THE RAIL

same time working their hardest at the disabled vessel. The peril was certainly great, for in such a storm the broken machinery could not be repaired, and the impossibility of steering left the *Touraine* at the mercy of the waves. All bearings were lost, and the storm carried them whither it would, and this lasted for ninety-four hours.

At the end of that time, when it was clear from the more moderate movements of the vessel that the tempest was drawing to a close, courage and energy revived. The wind fell, and though the swell continued for another day things were no longer hopeless, and the ordinary routine was resumed. It was known that the captain had shown great foresight and intrepidity, and everyone was aware that during the difficult crisis he had many times risked his life. So when he appeared at the first regular meal which followed the long interruption of four days, he was loudly cheered, and Sir Oscar Tilbury, in a lengthy speech, thanked him in the name of all the passengers, and presented him with a bouquet made of the camellias which he had kept so carefully for his own button-hole.

It was a delightful meal. Sir Oscar put so much fervour into his speech that at a pathetic gesture his scarf-pin was loosened and fell into the plate of Miss Betty, who sat beside him. She took it up, and wiped away the sauce from the malachite and gold serpent of which it was composed ; then, after examining it, returned it with a smile to its owner, saying, " What a beautiful trinket !"

"A thousand thanks, Miss Scott," returned Sir Oscar ; "that stupid pin is always falling out, and I shall certainly lose it some day"; saying which he replaced it in his necktie.

(To be continued.)

SPECIAL CORRESPONDENCE

Our Italian Letter

ROME, *February* 10th, 1905.

EVERY self-respecting correspondent feels the need of beginning his work by congratulating the editor and publishers of *Gibbons Stamp Weekly*. But I think I can do without that, for I have already sent in my good wishes, together with my subscription, as the best and the most practical way of encouraging publications. (Applause from Mr. Phillips.)

The land "where the orange-tree flourishes" is certainly not very favourable to an intense cultivation of the plant with its many branches, and with its flowers of every shade, called Philately. Putting aside metaphor, I must avow that collectors are by no means numerous here, and, one can add, that there are no great collections of stamps in Italy, for the best that we had have been sold abroad. The collecting of Italian stamps, and of those of the old States—which certainly form one of the most interesting groups—has naturally several devotees among us here. About fifteen collections of importance could be pointed out. But, here in Italy, scientific specialisation, which has such splendid experts in England, is not reached. On the other hand, we have some collectors who collect stamps on original letters, the example being set about twenty years ago by a collector whom I knew. In my opinion, this way of collecting, although it is often blamed for taking up a great deal too much space, is one of the most interesting, and seems to me destined to spread itself more in the future. Often we owe to stamps on the original letters a knowledge of several facts, and sometimes it has been due to stamps preserved on letters that a good chronological arrangement has been possible in the case of the different varieties.

Promised New Italian Stamps

I am applied to frequently by letter for information about the issue of the projected stamps which were notified some months ago, not only in the philatelic Press, but also in the Press at large. It will be remembered that it was a question of making something very striking. After the stamps of the " flowery style," which were reproached justly with having ornamentations of too heavy a kind, it was a question of symbolical designs—that is, a set to produce a sensation among the public, as it was said. There was an idea of reproducing on these stamps the development of means of communication.

The Designs

The set was to begin with a waterfall, the generator of motive power, and to end with wireless telegraphy. This would recall somewhat the ballet " Excelsior " of Manzotti. The artist Paolo Michetti, one of the leading Italian artists, was charged with preparing the designs, and people even went so far as to claim that his inspirer and adviser was his friend Gabriele D'Annunzio, the poet and novelist. A pretty ideal ; poetry and painting helping each other to create beautiful types of stamps. I have seen some photographs of the original designs, and it is easy to recognise in them the hand of a very great artist. Among other things I admired a portrait of King Victor Emmanuel III., standing out against a sky in which are fluttering some swallows, those faithful messengers. One sees that the artist had studied at first hand the portrait of the young and clever King, of whom he had in fact executed, by his orders, a large portrait in oils. But one can understand easily that when such subjects are reduced to the small size of a postage stamp, the effect is no longer absolutely the same, especially if the stamps are made by surface-printing.

Stumbling Blocks and Difficulties

Then, changes are introduced, touches up are given, and fresh studies are made. And while all this is going on, "dum Romae consulitur, politics, voila notre misère," as De Musset said, brings a fresh Minister to the head of the Department of Posts and Telegraphs, and then it is often a case of beginning all over again. There was some idea of bringing out the new set on the occasion of reducing the inland postage of letters. This has been promised a long time. But here also politics had to be reckoned with. It is well known that the rate of postage in Italy was 15 centesimi, about $1\frac{1}{2}$d., in 1863 and 1864, and that since January 1st, 1865, or for forty years, it has been 20 cent. This "provisional measure," as it was called in the Law of November 24th, 1864, was to have been revoked ; but the authorities could not agree as to whether the reduction should be to 10 or to 15 cent. In any case, a reduction was to be made, for among the proposals to be discussed at the Congress of the Universal Postal Union, which was to meet in Rome on April 21st, 1904, there was one to reduce to 20 centimes the postage of letters intended for the different countries forming the Union ; thus, if this proposal had been adopted, Italy would have found itself with the same postal rates for inland as for foreign letters going to the countries of the U.P.U. As it was, the Congress was postponed for a year by wish of the King of Italy. For some reasons unknown, the Congress has just been postponed again, and the date of its meeting has still to be fixed.

Still Undecided

It is believed that the discussion in the Chamber of Deputies with regard to the project for reforming the inland postal rates will take place soon, and although we have not a Henniker Heaton, a reduction will be passed without doubt. Then it will probably be a question of the stamps. I shall not fail to inform the numerous readers of this paper in time.

EMILIO DIENA.

THE STAMP KING

By G. DE BEAUREGARD AND H. DE GORSSE

Translated from the French by EDITH C. PHILLIPS

THE CAPTAIN APPLIED THE MATCH AND A REPORT SOUNDED

CHAPTER III (*continued*)

Showing how very slowly a Fast Steamer can go

THE remembrance of the dangers they had encountered together and the fears they had undergone had established a kind of intimacy among the passengers. There seemed to be none but old friends on board the *Touraine*. Miss Betty received her full share of attention, especially as in consequence of her fall down the stairs, when the sailor had hurried her from the deck—more anxious about saving her life than the manner of doing it—she had gone about with a painful lump on her forehead, which for two days needed the application of a bandage.

Sir Oscar, whose spirits had revived with the calm, surrounded his pleasant companion with more little cares and attentions than ever.

As for Victoria, who had not moved from the cabin during all this terrible time, she remained greatly depressed, but when Betty told Sir Oscar of her misery he exclaimed—

"Why, Miss Scott, how can you leave the excellent creature in such a condition? Permit me to fetch her to take a cup of coffee with us."

And without waiting for a reply he ran to the cabin, and only returned a good minute after Victoria herself had entered the saloon. She was much flattered by the attention he had paid her, and seated herself with great dignity in the midst of the chattering company.

"Do you know where we are?" asked the captain, going from group to group.

"No," was the universal reply. "Where are we?"

"In sight of the Azores!"

A general exclamation of surprise followed the announcement.

"Yes, indeed," repeated the captain, "in sight of the Azores; and if the storm had lasted three hours longer we should have stood a good chance of being wrecked on one of them."

After a shiver of fear for what might have been, the passengers rushed on deck, whence they could clearly see the islands in the distance.

The sea was calm, the air serene and very warm, for a breeze from the south had sprung up, before which the *Touraine*, whose repairs were not yet completed, drifted towards the north, while the islands, which had appeared but for an instant, were soon lost on the horizon.

Far from feeling any uneasiness at hearing the hammers striking on the steel rods, and seeing the workmen suspended above the water repairing the rudder, the passengers found these things, which were out of the ordinary course, quite a delightful change.

In comparison with what was past their safety now seemed absolute, especially as the help of three passing steamers had been refused. So they hardly ceased expatiating on the soundness of the *Touraine*, the "good *Touraine*," as they called her, patting her sides, coated with salt, as if to thank her for behaving so well.

The openings through which the engines could be seen, and the quarter-deck, from which a view of the rudder could be obtained, had now become the chief objects for a promenade. All were interested in the progress of the repairs, which had taken so much longer than was anticipated; they danced, they listened to the monologues in which Sir Oscar excelled. . . .

But one very curious thing had happened. About a score of people, the last-named gentleman among others, had lost their watches during the storm. The Englishman was loud in his lamentations at not being able to recover his, adding in explanation that it had been given him by Prince Albert as a reward for a successful diplomatic mission.

Everyone condoled with him on the incomprehensible loss, and he was still more looked up to for the important position he had held and for the prince's favour.

Moreover, Sir Oscar, except when the wind blew, showed a delightful amiability and cordial simplicity to which everyone rendered homage, and was, besides, such an agreeable talker that they all liked to be in his company.

It became known that, with a curious leaning towards intimacy, he loved small gatherings in which the conversation was restricted to two or three, so he was often invited to take a cup of tea in the various cabins—occasions which seemed to afford him great pleasure, and on which he always showed to the best advantage.

One morning, six days after their departure from New York, the captain announced that the rudder and engines would both be finished by mid-day.

"For my part," cried Sir Oscar, "I shall be quite sorry to end this stirring yet delightful voyage! But what must Lady Tilbury, who is waiting for me at Havre, be thinking?"

Each one was asking himself this question as he thought of a relation, friend, or acquaintance waiting for him over there, uneasy at the unheard of delay of the steamer, which was accustomed to making the voyage in exactly seven days.

"They will never imagine," said Sir Oscar gaily, "that we take our ills so patiently."

"Thanks in great measure to you," observed Miss Betty.

"You are the most indulgent of Americans as well as the most beautiful," returned Sir Oscar. They all applauded the sentiment, and were convinced that the noble Englishman had some nephew or cousin to marry, since the allusion he had just made to a Lady Tilbury, whose existence no one had suspected, showed that he himself was out of the running.

Towards ten o'clock the air suddenly began to grow cold.

"Hollo!" said someone. "Is the storm going to begin again?"

"No fear," said another; "one doesn't have a fine scene like that twice running. Besides, there's very little wind, and it doesn't seem inclined to change."

But they noticed that the captain on the bridge kept his glass constantly turned towards the north. He gave orders at frequent intervals, and at last with an air of impatience went down to the engine-room to inquire if the work was finished. Being told it would occupy three good hours yet, he raged against the slowness of the workmen, and threatened to have the lazy fellows put in irons if it was not all finished by twelve o'clock precisely.

Then he quickly mounted the bridge again without replying to the questions put to him on his way, and began searching the horizon once more, always in a northerly direction.

"What is the matter with the captain?" inquired one of the passengers. "He seems very uneasy."

"Has he lost the north, that he searches for it so earnestly?" was Sir Oscar Tilbury's playful insinuation.

Those who had glasses went and fetched them, and there was soon a long row of observers scanning the horizon to discover the object of interest.

The rest chatted and walked about at their ease, enjoying the calm and the unparalleled stillness of the atmosphere.

"Do you see away there that white point glittering?" inquired one of those with the glasses.

"Yes," said his neighbour. "Whatever can it be?"

In a few minutes the point grew, and became visible to the naked eye. It quickly enlarged in every direction, showing that it was approaching them with tremendous rapidity.

"An iceberg!" cried a passenger in accents of the liveliest terror.

"An iceberg?" said another calmly. "I shouldn't be sorry to see that nearer. I believe we are going to pass quite close to it."

"We are lost!" said the first speaker. "Look what an enormous mass is bearing down upon us. It is more than a mile in width. I have often seen these fields of ice, detached from the polar seas, which the currents bring into our latitudes. Nothing can resist them, and if we cannot manage to get out of the way——"

The prophet of evil had no time to finish his explanation, for the captain, in a voice of thunder, ordered the boats to be manned, the buoys and lifebelts to be distributed, and preparation made for any contingency.

The effect was overwhelming. Men and women rushed pell-mell upon the lifebelts, which some of the sailors were distributing, while others were uncovering the boats, executing the captain's orders with marvellous rapidity.

The most touching scenes were witnessed; members of the same family clung closely to each other, that they might die together; others, taking refuge in their cabins, shut their eyes, in order not to see death approaching. Betty begged Victoria to forgive her for having dragged her into this fatal adventure. As for Sir Oscar Tilbury, he was—no one knew where—occupied in putting his private papers in order.

The cold became more intense. The iceberg, which drew nearer every moment, had assumed fantastic proportions, and its shadow covered the sea for a great distance; it looked like a white island, studded with diamonds, bristling with sharp mountain peaks, and hollowed into great cavities, the ruggedness of which reflected the sun's rays blindingly. Now the gigantic field of ice was within two miles, its outline still growing more formidable and menacing. But, alas! like a paralytic, whose powerless members are incapable of flight, the *Touraine* resignedly offered her flank to the enemy.

The iceberg was not more than a mile away.

All the passengers were now kneeling, and tremblingly received the benediction of a priest and of a clergyman, who passed from one scattered group to another, giving absolution and heavenly consolation. There were no longer any cries heard. A stupefied silence had settled upon all, as with startled eyes fixed on the great white monster, drawing ever nearer, they realised that but a few moments could pass before the tranquil waves closed over their heads.

But one last and almost ludicrous resource remained for the captain. With extraordinary coolness he had the little brass cannon in the bows loaded, and himself directed it against the iceberg; he applied the match and a report sounded, of which the ice wall, now close at hand, sent back disdainfully the useless and pitiable echo.

It was over!

"*De Profundis*," began the priest, extending his hands over the prostrate crowd. A horrible sound, prolonged and sonorous as the discharge of a hundred pieces of artillery, was heard. There was a sensation as of the boat being pulverised and swallowed up in the depths of the ocean ; then more fearful shocks and more still, seemingly without end.

"Saved !" cried the captain from the stern, where he was standing. And at the word of hope heads were raised again.

They were indeed saved !

The immense field of ice, worn away, thawed, streaked with fissures and crevices by the warmth of the temperate latitudes, was broken by the concussion into thousands of small pieces, with which the *Touraine* was soon surrounded, remaining unmoved in the midst of their powerless clashing.

While this was still going on the captain was informed that steam was up, the engines put to rights, and the rudder repaired. He immediately gave the steersman the route, and seizing the lever which transmitted his orders electrically to the engineers, turned it on the brass dial till it rested on the words "Full speed."

Then the hissing steam took up its work once more, the screws set their great fins in motion, and the boat, urged forward, arrayed itself afresh in its double train of foam.

Another ovation had to be given to the captain, who had a second time saved so many precious lives. Sir Oscar had no more camellias, but as the sea was quite calm his loquacity was ready, and he improvised a new harangue, as full and convincing as the first, than which it had no less success.

At length, after so many vicissitudes, they arrived off Havre at nine o'clock in the morning, exactly fifteen days and three hours after leaving New York. Those on land had heard of the arrival of the *Touraine* from the semaphores at Ouessant and Barfleur, in sight of which they had passed, so the jetties were black with a swarming crowd of people who, after their long period of anxiety, watched the superb steamer approach in all her tranquil majesty.

When she was in the channel interminable and frantic shouts arose, which were answered by the joyful cries of the passengers, enchanted at being in shelter at last from billows and icebergs.

Then each rushed for his smaller baggage and prepared to land.

"I must find Sir Oscar and thank him for all his care of me," said Betty to Victoria.

But it was impossible in the midst of the general rush to get near him.

ARRIVAL AT HAVRE

"Never mind," said Betty resignedly, "I can thank him in Paris, since he has promised to come and see me there."

And she and Victoria, their bags in their hands, joined the file who were crossing the movable bridge and disembarked ; but as she stepped on the quay, catching sight of one of the lookers-on who had come to watch the arrival of the boat, Betty fell back into the arms of Victoria—which were full enough already —and a cry escaped her lips—a cry of but two words, but expressing more profound stupefaction than any longer phrase—"William Keniss !"

GOSSIP OF THE HOUR
By CORNELIUS WRINKLE

The Great Moguls Champion Class

WHAT a commotion I have raised, to be sure, over a simple suggestion that the Great Moguls should in future be pitted against each other. I am beginning

to think there must be a deal more in the suggestion than I imagined, for ever since, one after another, heads have popped up from the other side of the hedge claiming to have said that very same thing before. First it was Mr. Heginbottom, now it is Mr. Beckton in the *Philatelic Record*, and I understand my old friend Mr. Oldfield is also a claimant.

What does it all mean, this haste to father a simple suggestion of a harmless sort of body like myself? There must be more in it than meets the eye. If the idea has been kicking about in this way for so long, why has it not fruited? Chap at my elbow says, "Don't you know, Wrinkle, that one speaker after another may give expression to the same thoughts and only send the audiences to sleep, whereas another fellow may, with the same ideas, electrify his audience, and get them all on their hind legs, waving their handkerchiefs and cheering like one o'clock?" Ah ! Humph ! Is that so?

The Champion Class—a Certainty

However, I don't know that it matters a button who trotted out the suggestion in the hazy past, so long as it be acted upon at last. And since so much fuss has been made over the business, not only approving of the idea of a champion class, but even squabbling over the very parentage of the idea, it seems to me to have taken its place as one of those things that are no longer

THE STAMP KING

By G. DE BEAUREGARD AND H. DE GORSSE

Translated from the French by EDITH C. PHILLIPS

"HOW CAME YOU HERE?" REPEATED THE YOUNG LADY

CHAPTER IV

*Wherein William explains how being late caused
him to arrive the earlier*

THE incomprehensible and unprecedented delay of
the *Touraine* had made a great stir all over the
world, and given rise to a thousand suppositions,
each more pessimistic than the last, up to the very
moment when the steamer was signalled at Ouessant.

At first a collision was spoken of; then the idea grew
that she had struck upon a rock, and that passengers
and cargo were lost in the mysterious depths of the
ocean; later (and, as we know, this is what very nearly
happened), that she had met with one of those gigantic
icebergs which, at the approach of spring, detach themselves from the great polar beds and descend towards
the south with an awful speed which nothing can resist.

So it is needless to say with what joy the crowd had
hurried towards the jetty and landing-stage, to greet
the *Touraine* with frantic cheers, as soon as it was
noised abroad that the boat was in sight, and only
awaiting high tide to enter the dock.

The curious spectators were massed on the jetty;
the relations and friends of the passengers on the
landing-place. Of these latter particularly there was
a very large gathering.

Scarcely did a passenger set foot on shore before he
was surrounded by a group of people, who pressed
round him, embraced him, and with all sorts of inco-
herent and foolish exclamations testified their delight
at seeing once more the beloved one whom they had
feared was lost to them for ever.

But Miss Betty never expected anyone to meet her,

so it took her some time to recover from the stupefaction into which she was thrown on beholding William
Keniss. Victoria was no less surprised than her
mistress, and remained rooted to the spot staring at
John, hardly able to believe it could really be he.

"You here!" cried Betty to William at last, the
first moment of stupor over.

"Does it seem so very marvellous?" said he.

"Well," she said, "one hardly expects the instant
one lands in France to meet a person whom one
supposed to be still in America. How can it have
happened?"

"Can you not guess?"

The girl reflected for a few moments.

"I am so astonished," she began again. "I have
hardly realised yet that the *Touraine*, being eight days
late, must have been passed on the way by the next
steamer that left New York. The captain told us we
should find the *Gascogne* at Havre, though we ought
to have arrived long before her. No doubt you came
by that?"

"No, Miss Scott! No. I didn't come by the
Gascogne."

"Anyhow," said the girl, laughing, "you didn't
swim all the way from America?"

"Out of the question."

"Then—— I fail to comprehend."

William laughed at her expression of comic ignorance.

John affected an air of importance with Victoria,
who was no less surprised and much more delighted
at meeting her old friend again.

It was arranged they should breakfast at the Hotel
Frascati while waiting the departure of the Paris ex-

press ; and while Victoria remained with John to look after her mistress's luggage, William and Betty walked towards the hotel where the Stamp King had been staying since his arrival at Havre.

The girl demanded to be immediately enlightened on the subject of her companion's voyage, but he begged she would recount her adventures first, which she did with the best grace, without forgetting any of the terrors she had gone through, and at the end expressing once more her regret that the bustle of leaving the boat had given her no chance of seeing the gallant Sir Oscar again, to thank him for all his kind attentions.

It was a beautiful sunny morning in May, and the air was charged with a thousand scents of spring. Miss Betty had turned her veil up on to her hat, and for the first time perhaps, for he had no such clear impression of it before, William perceived how very pretty she was, with her clear blue eyes, in which a little part of the heavens seemed to lurk, and her hair so light and fine that the straying locks on her forehead and neck waved in the slight caressing breeze.

"I have been the one to talk ever since we met," she said.

"You do not expect me to complain of that?"

"I have given you my history. Now it is your turn."

"Oh, I cannot conceal from you, Miss Betty, that my journey was much less interesting than the one you have just told me about. The boat I came by had no adventures. We didn't meet with any icebergs——"

"Never mind. Tell me about your crossing all the same."

"Willingly. It will not take me long."

And still walking by her side William Keniss, not without appearing a little embarrassed now and again, spoke as follows :—

"On the night of the 27th of April, when I left the Philatelic Club, where we had passed such a charming evening, in the course of which you had been nominated a member of our Society, I returned home, and there I learnt that it was absolutely necessary that I should set out for Paris immediately, being called by important business——"

"Business?"

"Business, which the least delay might compromise. In a few minutes I was dressed—for I had gone to bed —had jumped, accompanied by John, into the first carriage that passed, and was on the quay. Unfortunately I only arrived in time to witness the departure of the *Touraine*, by which I had hoped to sail, and to see her being slowly swallowed up in the morning mist. I was, as you may imagine, intensely annoyed, and I was just going back to Hudson Street when by an unexpected chance I learnt from a sailor at the port that the *Campania* would weigh anchor three hours later for Liverpool.

"In spite of its being out of my way to come through England I found that I should save time, as the next direct liner, which was, I believe, the *Gascogne*, would not leave for Havre for another week. So I resolved to come by the *Campania*, and having booked my cabin and John's I patiently awaited her departure in a bar close by.

"There I was, then, on board the *Campania*. But after the exciting account you have given me of your passage I need not bother you with mine, in which there was not one notable incident. We only had, like you, a very violent tempest——"

"The same one, of course."

"And, like you on the *Touraine*, we on the *Campania* also believed that our last hour had come ; but you see it hadn't. We even arrived at Liverpool very little behind time.

"What is there more to tell you? From Liverpool the train took me to London in a few hours, and after spending an evening there, and a night—to— to rest——"

"To rest?"

"The next day I came by another train to Dover, whence I crossed straight to Calais by one of the steamers of the South Eastern Railway. Everything up to this time had passed satisfactorily."

"And now, I suppose, I am going to hear something terrible."

"Nay, though it was terrible for me at the time ; for I was no sooner in the express on my way to Paris than I read in the *Temps* an article on the delay of the *Touraine*. You can judge of my uneasiness, knowing you were on board——"

"Stop!" cried Miss Betty, distrustful in a moment. "How could you know that?"

"From your coachman ; yes, your coachman whom I met at the landing-stage," replied William with embarrassment, "he was returning from taking you to the *Touraine*."

"I am charmed," returned Betty, rendered sceptical by his evident confusion, "that this providential meeting should have made you conversant with my acts and doings. Well, you had just learned that the *Touraine* had not arrived in France. After that?"

"No other considerations could be taken into account from that moment. Knowing you to be in danger it was impossible to give any attention to the business which had called me to Europe, so instead of continuing my journey to Paris I resolved to go immediately to Havre, to be on the spot to hear the very first tidings."

"Really, how very good of you !"

"You see it is the very fact of my having left New York after you that caused you to find me here when you landed just now. I awaited your arrival hour after hour for three days with the greatest anxiety."

"Thank you !" said Betty, offering him her hand ; "thank you very much for your kind interest."

"Oh, don't thank me !" said he. "It is perfectly natural that I should take an interest in you."

The conversation had hardly reached this point when William and Betty arrived at Frascati's. The clock struck eleven as they entered the hotel vestibule. John and Victoria had arrived several minutes before. Seated on a terrace overlooking the sea they were carrying on an animated conversation, and to judge by the irritated face of the one and the discomfited air of the other, one would have said their marriage, from which, as we know, John hung back a little, was under discussion. But it was not that at all. Not that Victoria had lost sight of that matter, but that at the present moment she had other fish—or, rather, *an* other fish—to fry, and that fish was the unlucky John.

"Yes," cried she, "I will never forgive you for having been and told your master we were going to Paris, the very morning I came to let you know of Miss Betty's sudden determination——"

"But, Victoria——"

"There's no but about it ! Miss Betty will be furious with me when she knows it's my fault that Mr. Keniss is in France to try and prevent her getting that stamp she wants so badly."

"Will she really?"

"Will she? Of course she will ! Furious, I tell you, furious ! And not without reason. Oh, won't I hold my tongue another time !"

"At any rate it wasn't I who made you speak."

"That's the finishing touch ! You'll see, Master John, if I won't——"

And Victoria, in spite of her habitually phlegmatic disposition, was about to hurl some terrible menace at John, when the voices of William and Betty were heard as they entered the hotel.

The latter asked the manager for a room, and begged her companion to excuse her for a few minutes while she went to arrange her toilet.

"I will wait for you in the restaurant," he replied, "and make the best use of the time by arranging the menu for our breakfast."

THE STAMP KING

By G. DE BEAUREGARD AND H. DE GORSSE

Translated from the French by EDITH C. PHILLIPS

CHAPTER IV (*continued*)

Wherein William explains how being late caused him to arrive the earlier

"WOULD you also be good enough," said Betty, seeing a telephone in one corner of the hall, "to telephone to Paris for me, to the Hotel Bristol, and ask them to reserve a good room, for I quite forgot to telegraph just now?"

"Don't trouble yourself about anything," replied William, "I will see to it."

Betty went up to her room, and William profited by her absence to telephone to the Hotel Bristol, then to settle his own account at Frascati's, including the charge for the telephone and the breakfast he was about to have with his young friend, and for the room she was now occupying. Then he entered the restaurant and waited for her.

Miss Betty returned in a few minutes, and the two sat down to table. They talked of one thing and another till suddenly the girl, looking full into the face of her companion, said—

"My good friend, I am going to be very impertinent, but I want to know this instant what the business was that brought you to Paris."

William hesitated a moment, utterly taken aback by the unexpected question, but, reflecting that he would have to confess sooner or later, he returned—

"Well, when I saw, the last time we were together in New York, the mood in which you left the Philatelic Club I was very uneasy. After I returned home I could not shake off the presentiment that had taken hold of me, and after a good deal of reflection I concluded you meant to start for Paris."

"Indeed!"

"I immediately resolved to do the same myself; and after consulting the time-tables, seeing the day breaking, I rushed down to the landing-stage without luggage or any kind of preparation, just as I was. Unfortunately it was a long way from Hudson Street, where I live, and I only arrived in time to see the departure of the *Touraine*."

"But what did you want with me to make you in such a hurry?"

"I wished to dissuade you from undertaking a journey which seemed to me as unreasonable as it was useless."

"And why so, if you please?"

"Because this stamp, in pursuit of which you are running——"

"How do you know I am?"

William smiled as he returned—

"I know too well your tenacity, as well as your natural desire to conquer, to have any doubt about your object. You wish to find the second and, as I believed, undiscoverable specimen of the Maharajah's stamp. But since I was not able to prevent your departure, I shall at least try to render your search of no avail by finding and taking possession of the stamp myself, that my collection may never be equalled by any other."

"Well, really," said Betty, with a shade of annoyance, "that is more frank than kind."

"Pray do not condemn me so quickly. It is the philatelist who has just spoken. But in addition to the philatelist there is the true man and friend, who will follow you anywhere to protect you, to keep far from you all the annoyances and difficulties of what

will, no doubt, be a long journey; to be, in short, always at your service, save in that one respect."

"A duel then?"

"A duel, as you say, Miss Scott; but a courteous duel in which nothing shall be done by the one to hurt the other, and in which your adversary's one effort shall be to keep danger far from you."

Miss Betty could not do otherwise than accept the explanation, and smiling as she extended her little hand to William, she said—

"My dear Mr. Keniss, I am as much flattered at having you for an adversary as I am fortunate in having you for a companion. I hope I shall not prove myself unworthy of such a rival."

Then, breakfast being finished, they went down to the station, after William had excused himself eloquently for defraying all the expenses by representing to Betty that, as he was the first to land in France, he had the right to receive her on her arrival and do the honours.

He even arranged for a private compartment for her from Havre to Paris, and managed, as we shall see presently, that she should never once open her purse before arriving at the Hotel Bristol.

*　　　*　　　*　　　*

But now we must go back a little.

William Keniss, in giving an account of his journey, had omitted only one episode, but that one as full of importance as it was of interest.

The omission, moreover, had not been altogether involuntary, for as there was nothing to prevent him slurring over a circumstance which he preferred to keep to himself, the Stamp King had resolved to take this course; and the reason for his silence will be evident when we state that he had been on the track of the famous stamp.

This is what had happened.

On landing at Liverpool he and John had immediately taken the express for London, on their way to Dover, Calais, and Paris.

Anxious to learn the news, of which he had been deprived for a week, William bought the latest edition of the *Times*, the great English daily paper, supposed to be the most serious and best-informed of all in the United Kingdom. He read on, absorbed, never once looking at the country through which the train ran at full speed. Paying no heed to the route he did not so much as glance at Crewe, Stafford, Lichfield, Rugby, and only raised his head when the train thundered into the station at Northampton. By this time he thought he had perused the whole paper. But who can flatter himself with this idea when he has the *Times* in his hands?

As there remained a good hour and a half before arriving in London, William returned to his paper, and his eye was caught by an article he had missed before, headed "An Odyssey." Captivated by the mysterious title he settled himself comfortably and began reading again.

"Our readers have been kept informed of the troubles which have disintegrated the State of Brahmapootra, one of the few Indian territories still independent, and situated in the Himalayas. The *dénouement* of this tragedy still remains to be told. The Maharajah Badunabad——"

William felt his heart leap with emotion. What was this? A tragedy which concerned the Maharajah of Brahmapootra! The probable possessor of the second specimen of the gilt stamp. We can imagine with what avidity he continued reading.

"The Maharajah Badunabad," continued the article, "to whom the Viceroy had given a suite of bedroom furniture in pitch-pine, to make him favourable to the English, and cause him to sign a commercial treaty, ruinous to Brahmapootra, having had the imprudence to exhibit this present to one of his nephews, the latter resolved to become the possessor of it. Whence arose conspiracy, riot, rebellion, civil war, fomented by the young prince, to whom the very natural idea had occurred that he might as well take possession of the throne as well as the pitch-pine furniture.

"The Maharajah was compelled to fortify himself in his capital, Son-Po. But his subjects, weary of his

WILLIAM BOUGHT THE "TIMES"

abominable despotism, his exactions, and cruelties, thought a change of dynasty could hardly be for the worse, and delivered Son-Po to the usurper. So, while the latter made a triumphal entry into the city, Badunabad was obliged to flee, with his Vizier, Satrakas, and his Grand Talapoin, Trogustul. He profited by the occasion to take away with him the public treasure, consisting of precious stones and silver coins, worth, perhaps, as much as fifteen millions of gold mohurs, loaded on three elephants.

"The usurper would have been only too glad to let him go to get rid of him, but he had no intention of giving up the rupees. A troop of horsemen was sent on the track of the fugitives, who, when they saw they would otherwise be taken, abandoned the elephants and their precious burden.

"The Vizier and the Grand Talapoin, having now a great desire to remain in favour with the new ruler, offered to deliver up Badunabad, hoping to gain credit by their treason. But hearing their reward would be hanging, they speedily decamped, and from that moment showed unswerving fidelity to their original master. The three, arriving on English territory, hastened to implore the protection of British laws, which was given them in larger measure than they wished, for they were immediately embarked for England with a promise of an enormous pension. They protested, but the Government of her gracious Majesty, always anxious to maintain order in the world, insisted no less on making sure of them.

"The Maharajah and his two companions have just arrived in London, and are settled in a sumptuous mansion, furnished by Goole, Truxham, and Co., Limited (who had received telegraphic orders to this effect), in perfect taste and with oriental magnificence. The importance of this event will be patent to all. In fact, a detachment of British troops has already taken

Son-Po by assault, in order to repress the disturbance and protect those of our countrymen who are established there."

William could not conceal his joy on reading this news.

"So," said he, "another territory pilfered for the Queen. I ought to be able to profit by this——"

At this moment they arrived at Euston.

"We go straight to Charing Cross, I suppose, sir?" said John.

"No, indeed," said William. "I must see Badunabad first."

John shrugged his shoulders at the outlandish name.

"Of course," said William, laughing, "you haven't read the *Times*. Know then that the Maharajah of Brahmapootra, Badunabad himself, is in London, with his Vizier and his Grand Talapoin."

"Oh, the deuce!" ejaculated John, taken aback by the enumeration of all these titles.

"Don't you understand now?" said William. "The second copy of my stamp is perhaps in London. In any case I shall get all the information possible concerning it, since I am within reach of him who issued it."

The young American hailed a cab and, accompanied by his faithful valet, drove at such a pace to Goole, Truxham, and Co., Limited, in Cheapside, that they hardly had time to notice on the way the trees of Russell Square or the old houses in Holborn. Less than half an hour after leaving the station they reached Cheapside, and the reeking horse stopped short before an immense edifice, the windows of whose four stories shone like one enormous mirror in the rays of the setting sun.

A doorkeeper in white gloves and gold lacings came forward immediately.

"The offices are still open?" asked William anxiously.

"Yes, sir. Which department do you wish?"

William Keniss did not reply for a moment, being occupied in contemplating the dazzling face of the establishment, on which blazed, in letters two yards high, the names, "Goole" and "Truxham," and in smaller characters the many specialities of the house.

In this way one learnt, without even going inside, that they undertook pretty well anything: the buying and selling of estates, money lending and investing, furnishing novelties from Paris, libraries, furniture, carriages, linen, eatables, complete banquets, clothes, and every imaginable thing, whether necessaries, comforts, or luxuries. They supplied servants, horses, rooms, clerks, and secretaries, theatre and railway tickets; and organised trips and entertainments. In case of need they would have arranged marriages and procured friends.

"I wish to learn where the Maharajah of Brahmapootra is staying," said William at length.

"First floor, door No. 34."

John remained in the cab while William passed through a vestibule amidst a buzz of customers and employés, and mounted a staircase carpeted in red and lighted with huge electric globes. Each department had its own special place and was numbered, so that it could easily be found; and William soon arrived at No. 34.

"I am told," said he, "that I can learn here the address of the Maharajah of Brahmapootra."

"You are a creditor, sir, I suppose?" said the clerk.

"A creditor!" said William in astonishment. "Certainly not."

"Oh, all right, then."

And the clerk, without one unnecessary word, wrote a few lines on a card, which he gave to his client, who read, "H. E. Badunabad, Maharajah of Brahmapootra, Himalaya Villa, Park Lane, corner of Green Street."

William, having learnt all he needed, descended the

stairs, saying to himself, "What in the world made him ask me if I was a creditor?" Then, delighted at having attained his object so easily, he returned to the cab, which resumed its way, a little less rapidly than at first though, on account of the crowded state of the streets, which gives travellers a good opportunity for studying the various objects of interest which they pass.

These were, first, St. Paul's, the cathedral of London; then Ludgate Hill, the railway bridge, the two obelisks in Ludgate Circus, Fleet Street, with its numberless offices and its busy crowds. They also saw the Temple, and noticed on their right as they gained the Strand the Law Courts, with their battlements and Gothic turrets; St. Clement's and St. Mary's, two churches encamped in the middle of the street like two great kiosks; the Gaiety, the Lyceum,

the Vaudeville, Charing Cross Station, grand and monumental, with its curious campanile in the entrance court.

"This is where we start from for France—if we do start," said William to John.

The cab next crossed Trafalgar Square, passing by the great column on which is perched Admiral Nelson, the conqueror of the French fleet, who died in the very moment of victory. Leaving on their right the statue of George III. they drove along Pall Mall, the street of Clubs, and up Waterloo Place, at the bottom of which is the Duke of York on another column.

At length, after passing the trees of the Green Park in Piccadilly, the fashionable street of London, they turned to the right into Park Lane, and stopped before the dwelling of the Indian prince.

(To be continued.)

SPECIAL CORRESPONDENCE

News from Mysore

BANGALORE, *4th February*, 1905.

Stamp Collecting in India: White Ants

STAMP collecting in India is a very different thing from the same hobby at home. Here we have all sorts of disadvantages which are unknown in England: for instance, white ants may eat your collection; they think nothing of devouring a tennis racquet, a pair of brown boots, and a book or two in the course of forty-eight hours. A friend of mine once thought of chaining one up in his bedroom as a sort of watch dog. My friend is not quite truthful at times, and his excuse for not keeping that particular white ant was that it had eaten the chain. The white ant isn't really an ant at all, and it isn't white, but that is a mere detail, and the original name has stuck to it. It is the most destructive creature imaginable, and all stamps have to be carefully put away in a metal box, otherwise they are not safe. One frequently finds Indian stamps with small holes, particularly round the edge. These holes are caused by white ants, and if the stamps were valuable great loss would be the result.

Moisture: Another Enemy

Another disadvantage out here is the damp. During the monsoons, which bring—or ought to bring—the rain twice a year (they often fail, and then there is a famine), the amount of moisture in the air is very great, and stamps with gum adhere tightly to a page and frequently become stained or mildewed. To guard against damp we use air-tight metal boxes, but it is sometimes advisable not to look at one's stamps at all if the monsoon season is a very wet one.

No Stamp Dealers in India

Another and a very great drawback is that there are practically no dealers. You cannot wander into a shop and buy a shilling packet, or look through some approval sheets, as you can in England, and there are none of those nice little stationers' shops where sheets of stamps appear in the window.

Most Europeans in India Collect Stamps

On the other hand, we have certain advantages, for some of the Native Indian stamps, and those of Siam, the Straits Settlements, Hong Kong, and Ceylon, are much more common in India than they are at home; and another advantage is that the majority of Europeans collect stamps, and it is not an unusual thing to travel in a railway carriage and find your fellow passengers are just as keen as yourself. I have had many a long stamp chat with other passengers during the tedious thirty-six hours' journey, through the heat

of the Deccan, from Bombay to Bangalore; but if one commenced to talk "stamps" to the first man in a railway carriage at home he would think you were mad.

Indians are not British Colonials

It is a curious thing that so many collectors and even writers, who really ought to know better, will insist upon calling Indian stamps "British Colonials." India is very far indeed from being a colony; it is, in fact, one of the largest empires in the world, and is an integral part of the British Empire, but is no relation to a colony. What term should therefore be used for Indian stamps, since "Colonials" is utterly wrong? The best way out of the difficulty is to drop the word "Colonials" entirely, and use—for all stamps issued by any unit of the British Empire—the expression "Empire stamps," or "Empires," or "British Empires" (but please do not abbreviate into "Brempires"). This term would conveniently cover Protectorates and Native States, Dominions, Commonwealths and Crown Colonies, and States like Sarawak, which are protected by a defensive alliance, and which will be equally applicable in the future to the Federal States of South Africa, of Australia, of the West Indies, and of the Malay Peninsula, as it is at the present time for Seychelles and Natal.

To give an instance of my meaning, one frequently meets a collector who says, "I take only Colonials," yet nine-tenths of such people will show you page after page of Indian stamps, and will become very "fractious" indeed if told that they are not Colonials.

Another remarkable fact in connection with Indian stamps is that they are beloved by the schoolboy, and by the specialist, but are unpopular among ordinary collectors.

Indian Native States Stamps

The reason is fairly clear, however. In the first place, the issues of some of the Native States are among the most extraordinarily hideous productions in the world, and everybody knows there is a particular charm about certain things if they are only ugly *enough;* hence a dozen or so specimens from Datia, Dhar, Kishengarh, Bundi, etc., figure in every beginner's collection. As he gets older and more experienced he finds that many of these apparently rare stamps are either extremely common or vary so enormously that it is useless to go on with them: this condition lasts until experience has taught him that these stamps are vastly interesting and are, with of course a few exceptions (there are black sheep in every fold), a very respectable lot.

THE STAMP KING

By G. DE BEAUREGARD AND H. DE GORSSE

Translated from the French by EDITH C. PHILLIPS

THREE TALL FELLOWS WERE PLAYING AN ABSORBING GAME

CHAPTER V

Showing how, if money does not make happiness,
the want of it often causes misery

IT was a kind of palace, with a little flower garden in front and a magnificent porch. The double row of windows looked out on Hyde Park, and on the roof, which was surrounded by a balustrade, statues, placed at intervals, showed in elegant and graceful silhouettes.

"Come with me," said William, and followed by John he arrived at the main entrance and the porter's room. And here their astonishment began.

Through the glass partition they saw the interior of the room, where three tall fellows with blonde moustaches and distinctly English features, dressed in Hindoo garments and wearing silk turbans, were seated round a table playing an absorbing game with dirty cards. They were smoking enormous pipes, and were surrounded with bottles of ale and pewter pots, which they filled and emptied by turn with great gusto.

"These Hindoos are pretty well acclimatised already," said William. "They certainly belong to Badunabad's household." And he tapped on the pane.

"Come in," cried one of the players, without even turning his head.

"Does the Maharajah live here?" asked William, entering.

"Yes, but not for long."

At this retort, given in English with a thoroughly British accent, the three Hindoos burst out laughing, which completed the discomfiture of the visitor. However, he continued—

"Can I have a moment's interview with him?"

"If it's to demand money, certainly not," returned the individual who had already spoken.

"It is rather to offer him some," said William.

"Is it possible? In that case you arrive in the nick of time."

The behaviour of these three men seemed more and more strange to the young American, but he reflected that Indian ways might differ from ours, and that liberty in the Himalayas must be much greater than one generally imagined.

"Now, what do you want with the old chap?" said the first player, throwing down his cards after emptying a pint pot. "You can tell me, for I am the Lord Chamberlain of the palace."

At these words the hilarity of the three companions knew no bounds. They roared with laughter and shouted so loud that William was stupefied, and forced to wait till they were pleased to explain themselves more clearly than by these obscure and unseemly remarks.

"I," said another, "am the Commander of the Guard."

"And I," added the third, "am the Treasurer, which is indeed a sinecure!"

And they laughed louder than ever, leaving William in doubt as to whether they were mocking at him or at the master of the house.

"After all——" he began.

"I perceive, sir," interrupted the Lord Chamberlain of the palace, taking off his turban to wipe his eyes, which the excess of his merriment had filled with tears, "that you are not acquainted with the etiquette and the orders of his Highness——"

Interrupting himself with another laugh, he regained his composure and continued—

"Listen. The Maharajah fled in the first place with

the cash, but they recovered that, and he arrived on English territory without a farthing. The Government had promised him a superb pension, and on the strength of that promise he telegraphed to Goole, Truxham, and Co. to furnish this house for him in the style he was accustomed to, and to provide him with a sufficient following. We, whom you see here, are employed by the agency——"

"Indeed!" cried William. "Then you did not come to Europe with the prince?"

"Oh, dear, no! I am a Cockney of the Cockneys, born in Whitechapel; the Commander of the Guard, who is here before you, is a Birmingham man, and the Treasurer, also present, is a native of Ramsgate."

The three false Hindoos laughed again, and William, had his thoughts not been occupied with another matter, could hardly have resisted following their example. However, thinking it as well to learn all he could, he asked—

"But how about the costume?"

"Oh, they've dressed us up in this trumpery to remind our patron of his native land," said the Treasurer.

"His Highness," said William, with the utmost gravity, "brought some high functionaries over with him, if I am to believe the account in the newspapers."

"Oh, yes, you do well to mention them," chuckled the Commander of the Guard. "A sort of Vizier, who was, it seems, his minister over there, and his Grand Talapoin. Do you happen to know what a Talapoin is? It's a priest of Buddha. He was a very important personage in the kingdom of Brahmapootra."

"But from the accounts of travellers, as also from the situation and the very name of this kingdom, I understood they worshipped Brahma," said William.

"Yes, but Badunabad became a Buddhist to ingratiate himself with the Chinese, because he hoped for their support against the English. You see how much good it did him!"

"Well grounded convictions, certainly," said William, smiling.

"Wait till I tell you the rest," continued the Lord Chamberlain of the palace. "By the time their lordships arrived in London the house was ready, all the sham Hindoos at their posts, and they had nothing to do but to instal themselves here. Only—no pension. The Government, who no longer feared them, began to reflect. Bills arrived; we other dignitaries demanded our wages, but there's not a penny to be had. And with all that, a heap of salaams to make whenever one approaches them. The old fool of a Maharajah even threatened to have us impaled, if you'll believe me, because we refused to throw ourselves on our faces on the ground in his presence. We've had the greatest difficulty in convincing him that the Thames isn't the Brahmapootra. And they quarrel the whole time, he and his two rascals; each blames the other for their misfortunes, and they almost come to blows!"

As if in support of the declaration, a sound of hasty footsteps and overturned furniture was heard overhead.

"Do you hear them?" said the Treasurer. "They are discussing the affairs of the State."

This time even John joined in the burst of laughter, but William, who could not forget his object, soon returned to it.

"In any case," he said, "I wish to speak to the Maharajah. Can you manage it for me?"

"Oh, oh!" returned the Lord Chamberlain. "His Highness cannot be approached in this fashion. You must make formal request for an audience, which I will submit to the Vizier; he will submit it to the

Grand Talapoin, and the Grand Talapoin to the Maharajah, and if you are not a creditor, perhaps in six weeks' time——"

"Come, come," said William good-humouredly; "thanks to your good offices, I am sure in six minutes ——" And he slipped a sovereign into the hand of each of the dignitaries. The effect was instantaneous. While the Treasurer thanked him effusively the Lord Chamberlain rushed to the speaking-tube which communicated with the apartments above.

"Noble and powerful lord," shouted he, "there is someone here who solicits the inestimable honour of being admitted into the dazzling presence of his most magnanimous and most illustrious Highness."

Then, while his audience bit their lips to keep in their laughter, he put his ear to the tube and awaited the response.

"The Vizier," said he, "wishes to know if you are not an American."

"Why, yes," said William, still more astonished.

"Yes, noble and powerful lord," cried the Lord Chamberlain of the palace into the tube, "he who humbly solicits this favour is an American."

After listening again he added, addressing William, who had not yet recovered from the perspicacity of the invisible dignitary—

"The Vizier wishes still further to know if you are come in pursuit of an object of value."

"Yes, indeed."

The response to this came at once, and was to the effect that the visitor, or visitors, were to be immediately shown upstairs.

The Commander of the Guard, who was charged with the introduction of strangers, preceded William and John up the grand staircase, embellished with rich oriental colouring, which led to the first floor.

"They mean to try and palm some old rubbish on to you," he said as they went up. "Ever since they came here they've done nothing but look up second-hand dealers to sell the jewels they brought with them, and even their clothes. They've had nothing but their finery to bring them in any money. They have even tried to dispose of the furniture and tapestries, but we have an eye on them, and if we can't defend the entrance we can the exit. The agency has lost enough already."

William, who imagined that his guide said this with a purpose, and that he perhaps suspected him of wishing to take away some of the furniture, answered nothing, but continued on his way. When they reached the first landing, bordered with chased bronze balusters and with hundreds of rare plants arranged like a tapestry of foliage, the Commander of the Guard leaned over the staircase and called out to his companions below—

"Hi, there! don't meddle with my cards. I had a quint major!"

Then, turning to William again, he said, "I forgot to ask your name, and it's difficult to announce you without it."

"William Keniss, of New York."

"Very good."

On each side of the great door which led to the state rooms was a Scotchman, disguised in Brahmapootra garments, lounging on a stool and yawning enough to dislocate his jaws. One of the two, on seeing the new arrivals, rose, opened a folding door, and fell sleepily on his seat again.

"These are no better paid than we are, you see," said the Commander of the Guard. "All the same," added he, "if you want to make a good bargain play some pretty tricks when you see the good man. Salaam humbly; go down on your knees if you've a mind to, and give him plenty of titles. You'll get your trinket much cheaper."

(To be continued.)

THE STAMP KING

By G. DE BEAUREGARD *and* H. DE GORSSE

Translated from the French by EDITH C. PHILLIPS

WILLIAM CONTENTED HIMSELF WITH
A LOW BOW

CHAPTER V (*continued*)

*Showing how, if money does not make happiness,
the want of it often causes misery*

THEY had arrived at the door of the room called the Throne Room, where the Prince received.

The Commander of the Guard opened it, and with a deep reverence called out—

"The very humble and very suppliant servant of his most colossal Highness, Mr. William Keniss of New York."

This accomplished, and William, followed by John, having entered the room, he shut the door and ran to his interrupted piquet.

The spectacle of which the young American was now a witness was not of a nature to diminish his astonishment. The Throne Room, lighted by three windows looking on Hyde Park, was plunged in the early shadows of the closing day. But everything could still be clearly seen on account of its western aspect. Opposite the windows a large arm-chair was established under a canopy of crimson brocade, the floor being covered with a very fine Persian carpet. On the walls were trophies of arms and tapestries, embroidered in gold, which gave to the apartment an air of incomparable magnificence. From the platform on which the throne was placed rose two candelabra, delicately sculptured, filled with candles, and covered with lustres of great price.

But what William noticed first was the group of the three exiles.

Badunabad was seated in the arm-chair, which served for a throne, having on his right Trogustul, the Grand Talapoin, and on his left Satrakas, the Grand Vizier. The latter were standing. All three strove to maintain the most majestic and imposing demeanour. Not only had they, in the fullest sense of the term, what is generally known as a most venerable appearance, with all the attributes thereof—beards white and long, aquiline noses, profound looks, and royal physiognomies—but they were robed in splendid costumes, laced, embroidered, ornamented, with yataghans in their silk sashes, and turbans fringed with precious stones, the materials for which seemed to require the whole of Golconda.

William took a few steps, hesitating as to the correct thing to do, but reflecting that it was not necessary for a free citizen of America to hide his forehead in the dust, which was certainly sufficiently abundant on the carpet, he advanced and contented himself with a low bow, immediately imitated by John, who kept respectfully in the background.

"Are you the American?" inquired Badunabad in a grave voice.

"Yes, highest and most extraordinary lord," replied the young man, wishing at least to be polite.

"You see, miserable man!" groaned the dethroned sovereign, turning towards the Grand Talapoin.

"I beg that you will not insult me," returned the latter with some sharpness.

"Ah!" said Badunabad, raising his arms in a gesture both noble and desolate. "To hear one's self thus spoken to by a subject! Oh, my tortures! Oh, my pillories! Where are you?"

"Not here, happily!" murmured Trogustul. Then he added in a very low tone—

"Do have a little more dignity. You will cover us with ridicule."

The Maharajah gnawed his moustache and presently asked William—

"Have you the time to wait a minute or two?"

"As long as ever it pleases your incalculable Highness."

A silence followed which William, out of deference, dare not break. Suddenly Trogustul became lividly pale; he was evidently feeling very ill, and took a few steps towards a door at the further end of the room. The Maharajah rose precipitately and seized him by his tunic, but the stuff remained in his hand and the Grand Talapoin ran out of the room, closely followed by Badunabad.

William was not a little surprised to see that their backs were only covered with a thick shirt, and that their rich accoutrements consisted of a front part only, ingeniously fastened behind by strings, like a sort of breastplate.

Through the door of the adjoining room, which was left open, came sounds of a violent altercation, in which the voice of the Maharajah predominated.

"Oh, you cheat! You thief! You swindler! Be quick, or I'll strangle you!"

Satrakas had remained in his place, mute and impassive, and William, more and more bewildered, felt he must risk a question.

"Will you tell me, noble Vizier, what your magnanimous lord means by all this abuse?"

The Vizier hesitated a moment, and then suddenly making up his mind poured out his troubles.

"Oh, sir," cried he, seizing William's hand, "save us! We are in a horrible situation. No money, deep in debt, harassed with creditors. We have sold nearly everything. The backs of our robes even have had to go, and we have only kept the fronts that we may still appear with a little decency. To think that I should be reduced to making such an avowal!" And the poor man's voice trembled and tears rose in his eyes.

"All these jewels that you see," he continued, "are made of glass. The real stones have been sold. You see to what straits we are brought, through our fidelity to our guilty lord! It has deprived us of everything. We are dying of hunger in this palace! Our people refuse to serve us, and heap scorn upon us, so that Trogustul and I are illtreated both by our master and our servants."

"I sympathise most heartily with you," said William compassionately.

"One superb diamond remained to the Maharajah," continued Satrakas, "and he selfishly kept it back for his own personal needs. That is the one you have come for——"

"I?" interrupted William. "But I didn't come for a diamond."

"What! You are not the American whom the jeweller in Regent Street promised to send?"

"No, indeed."

"But, then, what do you want with us?"

A sudden idea struck William.

"It doesn't matter," said he. "I will buy the diamond all the same."

"Do you really mean that?"

"I swear it. And I will pay ready money."

"Then we must wait a little while."

"Why?"

"Because—this morning—weary of the egotism of our dear lord, Trogustul and I plotted to become the owners of it to improve our condition a little—and we succeeded. Trogustul was fortunate enough to seize it, and swallowed it straight away."

In spite of a strong desire to laugh William contained himself and listened for the end of this confidence.

"Unhappily the Maharajah had seen him. He immediately sent for a strong emetic and forced him to swallow it, threatening he would have him arrested as a thief. Oh, it was a terrible scene!"

In the next room the invectives continued, and the summons to make haste which Badunabad lavished on the unfortunate Trogustul. The narrative of the Vizier explained the sudden illness and unexpected flight of Trogustul, as well as the behaviour of Badunabad, which William had at first attributed to anger at the former's breach of etiquette.

John was so strongly tempted to laugh that he had to hide his face behind his master, who himself found it somewhat difficult to avoid smiling. Suddenly a triumphant exclamation was heard.

"Ah!" cried Badunabad. "Here it is! I have it! You see, thief that you are, that stolen things do you no good."

The moment after the Maharajah briskly entered the Throne Room, holding between his thumb and finger a beautiful diamond of the finest water, and of unparalleled shape, whose facets glowed in the fading light. William took up the stone gingerly, saw that it was a very valuable one, and said to the Maharajah—

"Most illustrious sir, what do you require in exchange for this jewel?"

"Whatever it is worth," replied the prince, who had quite regained his serenity.

"Will you accept twenty thousand pounds sterling?"

The roundness of the sum seemed to make a profound impression on the fallen monarch. Twenty thousand pounds! Thirteen thousand five hundred gold mohurs! A small sum truly compared with his former treasures, but attaining fabulous proportions in the present state of affairs.

"I accept," he said, with cold majesty.

"In that case I will conclude the bargain with your most magnanimous Highness. On one condition, however——"

"Ah! What is it?"

"That you will permit me also to buy a certain postage stamp, of which, I understand, one copy only remains in the hands of your Highness," and trembling with emotion he awaited the response of the potentate. There were so many chances that the stamp had been destroyed, mislaid, stolen, or left in San-Po when the capital was deserted so precipitately.

The Maharajah caressed his long beard thoughtfully.

"And how much would you give for this stamp?" he said at last.

"Whatever your Highness deigned to ask."

"It is of very great value, then?"

"To me, yes."

"Would you give as much as five thousand pounds for it?"

"Instantly."

At these words the Maharajah flung himself upon the Grand Vizier with cuffs and blows, crying, "Traitor, miserable creature, thief! Well might you give me such advice!"

"I will have you arrested for assaulting me!" cried the unfortunate man, sinking under the blows.

THE STAMP KING

By G. DE BEAUREGARD AND H. DE GORSSE

Translated from the French by EDITH C. PHILLIPS

CHAPTER V (*continued*)

*Showing how, if money does not make happiness,
the want of it often causes misery*

THE scene was a most painful one, and William dared not interfere, but at this critical moment Trogustul, looking weak and pale, entered the room and flung himself upon his master with savage fury. Badunabad, having now two adversaries to deal with, became more gracious and forgiving, and the commotion ended, but not before the sumptuous breastplates had become singularly disordered.

"Would you believe," said the Maharajah to William, "that that miserable Satrakas advised me to sell the stamp for a poor five hundred pounds to a certain Moulineau in Paris, who had learned, I cannot say how, that it was in my possession?"

"Then it is not yours now?" said William in a faltering voice.

"Alas, no!"

"And Moulineau has it?"

"Exactly."

"Very well. Then I'm off."

And suiting the action to the word, without even troubling to take leave, he turned on his heels and hurried towards the door. But the three Asiatics with one accord rushed after him, shouting in distracted voices—

"Hollo! ho! The diamond! He is running away with the diamond!"

William, who had already reached the ante-chamber, burst into a laugh as he heard their loud ejaculations.

"By jingo!" cried he, retracing his steps. "It is actually a fact that I was making off with their diamond!"

But the incident had made a stir in the house. The attendants, roused from their torpor, came in. The dignitaries below, not knowing what to make of the commotion, dropped their cards and mounted the grand staircase four steps at a time, and the whole household was soon assembled in the Throne Room.

"What's the matter?" said one.

"For goodness' sake make a little less noise," grumbled another. "One can't even sleep in peace."

"Don't trouble yourselves," said William. "I only forgot to pay for——"

"It's nothing, it's nothing——" interrupted Badunabad brusquely; and stooping to the ear of the young man he whispered in a tone of anguish—

"In the name of Buddha, do not let them know I am selling you a diamond! Those fellows are all capable of setting my creditors at me, or of plundering me themselves without ceremony."

Filled with pity for the evident anxiety of the potentate, William reassured the domestics and the dignitaries, who returned, the former to their nap and the latter to their piquet.

"Pardon my thoughtless stupidity," he said. "I will prove my good faith by immediately giving you a cheque for the amount in question."

The sad faces of Trogustul and Satrakas contrasted lamentably with the expression of triumph which illuminated that of the Maharajah. William noticed it, and remembering the Vizier's complaint he continued—

"Or rather, I am going to write three cheques of equal value, one for each of you, representing the third of the sum total, that is, six thousand six hundred and sixty-seven pounds."

"What is that for?" asked Badunabad uneasily.

"Highest, greatest, and most profound Sir," answered William, "it seems to me that you ought to share your last resources in brotherly fashion, and mutually help each other——"

"What is that to you?" cried Badunabad. "The diamond belongs to me—to me alone——"

"Your pardon, most mighty potentate. Your two companions having shared your exile it is only fair——"

"That is my business," protested the Maharajah.

"Very good," said William quietly, "then I will call your servants back."

"No, no, for pity's sake! Anything rather than that," implored Badunabad.

So the young American drew three cheques on Baring's bank and handed them to the three exiles, who were not slow to take possession of them, Trogustul and Satrakas with so resolute an air that Badunabad bowed to circumstances and said no more. He then took leave of the three noble lords, and driving to the nearest post office sent off the following telegram to M. Moulineau:—

"Hear you have second copy Brahmapootra stamp. Keep it; am coming and will buy it.—Keniss."

Then, still accompanied by John, he drove on to Charing Cross Station.

"May my message arrive in time," said he to himself as the train started for Dover.

Arrived at Calais he took his seat in the Paris express, after providing himself, according to his custom, with several papers; for although it was after midnight he had no inclination for sleep, and settled himself to read.

"I wonder," said he, opening the *Temps*, "if in this continental brother of the *Times* I am going to make some further discovery?"

And indeed as he read the first line he turned pale. His eye had fallen on the following despatch at the head of a column:—

"HAVRE, *April 30th*, 1896.

"There is still no news of the *Touraine*. As she was due to arrive here last Saturday, the twenty-fifth of April, and as so long a delay has never before occurred, a great deal of uneasiness is manifested. The officials of the company to whom she belongs are full of confidence, trusting in the powers of this splendid steamer, and are doing their best to reassure all who are interested in her fate."

He had not the courage to read another word, but sought vainly to think of something that could explain the strange delay. The idea of Betty in danger kept rising before him with agonising distinctness. He was astonished at himself for taking so much interest in one who was merely a fellow-philatelist, and even, when one came to think of it, a rival. Nevertheless, by the time they reached Amiens his resolution was taken.

"Get out," was all he said to John, "and take our things."

"What?" said the valet in astonishment. "Then we are not going to Paris?"

"Later on. Just now we are going to Havre."

"To Havre!"

When once he understood the reason John began to lament, though in his heart of hearts he would not have been deeply grieved had a good storm driven the too devoted Victoria back to New York. But it was not a bad heart after all, and, when he thought that the poor girl might really be in peril, he too began to tremble and to hope that after all it only meant a few days' delay. So without hesitation, in order to be at the fountain-head of news, and to be the first to receive the travellers—if it were God's will they should arrive after all—William Keniss and John pursued their way by Rouen to Havre, where, later on, William gave to Betty, as we have already heard, a sufficiently incomplete account of his interesting journey.

CHAPTER VI

How Miss Betty discovers that a courteous man is not always an honourable one

ON arriving at Saint-Lazare William told John to find Miss Betty's luggage and to have his taken to the Terminus Hotel, where he was going to stay. Then, turning to his travelling companion, he said—

"Now I am ready to see you to the Hotel Bristol."

"No, no!" she returned eagerly. "I cannot trespass on your kindness any longer. You have brought me safely to Paris; I can manage now very well."

"Then you wish to deprive me of a great pleasure?"

"Oh, I wouldn't do that for the world! Come with me if you like, but in any case we shall have to part in a few minutes."

Escorted by John and Victoria, who carried the smaller packages, the two young people had followed the stream of travellers, and now found themselves in the inner covered court, which led by a large gateway to the Rue d'Amsterdam. They took their places in the omnibus, leaving John alone at the station to execute his master's orders. But as the conveyance started along the Rue d'Amsterdam, on its way to the Place Vendôme by the Rue du Havre, Rue Auber, and Rue de la Paix, he heard his too faithful fiancée call out through the half-open door—

"And, above all, don't forget what you promised me in the train."

"Oh, all right," said John, "that's understood."

It will easily be seen that this referred to the wedding, by which Miss Betty's maid wished to terminate her engagement, which she began to find a hopelessly long one. It was the one thought that occupied the mind of this excellent young woman, and from Havre to Paris she had employed the time by driving poor John into the tightest possible corner, till he had solemnly promised to profit by their stay in Paris to settle, with a nice little ceremony, an affair which had already been hanging about so long.

So John was left standing, surrounded by travellers and luggage, in deep perplexity, feeling he could not much longer put off a duty which he was in honour bound to fulfil. The omnibus, meantime, had arrived at the Place Vendôme and the Hotel Bristol.

"Well, Miss Betty," said William Keniss, "we have arrived. It only remains for me to thank you for being kind enough to accept me as an escort from Havre."

"It is for me to thank you. You have been the most pleasant and agreeable of travelling companions."

"Why, you are already forgetting Sir Oscar Tilbury, who moreover did not come to France on purpose to oppose you."

"That is true. I forgot we were rivals, and that we had a duel to fight."

"Then *au revoir*, Miss Betty, and success to you, since hostilities have now commenced."

"*Au revoir*, Mr. Keniss."

William kissed her hand respectfully to show that, though a rival, he had an unchangeable regard for her, and she disappeared in the vestibule of the Hotel Bristol, accompanied by M. Pavilly, the manager, stiff and grave as usual in his black coat.

M. Pavilly was a man of exaggerated solemnity and correctness, strongly built, as all employed in a hotel should be, and celebrated not only for the luxury and good taste of his rooms, but still more for the delicate and refined science of his cuisine. He accompanied Miss Betty up the staircase which led to the apartments on the first floor, for which William had telephoned from Havre.

"I hope Miss Scott will be comfortable here," said he, opening the door of the ante-chamber. "These are the rooms we give to the Prince of Wales when he does us the honour of staying here. A fortnight ago they were occupied by the King of the Belgians. All the windows look out on the Place Vendôme, and you can see along the Rue de la Paix as far as the Place de l'Opéra. Perhaps Miss Scott would like to see for herself." And he drew back one of the blue velvet curtains which draped the windows.

"Yes," she said, "the view is indeed superb. I shall do very well here, very well indeed."

"Does Miss Scott wish for anything?"

"Nothing just now, thank you."

The manager withdrew, and Betty went to the window.

"Look!" said she to Victoria, who had followed her. "See how beautiful it is."

It was six o'clock in the evening, one of the liveliest, most curious, and most interesting hours in which to study this marvellous and unrivalled city of Paris. People engaged in trade or commerce are still at their work, and the street belongs almost exclusively to the world of fashion and the idlers. Betty went into ecstasies over the panorama which unrolled itself in the Place Vendôme, in the midst of which stood up proudly in the evening light the statue which Napoleon the First had had cast out of the cannons taken from the enemy.

The greater number of the equipages came from the Rue de Castiglione and the Faubourg Saint-Honoré, where are two or three of the most celebrated confectioners in the capital. Coupés and landaus had only to traverse the Place Vendôme in order to arrive at the Rue de la Paix, all the houses of which from the bottom to the top are inhabited by the most celebrated artistes of Parisian fashion—tailors, milliners, shirt-makers, linen-drapers, dressmakers, not to mention famous hairdressers, where ladies are obliged to enter their names weeks and months in advance in order to obtain an unhappy quarter of an hour of waving and curling. Under these circumstances it is easy to imagine the number of carriages which were stationed by each pavement all along the Rue de la Paix.

THE STAMP KING

By G. DE BEAUREGARD AND H. DE GORSSE

Translated from the French by EDITH C. PHILLIPS

SHE SEARCHED THE TRUNK TO THE REMOTEST CORNER

CHAPTER VI (*continued*)

*How Miss Betty discovers that a courteous man
is not always an honourable one*

AS Miss Betty and Victoria watched the scene, so new to them, night came slowly on. Little by little the shadows descended on the Place Vendôme, badly lighted by blinking gas-burners placed at long distances apart. But moving lights ran continually from end to end. They were the lamps of the many carriages which came and went, in two regular streams, on either side of the sombre and majestic column. Farther off, in the Rue de la Paix, lights approached each other, became confused, and blended together. Then they gradually parted again, seen less clearly now on account of the brilliant illumination which radiated from the shop windows to the middle of the street, forming a luminous vista, a fairy road to the Place de l'Opéra.

"No wonder they call Paris the capital of the world!" said Victoria.

"And you have seen nothing of it yet."

"But I hope to see a good deal more."

"We should have to stay some days for that."

"Why, surely we are going to stay a long time in Paris?" cried Victoria, horrified at the thought of a further move immediately after their long voyage.

"Well, yes—perhaps."

"Perhaps?"

"I shall not know until I have seen M. Moulineau to-morrow, and heard from him where the second copy of the Brahmapootra stamp is, for it was to find that I came to France, you know."

"Oh, yes, that is true ; and a wretched stamp it is, for it has already nearly drowned us, and now it may——"

"It may cause us to start off again to-morrow. In any case, don't let the future trouble you."

Victoria did not trouble about it exactly, but she thought, with a certain amount of apprehension, that if her mistress were going on again so soon it would put an end for the present, and no doubt for a long time, to the prospect of her marriage.

The voice of Betty, who was examining the rooms, and who had passed into the next one, roused her from her matrimonial reflections.

"Come and look here," cried the girl. "This is very nice and comfortable. You can sleep here and I will have the other room."

The suite was composed of two bedrooms and the sitting-room into which they had been shown by M. Pavilly. The windows of all three looked out on the Place Vendôme, and each had a door opening into the ante-room, so that they could be entered, if need be, from the outside without passing through the sitting-room. Miss Betty pointed out this advantageous arrangement to Victoria.

"And now," said she, "while I dress will you go down to the office and get me some sheets of paper?"

"You have letters to write?"

"No ; only a few telegrams, to let my lawyer and my friends in New York know about our journey. We left America so hastily that I had no time to tell anyone."

"The fact of the matter is they'll be very much worried about you, Miss Betty."

"Well, I can't help it. I quite meant to telegraph

on arriving at Havre. Even if that miserable *Touraine* had not been so late they would have been a week without news. So don't let us lose any more time."

Victoria disappeared, and soon returned with a blotting-case. Betty established herself at a table and began to scrawl. In a few minutes she stopped and handed seven or eight sheets of paper to Victoria, saying—

"Here, take these to the telegraph office."

"As I gave you all my own money to take care of, Miss Betty, I shall have to ask you for some to send the telegrams."

Betty put her hand into the little satchel hanging from her waist and uttered an exclamation of dismay.

"Oh, this is really too bad!" And, as she feverishly searched in every corner, she became deadly pale.

"Stolen—to the very last penny!" she cried. "Ten thousand dollars in notes all gone!"

"What? Stolen!" exclaimed Victoria, stunned at the news.

But Betty, losing no time, hurried to a trunk to look for her passport and some banker's drafts, payable to bearer, which she had thrown hastily in at the moment of her abrupt departure. Vainly she searched to the remotest corner. Nothing there! not even a sign of a paper.

"This is too much!" she cried, tapping on the floor irritably with her little patent-leather shoe.

"But who could possibly——" began Victoria.

"Oh, how do I know!" And she once more turned over all her linen, and even scrutinised the lining of the trunk, without any further result.

Then a cry of pain escaped her. In her haste she had pricked her finger till the blood came.

"What do you want to put needles among my handkerchiefs for?" she asked.

"But I haven't, miss," said Victoria.

"Then what is it?"

Wishing to discover the cause of the prick she searched again and found a scarf-pin, formed of a golden serpent twining round a slip of malachite.

"Why, that is Sir Oscar's pin, I am certain," she cried. "I remember it perfectly. It was always falling out of his tie, and I told him several times that he would lose it. But however does it come to be in this trunk?"

"Its owner must have let it fall in."

"But Sir Oscar never came into my cabin!"

"And yet it seems to me—— Yes —one day——"

"Stop! stop!" thought Betty suddenly. "Could he possibly be the thief? But no, of course not; he is too well educated, too nice! But, after all, there have been pickpockets as nice and as well educated. Of course there have; one hears of such and they may be seen any day. There are even swindlers who play the part of perfect gentlemen on purpose to mix with people and plunder them. Yes, the more I think of it the more suspicious Sir Oscar's behaviour during the voyage

appears. What an idiot I have been to let myself be deceived by the gallant manners of that indefatigable cavalier! For it certainly must have been he—it can have been no one else—who has robbed me! He alone was sufficiently intimate with me during all that long time on the *Touraine*."

A number of minute facts were recalled, one by one, by Miss Betty as she thus communed with herself: the time Sir Oscar loved to spend in other people's cabins, his fondness for the passengers who were supposed to be rich, the disappearance of watches during the tempest. And each of these little facts, in some new point, by some fresh detail, strengthened the suspicion in her mind, until it finally became transformed into an absolute certainty.

"Do you know who the thief is?" she said then to Victoria.

"No, miss. If I only *did* know——!"

"Well, it is Sir Oscar Tilbury himself. The clever rogue, in rummaging my trunk, dropped this pin, which, unfortunately for him, was always unsafe."

The honest girl could not suppress a start at such an unexpected revelation.

"Ah!" she exclaimed. "Then that explains why Sir Oscar made off at full speed when we arrived at Havre, without waiting to say good-bye to anyone."

"You saw him go?"

"With my own eyes! And he looked as if he wanted to lose himself among the crowd as quickly as possible. A very eel."

"Then there is no longer any room for doubt."

"I can hardly believe it! Such a very superior man, and so genteel!"

"This proves, my dear Victoria, that a courteous man is not always an honest one."

Miss Scott understood it all now. Sir Oscar was one of those cosmopolitan knaves who "do" the first-class trains and the large steamers.

"And to think that that wretched pickpocket promised to call and see me here!" she cried. "I would not advise him to come near me again, indeed I would not!"

In short, the young American had been robbed— hopelessly robbed, but as lamenting the fact would not put a penny in her pocket she set to work at once to find a way out of the difficulty. For a moment she thought of going to the correspondent of her banker in New York, but she soon reflected that he would not be likely to advance the smallest sum to a person who was unable to establish her identity. To borrow at the hotel was no less difficult; such a proceeding on the part of a young lady who had just engaged the most sumptuous rooms would cause her to be taken for a simple adventuress.

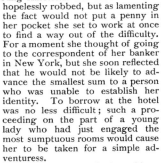

"Wait a minute," she said to Victoria. And, taking a sudden resolution, she drew from her ears two superb diamonds, and, holding them closely in her hand, went out into the Place Vendôme.

(To be continued.)

THE STAMP KING

By G. DE BEAUREGARD AND H. DE GORSSE

Translated from the French by EDITH C. PHILLIPS

CHAPTER VI (*continued*)

How Miss Betty discovers that a courteous man is not always an honourable one

NIGHT had fallen; carriages passed to and fro, and the brilliantly-lighted shop windows in the Rue de la Paix attracted her from afar. Betty gained this street, and perceiving the ostentatious display of the great jeweller, Courtalain, she entered without hesitation, and being accosted with that pompous obsequiousness of which "select" shopmen alone possess the secret, she said, blushing a little—

"Here are two diamonds that I wish to sell."

When they saw she had merely come to sell and not to buy the men drew back in affected disdain. However, one of them decided to look at the stones, and could not repress a movement of admiration at sight of the brilliants which the young American put into his hand. They were, in fact, two single diamonds of unusual size and brilliancy. Miss Betty had bought them the year before from one of the largest jewellers in New York, who, after coming into possession of the one, had had to wait several years before he could find a fellow to it. M. Courtalain himself was called, and, fixing his glasses on his nose, he studied Betty attentively from head to foot before he even looked at what she was offering.

"In the first place, who are you?"

"Miss Betty Scott, of New York," she answered almost timidly, for she was not in the habit of asking for money. Gathering courage, however, and annoyed at his impertinent air and evident suspicion, she continued somewhat drily—

"I only part with these jewels because I am the victim of a robbery, and find myself absolutely without any money. Kindly answer me one way or the other, and, if you wish to take them, tell me what you will give."

M. Courtalain studied the diamonds closely for some time, and Betty occupied herself in examining the many trinkets before her—bracelets, necklets, brooches, rings, blazing in the varied colours of amethyst, topaz, beryl, turquoise, and opal, arranged on the velvet counter like the flowers of a dream. At length M. Courtalain looked up and said, with his inquisitorial air—

"Twenty thousand."

"Twenty thousand francs!" cried Betty. "Why, I gave sixty thousand for them."

"That is your business, mademoiselle. I cannot give a halfpenny more."

But Miss Betty was very loth to part with her earrings at so absurdly low a price.

"Just see how lovely they are!" she insisted.

"Pretty fair, pretty fair," returned M. Courtalain with a preoccupied air. "Unfortunately business is bad and——" He finished the sentence by handing the diamonds back to Miss Betty as if he had given up all idea of them since she was not satisfied with his price. But she reflected that after all twenty thousand francs was better than nothing, so closed with the offer.

M. Courtalain's face brightened and he became exaggeratedly polite.

"And to what address shall I send the money?" he asked.

"Why, sir, I will take it with me."

"Ah, no; I am not permitted to give it to you here."

He explained that, on account of frequent thefts, the law obliged him to pay at the residence of the former owner; it was necessary to take every precaution; in fact, he said as much as he could to make Betty feel thoroughly uncomfortable, until, in order to escape, she said she would be at home at the Hotel Bristol between two and three o'clock on the following afternoon. Once outside she drew a long breath. She would very much have liked her money at once, but the certainty of having it soon gave her a feeling of calm and security. So she returned tranquilly to the hotel, where an extraordinary and very unlooked-for surprise awaited her.

M. Pavilly, who had learned that our travellers had just arrived by the *Touraine*, was so proud of having in his house two of the passengers of the boat whose adventures were still the news of the day, that he had the restaurant, where Miss Betty was to dine, ornamented with plants of every kind and many-coloured Venetian lamps. The room thus presented a fairy-like aspect, with its varied foliage and illuminations. In one corner a little platform had been erected, on which a dozen performers in sky-blue breeches and red jackets struck up a lively tune as she entered the room, and followed it with the best pieces in their répertoire. Miss Betty, arriving in Paris for the first time, would have liked to believe that such luxuries were usual in the large hotels, but she was speedily undeceived and taught that this little fête was specially organised in her honour, for the moment she entered ladies and gentlemen rose with one accord, at a sign from M. Pavilly, and greeted her with a round of applause, which continued until, blushing and deeply moved, she took her seat at one of the tables.

"If only all these people knew," thought she, "that Miss Scott, the little New York millionaire, had not a dollar in her pocket!" And at heart she was very much annoyed to find herself the object of all this curiosity. So she finished her dinner as quickly as she could, and, after thanking the company for their kind ovation and asking M. Pavilly to bestow some of his best champagne on the performers, she hastened back to her rooms, unable, however, to escape a final and still louder burst of applause. Then she went to bed. And the fatigue of the journey, joined to the many emotions of the day, soon hushed her into the profoundest slumber.

CHAPTER VII

In which William, having taken the strings in his hand, continues to pull them

VERY early the next morning Betty awoke, and, as soon as she was dressed, started off to see M. Moulineau. The streets, brightened by the sunshine, already presented an animated appearance. It was the hour when the young workwomen come in from the populous suburbs to their shops and workrooms. On the pavement were busy streams of people coming and going. A few, as they passed, exchanged a hasty greeting, as if they were in the habit of meeting at the same point in their journey every day. Miss Betty had only to go across the Place Vendôme to reach the Rue de la Paix. At almost every step she stopped to admire the shop windows, obtaining an idea of all the treasures hidden within, and a cursory view of the latest Paris fashions, so celebrated all over the world.

BETTY PERCEIVED THE OSTENTATIOUS DISPLAY OF THE JEWELLER

She longed to go in and buy everything she saw, but recollecting that she had no money continued on her way regretfully till she came to the next window, when the same thing was repeated.

"That will do for later on," she thought, and, remembering that she was in a great hurry, she tore herself away and hastened on for a few seconds. But soon she lingered again, unconsciously, so great is the fascination of those wonderful windows of the French capital to provincials and foreigners who come to Paris for the first time. In this way Miss Betty wasted half an hour before she arrived at the Place de l'Opéra, and, as she gained it, William Keniss also arrived from another direction.

The evening before the young philatelist had sent his faithful John to inquire at what hour M. Moulineau would be visible the following morning, and had learnt that, although the establishment opened at eight o'clock, M. Moulineau himself did not arrive before nine. So William, waking early, found himself on the Boulevard at eight o'clock, and whiled away the time till he could present himself at M. Moulineau's by visiting a tailor, a shirt-maker, and a boot shop in the neighbourhood to supply his wardrobe, as he had left New York without any luggage whatever. Then he turned towards the Boulevard Montmartre. Thus it happened that he reached the Place de l'Opéra at the same time as Miss Betty.

The latter had paused at the corner of the Boulevard des Capucines to admire a display of photographs, when William caught sight of her. She was so absorbed that, though he was only a few feet away from her, she never saw him. "By Jove!" thought he, "my rival has lost no time, and I have almost let myself be distanced by her. I must make haste!"

Turning, he crossed the street without being seen, and hastened along on the opposite side till he gained the Boulevard des Italiens and then the Boulevard Montmartre, which he followed till he arrived at No. 6, the address of M. Moulineau.

This house was established in Paris by M. Alfred Moulineau in 1860, and, thanks to his unceasing efforts, it soon became the most celebrated and best-known stamp business in the world. M. Moulineau was, in fact, a man of remarkable intelligence, and you could see at a glance that he was still endowed with tremendous activity, though now sixty-five years of age. His years, moreover, seemed to weigh but lightly upon him, and he carried himself as gallantly as possible, in spite of his small stature. When his height was taken at the age of twenty-one he measured scarcely five feet three, and, unhappily for him, he had grown no taller since that time. But this could only be noticed when he was standing up, for his body, being very long, gave him, when seated, a much more imposing appearance, which consoled the excellent M. Moulineau not a little.

But if he felt a grudge against providence for not allowing him a few inches more, he was proportionately grateful for the remarkable face with which he had been endowed. He possessed, in fact, a very fine head; not exactly an extraordinary one, but such that, with his beard combed fan-shape on either side of his chin, its owner thought it good enough to be printed on stamps of various colours and freely distributed.

"And who can say," he would often repeat jokingly, "that I have not the air of a President of the Republic or of an Emperor!" And, if you wished to please him, you would reply—

"I believe you, M. Moulineau, and it is not only on your stamps that you have the air of a President or an Emperor, but in reality." Upon which the good man would draw himself up to his full height and appear, indeed, just a little taller.

But however this may be, we must repeat that M. Moulineau was a man of superior intelligence and activity. His intelligence might be read in his eye, which was always on the alert. His activity was shown in the singular vivacity which would scarcely permit him a moment's repose. In fact, at whatever time you surprised him he would be found busily at work, occupied with a dozen things at once without in the least confusing them. On this particular morning M. Moulineau had just entered his study when one of his clerks handed him William's card.

"Mr. William Keniss!" cried the great stamp dealer. "Show him in; show him in immediately."

As William entered he rose from the desk at which he was seated and, with a beaming face, went to meet him.

"I have great pleasure in greeting our best customer," said he. "I am happy that your presence in Paris should have procured me the honour of this visit. Will you be good enough to take a seat?"

William sat down in the arm-chair which M. Moulineau pointed out as he took his own seat again.

"Monsieur," began the young American, "I will at once give you in detail the reason of my visit, for which my telegram from London will have prepared you. You sent me, some time ago, a very fine copy of a stamp——"

"The Brahmapootra one?"

"The very same."

"Was I wrong? Do you not like it?" asked the stamp dealer anxiously, for William's somewhat solemn entrance had caused him a little uneasiness.

"On the contrary, you did quite right. But did you not tell me there were two copies of this stamp?"

"Yes, indeed, and you may believe me it is a fact."

"I have had that confirmed in London a few days ago, by the Maharajah of Brahmapootra himself."

"What!" cried M. Moulineau in a wounded tone, "you have thought it necessary to go and confirm the truth of my assertion. Oh! Mr. Keniss, such a lack of confidence grieves me deeply, deeply."

"Be comforted," said, William, laughing. "I have not doubted your good faith for a single instant. The proof of which is, that I only went to see the Maharajah to ask him if he would be good enough to let me have the second stamp of which you had told me."

"Ah, yes. I guessed something of that from your telegram."

"To find this stamp I had no intention of applying in the first place to the Maharajah, of whose address I was ignorant, but to you, my dear M. Moulineau, who had yourself told me that the Maharajah had kept it. It was consequently just and natural that I should charge you with the purchase of it. Only it happened that, in passing through London, I discovered by chance that the Maharajah had just arrived there, upon which I hastened to him at once—only to learn that he had sold to you a few days before the stamp I want, and which I have come to ask you for."

"It is——"

"Yes, yes, I know. It is the last that can be put on the market, and it is impossible for you to let me have it at the price of the other. But when I tell you I will pay double, treble—anything you ask!"

"I understand very well, but——"

"There is no but! Surely you understand me? Either one is a philatelist or one is not; and you know what a passionately devoted one I am! So since there is a stamp in the world of which there are only two copies, you know I must have them! You hear? I must! So tell me your price at once."

"My price!" cried M. Moulineau, glad to be able to get in a word. "I only wish I could fix it, but——"

"But?"

"But unfortunately I cannot."

"What!"

"The stamp was sold and sent off an hour before your telegram reached me."

"Sold!" cried William. "And to whom?"

"To a philatelist of recent date; Prince Albrandi, of Naples."

THE STAMP KING

By G. DE BEAUREGARD AND H. DE GORSSE

Translated from the French by EDITH C. PHILLIPS

"TOO LATE!" SAID THE DEALER

CHAPTER VII (*continued*)

In which William, having taken the strings in hand,
continues to pull them

M. MOULINEAU then opened a drawer in his desk.

"All I can do for you, therefore, is to give you a few of these little photographs which I had taken, that I might add the Brahmapootra stamp to my catalogue."

William took them, and saw that they were veritable works of art.

"If only I could have foreseen this," he said, with evident annoyance, "I should have sent to you at once asking you to keep me the second copy. However, it is too late, so we will say no more about it. Would you mind telling me, though, the price you asked for it?"

"A hundred and fifty thousand francs."

The young man nodded and was silent for a few moments, apparently in deep reflection. Evidently he sought some means of counteracting this unexpected blow of fortune. The matter seemed rather hopeless at that moment, for Miss Betty as well as for himself.

"You will promise me one thing?" he said to M. Moulineau.

"I ask for nothing better, if it be possible. To what does it refer?"

"Give me your word of honour that you will tell no one—you quite understand—no one, that the second copy of the Brahmapootra stamp is in the possession of Prince Albrandi, at Naples."

"If that is all," said the merchant, "I can easily satisfy you. I promise, on my word of honour, that no one, absolutely no one, shall learn it from me. And now may I ask your reason for making me take such a solemn oath?"

"For the very simple reason that I count on persuading the Prince to sell me his copy, and that I have a rival, a member, like myself, of the New York Philatelic Club, who has come to France for the same purpose, and is herself prepared to buy it at any price. This rival will, no doubt, come to you this very day for news of it."

"And you wish me not to put her on the scent?"

"Certainly. Have I not your word for it?"

"Sleep in peace, dear Mr. Keniss. When the lady appears I will be most circumspect. And pray allow me to wish you good luck."

William took up his hat and prepared to depart, but M. Moulineau stopped him.

"I hope you are not going, my dear sir," said he, "without inspecting my house. You must see, if you have not already seen, what a great stamp business is like, in Paris at least; for, of course, in New York you, the Stamp King, have seen enough of them."

"I should like it of all things," said William.

"Then follow me."

CHAPTER VIII

In which William Keniss, Stamp King though he is,
passes from one surprise to another

M. MOULINEAU opened one of the doors of his study and led William into the adjoining apartment. On the walls, covered with rich tapestries, were hung, as ornaments, dishes, plates, panels, pictures, composed of innumerable and many-coloured bits of stamps, arranged in patterns with infinite care. There were also, here and there, special frames, fastened with tiny padlocks, in which were exhibited under glass some of the rarest and most curious of stamps. A few of these specimens were still on the original envelopes, yellowed by age.

Large tables were arranged before the windows, at each of which a young girl was seated in conference

any quantity. The rarer ones, of which we have but one, two, or three copies, are in a special safe in my study. But all the others are here, arranged in order in little linen envelopes, each containing two or three hundred stamps all alike. This is our 'small reserve.'"

"What a number of these drawers you must need!" said William.

"Not as many, perhaps, as you would think, for there are some countries whose stamps are not numerous, and take up but one or two drawers, but that is only a minor detail. I must tell you, though, that I was obliged to have a hundred of these sets of drawers made, which are all in this room and the following one. They are mounted on castors, as you see, so that at night they can be easily pushed back into their respective safes, for no insurance company can be found to insure us against the risks of fire."

ALL WERE ABSORBED

with a customer, dotting down in a note-book the prices of the stamps which he picked out, one by one, from the pages of a large album. And what a strange collection of collectors it was!—young nobles, old maniacs, and business men. And all were absorbed in the fastidious work in which they were engaged, and in amazement at the philatelic marvels unfolded before their eyes.

"When our customers send in an order," said M. Moulineau, "we do not take the stamps from these albums," indicating the ones whose leaves were being slowly turned by the various individuals, "but from what we call our 'small' and our 'large reserve' stock."

So saying he led William into a second room of sterner appearance. It was surrounded by huge safes, the doors of some of which stood ajar.

"This is our chief stock," said M. Moulineau. "Here we keep all the stamps which we possess in

"I cannot help admiring the order and skill which have organised all this," said William. "But, even so, I cannot imagine how, considering the immense number of stamps that exist, you know where to find the particular ones your customers want. I know my father had a number of little ways of doing things of this sort, but I never understood them in the least."

"Oh, it is very simple. You know how we manage, as we have had dealings together for so long. All the stamps which I think worthy of being catalogued—and in this work, which has taken me long and patient years, I have not troubled much about little absurd details of paper, watermarks, shades, and I don't know what besides—all the stamps, then, that I think worth cataloguing are numbered in order in the catalogue. So when anyone sends me an order he gives this number instead of a minute description of the stamp, which would, no doubt, cause constant mistakes."

THE STAMP KING

By G. DE BEAUREGARD AND H. DE GORSSE

Translated from the French by EDITH C. PHILLIPS

CHAPTER VIII (*continued*)

In which William Keniss, Stamp King though he is, passes from one surprise to another

THE two men then ascended a little winding staircase in the shop and reached the next floor. The first room they entered was, like the one below, surrounded by immense safes. M. Moulineau opened one of them, and William saw, carefully arranged on shelves, a number of envelopes, much larger than those of the "small reserve," and labelled with the number of stamps within. They each contained several thousand all alike, and bulged more or less according to the number they enclosed. These were the envelopes of the "greater reserve."

"And it is on these we draw," M. Moulineau observed, "when those you saw below are exhausted." And as William expressed his astonishment at the colossal quantity of stamps, he continued: "Wait awhile; wait awhile ; you have scarcely seen anything yet."

And, in fact, a very extraordinary scene awaited our visitor in the next room, where twenty or thirty women were seated at a large table, extending the whole length of the wall. Each had an enormous bag at her feet, out of which she took handfuls of stamps, which she sorted and arranged on the table into numbers of tiny, many-coloured heaps.

"But how in the world do you obtain all these?" cried William, stupefied at the sight.

"From our correspondents in different countries," returned M. Moulineau. "They not only send us new issues as soon as they appear, but sacks like you see here, full of all the stamps in use which they are able to procure. Naturally, when they are not rare stamps, for instance, the ordinary European issues, we only buy them by weight at varying prices, but generally very low ones. Even then we receive a great many more than we want. In France, Italy, Spain there is not a single convent or religious community which does not collect stamps in thousands to sell to dealers. As soon as they arrive they are sorted, as you see, by my emyloyés, and sometimes among the number they discover one interesting one which pays for the lot, otherwise almost useless

"And the other stamps, the commonest ones? Surely you don't keep them all in your reserve?"

"Oh, no, that would not be possible. We sell them again by weight, in the same way as we bought them, to people who use them to make ornaments—plaques, and such-like. If you wish to buy any we have a certain amount here, you see—fifty millions, at least." And M. Moulineau opened the door of a large closet, the floor of which was covered, to a height of two yards and more, with millions and millions of stamps.

In one corner was a large shovel and an imposing

M. MOULINEAU OPENED ONE OF THEM

pair of scales, used for piling them up and weighing them.

"I never saw anything like it!" said William in the utmost amazement. "The New York dealers have nothing of this sort."

M. Moulineau smiled. "You see now," he said, "what a large stamp business is in Paris. And, believe

SACKS FULL OF STAMPS

me, it is no sinecure to manage it. I have to be always on the alert; not a moment's repose, not a moment's hesitation. Not a day passes now without a new issue in some country more or less· unknown and far away. And if they go on in this way much longer only the philatelists who are millionaires like you will be able to afford the luxury of collecting stamps. As for the others, the smaller ones, they will certainly have to give up this instructive and delightful pastime because of the impossibility there will soon be of collecting even the common ones, which become, alas! more numerous every day. But I don't know why I should speak of this state of things; you know all about it as well as I do."

While talking the two men had returned to the sorting-room.

"Look!" said M. Moulineau, snatching up some of the stamps from the table and waxing warmer every moment. "Look at these Commemorative stamps that Portugal issued last year, to glorify the seventh centenary of St. Anthony of Padua. They are all surcharged, too, for the Azores. On some of them you can admire the portrait of the saint—it seems to be very like him. Others represent some of his principal miracles—his preaching to the fishes, his ascension; the most amusing thing being that, on their backs, under the gum, they have printed a prayer to St. Bonadventure. The Portuguese Government have even issued a whole series of stamps which they had previously had blessed! These, naturally, were sold at double their value!"

"And yet it is difficult for philatelists to recognise them."

"Then this year we have had: in Italy, the cards commemorative of the entry of the Piedmontese troops into Rome; in Peru and Ecuador, stamps destined to cause the memory of intestine strife to live in the hearts of the people; in the Transvaal stamps commemorative of what——? Of the establishment in the State of a halfpenny post!"

"Ah! These commemorative stamps will become a little too numerous before long," said William.

"We shall be invaded, inundated, submerged by them! Australia was the first to open fire; then it

was England's turn, in 1887, to celebrate the fiftieth year of Queen Victoria's reign; then the United States launched the Christopher Columbus stamps, in honour of the four hundredth anniversary of the discovery of America. Afterwards, ah! afterwards things have gone on at a fine rate, as you know. We have had the stamps with which the little Republic of San Marino celebrated the foundation of its national palace; those with which Portugal celebrated the five hundredth anniversary of Don Henry, the navigator; Bulgaria, the baptism of Prince Boris; and finally the Exhibition stamps of Antwerp, Brussels, Venice," etc., etc.

"There certainly are some countries which abuse their privileges."

"Some countries! Why, those that yield themselves to this shameful speculation are innumerable: the Argentine Republic, Colombia, Honduras, Nicaragua, Peru, the Belgian Congo State, the Spanish West Indies, the Philippines! I should never come to the end were I to mention them all. If they would even be content with issuing ordinary postage stamps! But no, they must have Unpaid Letter stamps, Official stamps, Telegraph stamps!"

"It is hard indeed to say where they will end."

"We cannot say. There are some governments which sell, without any shame, whole issues to certain not over-particular dealers. Witness the greater number of the Egyptian stamps sold to one of my fellow-dealers this last winter. But a reaction against such abuses cannot long be delayed."

"Obviously."

"I hear, too, that in order to defend themselves collectors have just formed a society in London, called the 'Society for the Suppression of Speculative Stamps,' designated by the four letters, 'S.S.S.'"

"It is quite true."

"They say, too, that the Philatelic Congress at Mannheim recently protested in strong language against such jobbing."

"That is equally true. . . . And do you hope it will bring about any good result?"

"How can I tell? I do not know in the least. The only certain thing is that neither Society nor Congress has power to impose its will on States which, having come to the end of their resources, can replenish their funds with a new issue, or, which is more economical, content themselves with putting some inartistic surcharge on their current issues. Oh, those surcharges! They ought to be despised, scorned by every collector! They are of no interest whatever! If I made a collection on my own account I would give them no more place than I would give the German, Russian, or Chinese locals, which have never been in legal use at all, and are but the parasites of philately."

As the dealer pronounced this fulminating diatribe one of his clerks came in and handed him a visiting-card.

"It is a lady," said M. Moulineau to his visitor, "who wishes to speak to me at once. Shall we go into my study?"

"With pleasure," returned William with a quiet smile, for he felt convinced that the lady was no other than his young friend, which was, indeed, a fact. The girl was waiting in M. Moulineau's room when he entered, accompanied by William. She could not repress a slight gesture of disappointment at seeing her rival first in the field. But she recovered herself and greeted him with a smile.

"You here, Mr. Keniss?"

"Yes, Miss Betty, and very glad to have the pleasure of introducing you to M. Moulineau, for you are not yet acquainted, I believe, with the celebrated M. Moulineau?"

"I have not that honour," said the girl, bowing, while the stamp dealer also made a profound inclination.

"Miss Betty Scott, of New York," continued

William, "is a great philatelist. She has been collecting for six months at the most, and yet during that time she has formed a collection almost equal to mine."

M. Moulineau thought he could not have heard aright, and opened his eyes to their fullest extent.

that she might understand his visit had been both interesting and profitable—

"I have been here for half an hour, Miss Scott, and have had a chat—a long chat—with M. Moulineau. Have I not, M. Moulineau?"

"Yes, yes, Mr. Keniss, yes, certainly."

HE HANDED THE PHOTOGRAPHS TO THE YOUNG LADY

"A collection almost equal to yours, did you say?"

"Yes, very nearly equal."

M. Moulineau, stupefied, muttered to himself, "In six months! Most extraordinary!" while William turned to Betty and said, laying stress on his words

Betty bit her lips in increasing mortification.

"Yes," she said, "you are before me this time."

"And, believe me, I am already cursing my lucky star. But I will not keep you longer"; and he saluted respectfully and retired.

(To be continued.)

PHILATELIC SOCIETIES

Enterprise Philatelic Society

Secretary : A. C. Constantinides, Woodview, Archway Road, Highgate, London, N.

Meetings : Monthly, Devonshire House Hotel, Bishopsgate Street, London, E.C.

THE twenty-third ordinary monthly meeting took place at the Devonshire House Hotel, Bishopsgate Street, E.C., on Wednesday, April 19th.

Present : Messrs. E. A. Klaber, E. W. Butcher, G. H. Ordish, P. Farnan, W. B. Edwards, B.SC., D. C. Tewson, G. H. Simons, A. H. Harris, H. W. Westcott, W. H. Eastwood, H. Wills, A. C. Constantinides, and five visitors.

Mr. Klaber (Vice-President) occupied the chair at 6.30 p.m., when the minutes of the previous meeting were read and confirmed.

The name of Mr. Paul E. Lehmann, of New York City, was added to the membership roll.

The resignation of Mr. Harper from the office of

Librarian rendered vacant one seat on the Committee which had been held by virtue of office, but Mr. Harper was unanimously elected to retain the duties of a Committeeman.

The following votes of thanks were passed by the meeting :—To sundry members for donations to the Library ; to the Fiscal Philatelic Society for several copies of the official catalogue of their recent Exhibition for distribution amongst the "Enterprise" members, and to Mr. Edwards and the Rev. O. W. Clarke for donations to the Forgery Collection.

The first part of the programme was provided by Mr. W. Schwabacher, who had kindly promised to dilate upon the joys appertaining to the collecting of Fiscals. This gentleman gave an extempore discourse, and illustrated his remarks by a marvellous array of the Fiscal stamps of Mexico. Sheet after sheet of the handsome stamps were passed round, and elicited the undisguised admiration of all present. Mr. Schwabacher's humorous remarks raised many a

THE STAMP KING

By G. DE BEAUREGARD AND H. DE GORSSE

Translated from the French by EDITH C. PHILLIPS

SHE SAW AN ANNOUNCEMENT

CHAPTER VIII (*continued*)

*In which William Keniss, Stamp King though he is,
passes from one surprise to another*

BETTY, left alone with the stamp dealer, explained the object of her visit.

"Sir," she began, "I do not know if the gentleman who has just left us has told you of the philatelic duel in which we are engaged. A little time ago you sold Mr. Keniss a stamp from the Maharajah of Brahmapootra?"

"Quite true, Miss Scott," returned M. Moulineau, convinced now that this was his customer's rival.

"Of this stamp, you say, there exist but two copies?"

"The one belonging to Mr. Keniss—and another ——"

"Can you possibly get the other one for me? I have come to you on purpose to ask this of you."

M. Moulineau felt so embarrassed that he hardly knew how to reply.

"Do you know, Miss Scott," he said at last, "that is exactly what Mr. William Keniss came to ask me to do? I can only answer you as I have just answered him."

"Well, tell me quickly."

"Some days ago I sold the second copy to one of my best customers."

"Sold it! To whom?"

"Forgive me if I do not tell you that, Miss Scott. I have given my word of honour not to divulge to anyone the name of the new owner of the Brahmapootra stamp. You see how impossible it is for me to break this engagement."

But Miss Betty could not bear to be beaten.

"You have given your word of honour," she said. "Would it be indiscreet if I asked you to whom?"

The dealer reflected again. He was evidently fighting against himself, and considering whether he ought to answer the question so adroitly put.

"Yes, Miss Scott, it would, I fear, be indiscreet," he said at length.

"Then there is no more to be said," returned the girl. And she rose to take her leave of M. Moulineau, feeling very cross, for she had no doubt it was William who had extracted the promise from him.

"If only I could be of service to you in some way in this matter," began M. Moulineau, who was a most obliging man, and deeply grieved at not being able to satisfy the curiosity of the charming philatelist.

"I do not at all see how," returned Betty.

"I do! I do!" cried M. Moulineau, struck with a brilliant idea. "Have you a *fac-simile* of the stamp you are seeking?"

"No."

"Then permit me to offer you some." And, opening the drawer of his writing-table, he took out five or six little photographs of the Brahmapootra stamp, like those he had already given William Keniss, and handed them to Betty. This did not commit him to much, and gave him an opportunity of being kind at a very small cost.

"Moreover," he continued, "here is the last number of the little journal I publish every month—*L'Echo de la Philatélie*. You will find in it a very minute description of the stamp which interests you, with circumstantial details as to its colour, paper, etc."

"Thank you," said Betty, taking the photographs and the journal. "Your little present may some day be more useful to me than you think."

And the infatuated philatelist left M. Moulineau,

SHE ACQUAINTED M. PICQUOISEAU WITH HER OBJECT

assuring him of her gratitude for the way in which he had received her, but a little discomforted as she thought how much better it might have been for her had she risen an hour earlier, or loitered less at the shop windows. And in deep meditation she once more gained the Boulevards.

CHAPTER IX

In which Miss Betty determines to use strong measures

IT can be easily imagined that Miss Betty's reflections were not happy ones. She wandered on at random, seeking for some means to ward off the blows of fate, which seemed obstinately to fight against her. Vexation with William for having got the start of her, and especially at feeling herself the victim of his foresight, absorbed her completely.

"What can I do? What can I do?" she kept saying to herself.

Passing through a by-street she happened to see in gold letters the announcement—"Picquoiseau, Intelligence Agency." It gave her an idea.

"I'll do it," she said, after a moment's hesitation. "I will have William Keniss shadowed, so that, if he goes after his stamp, I shall hear of it, and perhaps, with the help of a little audacity, get the better of him." And she entered the house containing the offices of the intelligence agency.

A staircase mounted, a ring of the bell, one minute's waiting in the ante-room, and she was ushered into a room, elegantly though plainly furnished, one wall of which was occupied by rows of little green boxes all numbered. This was the private office of M. Prosper Picquoiseau.

The chief rose as she entered, and Miss Betty beheld, behind a table piled up with numerous and important papers—intended, perhaps, to throw dust in the eyes of clients—a tall man, thin and spare, with a head angular and flattened as that of a bird of prey, and whose twinkling eyes never looked one straight in the face.

"What an ugly man!" thought the girl.

"Madame," said M. Picquoiseau, "will you have the kindness to take a seat, and tell me the purpose which has brought you hither?"

The young American, seated opposite M. Picquoiseau, soon made him acquainted with her object.

"I want a gentleman followed, and I want to know, day by day, hour by hour, what he does and where he goes."

"Nothing is easier," returned the chief. "You have only to give us the address and description of the gentleman, madam, and every morning and every evening, or several times a day if you wish it, and at whatever hours you please, you shall receive notes, relating all the goings and comings of the person in question. For all lesser details you can make what arrangements you like with one of the detectives whom I will place at your service. Will you kindly give me your name and address, and the name and address of the gentleman to be shadowed?"

At this Betty hesitated. She felt, all at once, that it was not a nice thing she was doing. But it was too late now to draw back, so she gave the chief the information he asked for.

"I should like three reports a day," she added—"one in the morning, one during the day, and one in the evening."

"At eight o'clock, twelve, and nine?"

"Yes, that will do." And Miss Betty rose to leave.

M. Picquoiseau, who had also risen, detained her with a gesture.

"I beg your pardon for mentioning such a subject," said he, "but it is customary, in confiding a matter of this sort to a detective agency, to pay a certain deposit at the office. I shall be obliged if you will kindly conform to this little formality before you go."

"Oh—certainly—sir——" returned Betty, blushing to a deep crimson.

M. Picquoiseau was already pointing out the way to the office when Betty, summoning up all her courage, said bravely—

"I have not the money with me at this moment, but if you will send someone to me this afternoon I will hand him the amount. Please tell me how much it will be."

"In your case, madam, only five hundred francs."

"Very well. I will send the five hundred francs by your messenger."

"At what time should you wish him to come?"

"At half-past three. Mr. Keniss will be with me at that time, and your detective, if it be the one who is to shadow him, can see for himself what he is like, and follow him at once."

"Very good, madam; that is settled then?"

It was nearly twelve o'clock when, the matter being thus arranged, Miss Betty left M. Picquoiseau's room, and she immediately resumed her way to the Place Vendôme, delighted with herself as she thought how her little plot would hinder Mr. Keniss from profiting by the advantage he had gained. But though it was now high time for her to return to the hotel, the luncheon hour being near, Miss Scott stopped once more at the post and telegraph office in the Rue Choiseul, which had been just pointed out to her by a sergent de ville. There she inquired the cost of a telegram within the city, and, finding she could send by pneumatic post for fifteen or thirty centimes, according as she chose an open or a closed card, she despatched the following, after a careful examination of her pocket had brought to light a few pence, which the gallant Tilbury had disdained:—

"MR. WILLIAM KENISS,
  "HOTEL TERMINUS,
    "RUE ST. LAZARE.

"DEAR MR. KENISS,—Will you be kind enough to come and see me this afternoon between three and four o'clock? I absolutely must speak to you.
  "With kind regards,
      "BETTY SCOTT."

After which she hastened to the Hotel Bristol.

THE STAMP KING

By G. DE BEAUREGARD AND H. DE GORSSE

Translated from the French by EDITH C. PHILLIPS

CHAPTER IX (*continued*)

In which Miss Betty determines to use strong measures

IN the meantime what had William Keniss been doing? On leaving M. Moulineau he had hailed a fiacre and driven to the Bois for an airing. His rival, Miss Betty, being ignorant of the fate of the Brahmapootra stamp, he hoped to have time to study Paris at his leisure. So he drove this morning towards Longchamps and the Cascade—the most tranquil and delightful drive—admiring the little glimpses of landscape opening up before him as the carriage continued its course along the pretty shaded alleys of the Bois de ·Boulogne.

But as he was returning towards the city, an idea suddenly occurred to him.

"Suppose, by chance, Prince Albrandi has disposed of his stamp! I never thought of that. It would be useless then for me to go to Naples. I must get to know somehow."

So when they reached the post office in the Rue de Marignan the young philatelist went in and, at the very moment when Betty was addressing her message to him, sent off the following telegram :—

"PRINCE ALBRANDI,
"STRADA NUOVA DI POSILLIPO,
"NAPLES.

"Have you still in your possession the Brahmapootra stamp sold you by M. Moulineau? I should like to know, as I am myself an ardent philatelist. Pray excuse the liberty I take, and allow me to thank you in advance for your kind answer.

"WILLIAM KENISS,
"HOTEL TERMINUS,
"PARIS."

And the Stamp King returned to his hotel, where, during luncheon, he received Miss Betty's pneumatic card.

CHAPTER X

How Miss Betty received three simultaneous visits which she would have preferred to have in succession

BETTY had scarcely left the table before she began to count the minutes, so full of impatience was she. Victoria having asked leave to go and see her friend John, she had given it, on condition that she returned in time to show in the expected visitors. For we must remember that the little American had made three appointments for that afternoon ; the first at about half-past two with M. Courtalain's man, who was to bring her the twenty thousand francs for her ear-rings ; the second at half-past three with M. Picquoiseau's agent ; and the third between three and four with her rival, William Keniss.

"I do hope," she said to herself, "that the three will arrive in the right order, or I shall find myself in a difficulty."

The maid, having promised not to be long away, went out. Just as two o'clock struck William arrived, to Betty's surprise and annoyance, for her maid had not yet returned.

"I am too early," he said, "but I hope you will forgive my eagerness."

"Not a bit too early," returned Miss Scott, devoutly wishing she could send him away. But it could not be done, so she must play her part.

The conversation touched only on quite insignificant matters to begin with. Betty and William both found it an uncomfortable interview. The girl's lips burned with a question she dared not utter, but which he felt, all the same, in every insignificant word. So they both avoided any subject which could lead the talk in the direction of philately. They spoke of everything and of nothing : of what they had read in the morning papers, of how delightful the weather was for May, and of the impressions made upon them by their first walk in Paris, but not one allusion to their respective visits to M. Moulineau that morning.

And all the time Betty was giving signs of the liveliest impatience. "Victoria has not come back," she was thinking. "She will never be here by the time the jeweller sends me my money."

After a few moments' conversation, which was all the more laboured because Betty was trying to invent some excuse for her pressing invitation, one of the hotel servants appeared.

"There is someone in the next room who professes to be expected by you, miss," he said.

"Tell him I am coming," returned Miss Betty. Then to William, "Will you kindly excuse me for a few minutes? I really must see this person."

"Oh, by all means, Miss Scott ; I will look over the paper while you are away."

Betty left the room, and William dipped into a soporific leading article, which would soon have sent him to sleep had not scraps of conversation continually reached him through the door of the next room, which the little American had thoughtlessly left ajar. He caught such phrases as these, spoken by one or the other in an earnest tone, and he vainly sought the meaning of them :—

"With regard to the deposit——? "
"Five hundred francs. I have a receipt——"
"Ready to pay—— Wait a few minutes ; someone is coming——"

It was, of course, M. Picquoiseau's agent who was carrying on a conversation with Miss Betty.

Then she heard a door in the next room open and shut, so without passing through the sitting-room, where William was waiting, she went to the third room to receive the new-comer. But she did not remain with him more than a few minutes, and, having sent him away, returned to her other visitor.

"What can she be plotting?" wondered William Keniss, astonished at the few words he had overheard and at Betty's journeys to and fro.

But the Stamp King was not to remain long in doubt on the subject, for a young man, after two timid little knocks, opened the door and looked in.

"I beg your pardon for disturbing you," said he. "Could you tell me where I shall find the lady with whom I have just been talking in the next room? I forgot to get her to date the receipt for the twenty thousand francs I brought her from M. Courtalain, the jeweller in the Rue de la Paix, for a pair of ear-rings she sold him this morning."

"You surely don't mean that Miss Betty Scott has sold her diamonds!" cried William.

"Why, yes, I do. It seems she found herself without any money, as it had all been stolen during her voyage from New York to Paris."

"Stolen!" murmured William. "And she did not apply to me!" And, turning to the jeweller, "Be good enough, sir," said he, "to give me back the receipt signed by Miss Betty Scott. Here are twenty thousand francs in return for it."

"What!"

"I shall be much obliged if you will consider the bargain made by the young lady null and void."

"But I do not know whether M. Courtalain will agree."

"He will agree. If he demands any compensation, tell him I will call upon him almost immediately. Meanwhile, it is scarcely necessary to say that I wish you to bring back, as quickly as possible, Miss Betty's ear-rings, which she has sold and I have bought back."

"It shall be done as you say, sir."

Scarcely had the jeweller retired when the door of the next room, where Miss Betty was holding her conference with M. Picquoiseau's man, opened wide, and revealed to William the person whom he had heard talking with the little American. He was a man of about thirty, not over-well dressed, and not of a particularly prepossessing appearance. In crossing the room to go out he looked fixedly at the Stamp King, so much so that the latter could not help saying to himself—

"Who is this fellow who stares at me so? Can it possibly be——? But no, not possibly."

In fact, a vague suspicion had begun to rise in William's mind. He had a feeling as if a snare were being wound around him, and yet no definite idea as to what form it was taking. But a smile from Betty, who re-entered the room after seeing the unknown to the outer door, drove away all apprehension.

"Do forgive me for having left you so long," said the girl. "I had an important little matter of business to settle, but it is finished now. I am entirely at your disposal."

William was debating with himself as to whether he should let her know how he had bought back her ear-rings, the fear of offending her making him hesitate. But, on the other hand, it would not do for her to be unprepared when M. Courtalain sent back her diamonds, so, all things considered, he thought it best to speak.

"Miss Betty," said he, "M. Courtalain's man, who was here just now, forgot to ask you to date the receipt, so he came in here to look for you, and, naturally, found me instead."

"He found you!"

"By a word from him I gathered what had happened——"

"And ——?"

"I took the liberty, by returning the price of the ear-rings, to break off a bargain which you must have been sorry to make."

"That is most provoking of you!" cried Miss Betty, whose face, as William spoke, had passed through all the varying shades from most delicate pink to deepest scarlet. "So I have become your debtor in spite of myself?"

"Well, Miss Betty, I suppose I must accept the position of creditor, though it would have given me far greater pleasure had you never again mentioned such an insignificant debt."

"My dear Mr. Keniss, allow me——"

"Yes, of course, I know you could not consent to that. From this date, therefore, the fifth of May, 1896, Miss Betty Scott, of New York, owes Mr. William Keniss, equally of New York, the enormous sum of twenty thousand francs, which she will repay without interest whenever it suits her. Now are you satisfied?"

"You do well to make a joke of it, but I am furiously angry."

"What, angry with me, your friend, because I believed my respectful affection for you gave me the right to help you? Wasn't that our compact?"

"Oh, well, let it be so. I forgive you."

"Ah, now you are charming."

"But all the same, another time, before arranging my affairs, you might at least consult me."

"I promise you I will."

Then, to show him she bore no malice for what had happened, she gave him her hand, which he chivalrously bent and kissed.

"If you should happen, when you go back to the Terminus Hotel, to see Victoria, who has gone to pay her friend John a visit, I should be much obliged if you would kindly tell her I am very much displeased. She promised to be back by two o'clock."

"And it is after three, and I must go. Good-bye, Miss Betty."

"Good-bye—and thank you."

Then William began to think that perhaps she was too timid to make use of him, and instantly he demanded why she had sent for him, and if she would like him to take her out somewhere. She stammered out a vague explanation, and, with signs of embarrassment, begged him to excuse her, urging that, being in France, they must conform somewhat to the custom of the country. So he took leave of her, feeling that her conduct was both strange and mysterious.

(To be continued.)

APPROVAL SHEETS AND COLLECTIONS.

New Sheets of stamps for beginners and medium collectors. We have just been arranging our Approval Sheets of Stamps on an entirely new and much simpler plan than formerly. The Stamps are mounted on Sheets, containing an average of 100 Stamps per Sheet. They are all arranged in the order of our New Catalogue. First, Great Britain and the Colonies, then all Foreign Countries. These Sheets contain about 5,000 different Stamps, and a Sheet of any particular country will be sent on demand. The Sheets arranged to date are over forty in number, and contain all Great Britain and the Colonies, and all Foreign Countries.

THE STAMP KING

By G. DE BEAUREGARD *and* H. DE GORSSE

Translated from the French by EDITH C. PHILLIPS

CHAPTER X (*continued*)

*How Miss Betty received three simultaneous visits
which she would have preferred to have in succession*

ON leaving the Hotel Bristol he saw, a few paces off, at the base of the Vendôme Column, three men walking up and down, as if waiting for someone. He recognised one of them for the fellow whom he had seen a few minutes before with Miss Betty, and who had stared at him so rudely. As soon as he appeared this man pointed him out quietly to his two companions, and, by the way in which they also studied him, the American felt certain they were detectives of some sort. And he was by no means pleased to find they were shadowing him. When he stopped at M. Courtalain's to settle about the ear-rings they waited for him on the opposite pavement, and, as soon as ever he had taken a step outside, they followed him again with the same persistence.

"They make such a show of spying upon me," thought William, "that it would almost seem as if they do it purposely. I see what it means. Not only am I shadowed, but I am to know that I am, so as to take away from me all desire for action, for the good reason that if I make the least move Betty will immediately hear of it, and hasten to thwart me and profit by it herself."

But at this moment he arrived at the Terminus Hotel, and lost no time in entering.

SHADOWED BY THREE MEN

CHAPTER XI

Wherein John meditates a terrible vengeance

VICTORIA, having received Betty's permission to go out, hastened to the Terminus Hotel, wasting no time in playing truant in the Paris streets. She had deeply considered the question of her marriage with William's valet since the evening before, and felt that she had things of the highest importance to say to him. John was exerting himself in putting his master's clothes in order when Victoria arrived and breathlessly rang the bell of their rooms. As the authoritative peal echoed through the whole hotel the good fellow started so that he let fall the coat he was brushing. But as soon as he recovered from the shock he hurried to the door, thinking it must be Mr. William Keniss returning unexpectedly.

As he opened the door a still greater shock caused him to fall back two or three steps, and nearly threw him on the floor. Victoria, always in exuberant spirits when she found herself in the presence of the man to whom she had lost her heart, had thrown herself without warning into his arms. And John, being quite unprepared for such an event, could only stare open-mouthed, incapable of manifesting his surprise in any other manner.

"That's a nice way of coming in!" he cried at last, when he could find breath enough.

"Then you didn't expect to see me?" returned Victoria.

"Well, well——"

"Well, what?"

"Well, I didn't expect you—so soon !——"

"Then does my coming displease you, sir?"

"No, no! What ideas you do get into your head, my dear Victoria!"

"Well, you don't look as pleased as you ought to be at my visit."

"What makes you think I am not pleased? I am delighted—enchanted——"

"No one would imagine it."

"I can't fire a salute from a cannon every time I see you. In the first place, for the very good reason that I am not in the habit of carrying such an instrument about with me. But come into this room and tell me what brings you here."

"What brings me! He wants to know what brings me! The ungrateful man! And what do you think would be likely to bring me, Master John, if not the thing in which we are both so deeply interested?"

"Our marriage?"

"Of course."

"Are you afraid, then, that I shall forget it? The thought of it is never out of my mind."

"I don't believe you."

"Must I give you my word of honour?"

"Yes."

"Very well; you have it."

Such were the first greetings exchanged that day between John Cockburn and Victoria Crockett, and, if we might be allowed to draw a conclusion from these few words, we should say that Mr. William Keniss's valet, honest fellow though he was, occasionally gave his word of honour somewhat lightly. We know that John quite intended to marry Victoria, whose nice little dowry was far from distasteful to him, but he was in no great hurry for the nuptial ceremony, holding that there are some things, even some agreeable ones, which may be put off for a time without inconvenience. And marriage, as we have seen, was, in his opinion, one of these things.

Victoria, on the other hand, in spite of her lost youth, loved him with an ardent love, and was so afraid, too, of becoming an old maid that she would have married him straight off had it been possible. So Miss Scott's hurried departure, coming at the very moment when John, tired of resisting her importunities, was on the point of giving in, had hurt her deeply. Her wedding had been indefinitely postponed, perhaps broken off altogether. She had asked herself if it were possible John should forget her entirely, in spite of his many promises. For she doubted the truth of the old proverb—"Absence makes the heart grow fonder."

So it was in a very unhappy frame of mind that Victoria had crossed from New York to Havre, where, however, one of the greatest joys that had illuminated her existence was awaiting her, for there she met again, in the most unexpected way, him whom she feared she had lost for so long.

"So it is really true there is no change with regard to our marriage?" she began again, while John continued his work, walking backwards and forwards in the room.

"Why, Victoria, what do you want changed?"

"Nothing at all; but I am afraid——"

"Why?"

"Because you men are so changeable."

"Other men may be, but I am not."

"Oh, you are no better than the rest."

"Yes, I suppose I did."

"Doesn't it seem to you the most natural thing in the world? How can we tell when we shall get back to New York?"

"On the other hand, how can we tell how long we shall be in Paris?"

"What do you mean by that?"

"Why, we can't get married in that way, straight off the reel. There are innumerable formalities to be complied with in France as well as in America—more even in France than in America. And for that purpose we must have plenty of time before us. Now it seems to me that this isn't our case, for either you or I may have to leave here at any minute—to-day, to-morrow, the day after to-morrow. How do we know when?"

"All the same——"

"No, Victoria; take my word for it we can't get

JOHN WAS OCCUPIED IN BRUSHING HIS MASTER'S CLOTHES

"Thank you—on my own account first and secondly on theirs."

But Victoria, seeing the conversation was not taking the direction she wished, could not repress a movement of impatience.

"Look here, John," she cried; "this is not the time to be witty. We are talking of serious things."

"I quite agree with you."

"Before we left New York we had settled, you know, to have the banns published."

"Yes, I remember."

"And by this time we should probably have been married."

"Very likely."

"So I've thought of something."

"What is it?"

"As we didn't get married in New York, why shouldn't we in Paris?"

John stopped in his work with such a jump that he nearly knocked his head against the ceiling, while a look of the deepest surprise spread over his face.

"*What* did you say?" he demanded.

"It isn't necessary to repeat it. You heard quite well."

married in Paris. We must wait till we get back to New York; for I promise you the wedding shall take place as soon as ever we return."

"You swear it?"

"Yes, I do."

The future husband and wife being, as we know, devoted to bezique, now settled themselves at a table and began a game. At first chance favoured John, who almost immediately scored a hundred for aces and a two hundred and fifty. Then for a few minutes they played on without being able to declare anything, and the game was becoming monotonous, when Miss Betty's maid threw down a king and queen of trumps, crying—

"Forty for a royal marriage."

John could not resist so good an opportunity for a joke.

"Really, my dear, you can't think of anything but marrying people to-day," he said.

It was not, perhaps, a very witty remark, but Victoria was so delighted at having scored forty that she laughed long and loud.

At this moment a bell rang.

THE STAMP KING

By G. DE BEAUREGARD and H. DE GORSSE

Translated from the French by EDITH C. PHILLIPS

CHAPTER XI (*continued*)

Wherein John meditates a terrible vengeance

"THAT must be the master!" cried John, running to open the door, while Victoria covered the table with a newspaper to hide the cards. But she took care first to glance at her opponent's, which were turned face downwards, not with any intention of cheating, but because she had so much curiosity in her composition that she was incapable of resisting it, especially when playing bezique.

"False alarm!" said John, reappearing.

"What was it, then?"

"A little telegraph boy, who brought this for Mr. Keniss."

"Then let us go on."

"By all means."

The game began again in earnest. Victoria regained the ground she had lost by scoring the five hundred, then sixty for queens. As for John, he sacrificed several marriages, one after the other, for the sake of getting forty for knaves, which was not exactly brilliant play.

A terrible and excited strife continued from that moment between the two players. John held in his hand a magnificent two hundred and fifty, but to score them he must take a trick, and Victoria put forth all her efforts to prevent this, and succeeded, by dint of throwing away, one after another, all her trumps. One consolation only remained for the unhappy John, the last trick, for which he was able to take ten, a very small compensation for the loss of two hundred and fifty.

"To think I should hold that sequence in my hand and not be able to score it!" he cried.

The two then counted up their respective tens and aces. Each of these counting ten, John was able to mark a hundred and ten, and Victoria fifty.

"Now how many have you?" she demanded.

"Seven hundred and seventy. And you?"

"Nine hundred and eighty."

"Then you have won!"

"I'll give you your revenge."

"All right."

And they were just about to begin a second game when they once more heard the bell.

"This time it must be the master," said John.

Victoria hastened to dispose of the cards in one of the table drawers while John went to the door. It really was Mr. Keniss who entered.

"You will get into trouble, my good Victoria," said he. "I have just come from the Hotel Bristol, where I left Miss Scott very much annoyed at your long absence."

Seeing by a glance at the clock that it was nearly four, Victoria uttered a cry and disappeared, without staying for any adieus. John, who had followed her flight with a look of indulgent compassion, returned to his master, to whom he gave the recently-arrived telegram. William hastily opened the blue paper, and his eyes shone as he read—

"WILLIAM KENISS,
"TERMINUS HOTEL,
"PARIS.

"Have still Brahmapootra stamp in album. Greeting. PRINCE ALBRANDI."

"Ha! ha!" thought he. "Now I can stay in Paris as long as I please, to spite those two bloodhounds who are following me." And turning to his valet he said, "I have some news for you, John."

"Might I ask, sir, if it has anything to do with our journey, and with the stamp we are in pursuit of?"

"Yes, my friend, it has." And the good news having put the Stamp King in the humour for confidences, he recounted the whole of his day's adventures to John, from his visit to M. Moulineau to his recent call on Betty. Then he told of the strange way in which he had been followed, which was a great shock to the susceptible fellow.

"That is too bad," he said, "and I never could have believed Miss Scott capable of such behaviour! We are neither thieves nor assassins."

"So it seems to me. But if that is what hurts and offends you, my dear John, I can reassure you. It is not only assassins and thieves who are shadowed. Sometimes, for different motives, people have the highest and most important personages followed; political men, for instance, especially members of the Opposition, whose intrigues the Government may have cause to dread. So you see we are, perhaps, in excellent company."

"Oh, in that case it is different. But all the same, I shouldn't have thought it of Miss Scott. I did expect better things of her."

"What would you have?" said William philosophically. "One must defend one's self the best way one can. Every stratagem is admissible in war, even spies. So don't be more royal than the King; and, since I treat the matter as a comedy, don't you think it a tragedy. Moreover, we have nothing to fear, for we shall get the better of our spies."

But this did not prevent John letting various sinister designs pass through his mind. He wondered if he could provoke the rascals to single combat, or harass them to such an extent that they would be disgusted with their calling from that time forward. William Keniss began to suspect these Machiavellian meditations, and set himself to calm them.

"Here is something that may interest you, you

A SPY

collector of forgeries and reprints," he said, presenting him with one of the photographs of the Brahmapootra stamp which M. Moulineau had given him that morning.

"It is a very fine copy," said John, examining it with the air of a connoisseur. "I see M. Moulineau is going to make a good thing out of these imitations from customers who cannot get the originals."

"You forget, my lad, that M. Moulineau is a very honest dealer."

"Oh, I have a very limited confidence in dealers myself. When I used to make a proper collection I discovered in New York an old broker, from whom I thought I got splendid bargains. Not a week passed without his selling me, on the pretext that it was a special opportunity, some very rare stamp for a few cents. So I made up a magnificent album, which made my friends ready to burst with envy. One day, being short of money, I determined to sell my collection, so I went and found another dealer, before whom I displayed it triumphantly. He carelessly turned over the pages and then, in the most natural tone in the world, said, 'But, my friend, these are all forgeries.' You can imagine what an idiot I felt, sir. At first I nearly fainted ; then gathering my wits together, I went off to the broker who had deceived me so infamously, and, I can tell you, the old Jew heard of it that day ; I called him a liar and a cheat, and threatened to bring an action against him and have him arrested! The scoundrel never for an instant lost his calmness and serenity, and what do you think he replied, sir? But you would never guess."

"Tell me, then."

"He said he had never told me there was one original among all those he had sold me, and I was a fool to think there was !——"

"So I suppose from that time you began to collect forgeries?" interrupted William.

"Yes, sir, and I have found means to get something out of them, for several times over they've sold me real stamps under the impression they were forgeries."

Mr. Keniss laughed heartily at this frank avowal.

"Be off," he said. "You are making me forget with your chatter that I have several letters to write. I do not need you just now, so you can go out if you like."

John did not wait to be told twice, and, putting away the photograph of the Brahmapootra stamp in his pocket-book, he started for a stroll through the streets. On the way he reflected deeply. He had no doubt that he would be followed as well as his master, and he—who was so touchy in the matter of his liberty that he was continually putting off the day of his marriage, though desiring it in his heart—chafed against the idea of having his footsteps dogged by some scoundrel of a spy, and his least movement reported to Miss Betty Scott.

As he strolled along the narrow pavement of the Rue de Provence his eye lighted by chance upon a little white placard fixed to a door, and bearing these words, drawn by hand :—

"SKILFUL ENGRAVER, *working at home, wishes for work. Apply within.*"

Mechanically he stopped, remained a few seconds plunged in thought ; then, crying "I have it ! What a good idea !" he disappeared up the dark passage.

CHAPTER XII

Showing how lost time is sometimes merely time gained

THE engraver, M. Auguste Crabifosse, a very clever workman, formerly employed in the workshops of the Bank of France, occupied a very small and modest apartment on the fifth floor. He welcomed very courteously the client who had fallen from the skies—up ninety-six stairs—and showed him into the room where he was accustomed to work. The dimensions of this room were restricted, but it was very clean, and, above all, very light, for part of the roof was of glass. The middle of the room was occupied by an immense work-table, on which were piled all manner of instruments—chisels, gravers, files, and hammers, planks of wood, ingots of lead, slabs of steel and of copper, and finally, a number of little basins of different sizes, filled to the brim with liquids of varying shades.

"I just caught sight of your writing, sir," said John, "as I was passing along the street. You are out of work just at this moment ?"

"I was, two or three days ago," returned the engraver, "but that announcement has already brought me several important orders."

"Pressing ones ?"

"As a general rule, sir, orders always are pressing."

"I meant by that, would it be possible for you to undertake, at the same time, a small piece of work which is wanted in a great hurry ?"

"Certainly, it is always possible to arrange that. But still it is necessary——"

"That the work should be well paid for, to make up for the overtime you must put in to get this fresh order finished without interfering with the others ! Well, M. Crabifosse, there will be no difficulty about that. I am prepared to pay whatever you think right."

"It is easy to see, sir, that you are quite accustomed to business arrangements."

"Oh, no ; I am simply an American, and, as you know, all Americans are sharp. See, this is what I want done."

And John took from his pocket the photograph of the Brahmapootra stamp given him by Mr. Keniss, and explained to the engraver that he wished for an exact copy from which a stamp might be printed in gold, on a particular paper, with a special perforation ; in fact, such an exact copy that it might be taken for the original. The idea of the astute, cunning fellow was a very simple one—merely to obtain a forgery which might be mistaken for the original stamp, to let it fall into Miss Betty's hands by some means or other, and so persuade her to return triumphantly to America, while Mr. Keniss could at his ease proceed with the purchase of the real one.

This was not, perhaps, a very refined or delicate calculation. "But it's not necessary to be too particular with a lady who can set spies on us," thought John.

(To be continued.)

THE STRAND POSTAGE STAMP ALBUM.

Well arranged, reliable, and thoroughly correct. Seventh edition. 100 Postage Stamps, all genuine and different, and of a catalogue value of over 8s., are presented with each Strand Album. The book, which is printed on an unusually good quality paper, is bound in a new and specially designed cover. The shape is as illustrated, and the size a new and convenient one, viz. 9½ inches by 7½ inches. Sufficient guards have been inserted so that when the Album is full the covers shall be level with each other, and not bulged, as is often the case in imperfectly constructed books. 300 pages, post-free, 2s. 11d. ; abroad, 3s. 4d.

Stanley Gibbons, Ltd., 391, Strand, London, W.C.

THE STAMP KING

By G. DE BEAUREGARD AND H. DE GORSSE

Translated from the French by EDITH C. PHILLIPS

JOHN EXPLAINS TO THE ENGRAVER WHAT HE REQUIRES

CHAPTER XII (*continued*)

Showing how lost time is sometimes merely time gained

AT first M. Crabifosse, with a great show of dignity, flatly refused to assist in the forgery, and John had to relate in detail the whole matter, promising that he would take but one impression, and that in the presence of the engraver, and protesting that it was a joke rather than a deceit, before the scrupulous workman would consent to execute the order. But at length, becoming interested in the enterprise, he no longer disdained to give John the benefit of his skill, and even wanted to give him a few hints on the art of engraving, and on the way in which stamps, real stamps, are made in the magnificent buildings in the Boulevard Brune, in Paris, where the State works, as everyone knows, are situated.

John cared little enough about it all, but thought it might be as well to seem to take the liveliest interest.

"I am going to make you a chemical engraving on zinc," said M. Crabifosse, "as that will be quite the best thing for the purpose."

"Are there then several sorts of engraving?" asked the artful fellow.

"I should think so, indeed," said M. Crabifosse. "First of all there is chemical engraving on zinc, as I just said, and wood engraving. These are generally used for illustrating books, for which purpose not a very great number of copies are required. But that would not do for stamps, you see, since we want millions and millions of impressions of those."

"Then an engraving on wood is not reproduced by a galvanoplastic method," insinuated John timidly, though glad to be able to put in a word to show he had some knowledge of the science.

"Yes, in almost identically the same way. But the type would deteriorate if too great a number of prints were taken from it. So it is often necessary for the engraver to use a harder metal, steel being generally employed on account of its cheapness. Types made in steel can stand enormous pressure without wearing at all, and they can be reproduced in as many blocks of steel or any other metal as are wanted. This is how it is done.

"When the steel block comes from the hand of the engraver it is, relatively speaking, soft, since it has had to be shaped with the hammer and cut by the graver and file. It then has to undergo the process of *tempering*, which is done by bringing it to a great heat and then plunging it into a bath of cold water, which cools it suddenly. By this means the steel becomes hard and elastic ; it is *tempered*. The block of steel has now become what is termed a die or mould, and here the work of the engraver ends. The die or mould—call it what you will—is engraved in relief like ordinary type, which also consists of so many little dies.

"It remains now, when a large number of impressions are needed, to reproduce the original die. This is done by impressing it, by machinery, on another block of untempered steel, on which a similar impression is formed. Then this second steel block is tempered, and now forms what is called a matrix, from which as many other dies as are required can be taken in relief, either in copper or soft steel, which must afterwards be tempered. These are now identical with the original die, but, instead of steel, these latter dies are often made of gutta-percha, as, for instance, those from which the French stamps are struck. And now I will tell you how this is done," continued M. Crabifosse, encouraged by the number of nods and other signs of approbation with which John received the information.

"The original design is given to the engraver in a drawing, about eight times the size that the stamp is to be. He engraves it on wood, or in *taille-douce*, three or four times the right size. Then a proof of this engraving is photographed to reduce it to its proper dimensions, and from this the first steel block is made, as I told you. In this block the space for the figures indicating the value of the stamp is left empty. From it fifteen blocks are made in lead, on which are inscribed the fifteen values existing in the French postage stamps, namely 1, 2, 3, 4, 5, 10, 15, 20, 25, 30, 40, 50, 75 centimes, 1 and 5 francs. These fifteen fresh blocks constitute the original dies, and are carefully preserved; a number of gutta-percha blocks are made from them, and are grouped together in formes of three hundred for each sheet.

"Now this sheet, on which the three hundred stamps are printed, is of special paper, and probably tinted before receiving the impression, in order, by

have got an idea how it is all done. But I'm rather in a hurry, so I shall be glad if you will tell me the time necessary for your work and the price you will charge for it."

After a moment's reflection M. Crabifosse said it would only cost a hundred and fifty francs, and that eight days would be sufficient to complete it.

"All right," said John, as he took his departure. "Be as quick as you can, but make a good job of it."

After this the days seemed to pass both slowly and wearily to William Keniss as well as to John. John would not go near M. Crabifosse, thinking it would be useless, and besides, he had no doubt his master's rival had set some horrid creature to dog his footsteps too. And yet, being forewarned, he was

HE EXPLORED ALL THE WONDERS OF PARIS

using a special ink on a special shade of paper, to make washing or forging almost an impossibility.

"Finally, when the impressions have been taken by means of special printing presses, the stamps are perforated by a row of pins arranged in a straight line, which pins, being fixed in a frame, go through the paper all at once, and with marvellous precision, into a number of holes arranged in a plate under the sheet. After the first line of holes has been pierced in the paper, forming the first row of perforations, the sheet advances automatically the width of a stamp, when the pins, descending again, pierce the second line, and so on. Then they are gummed and dried and are ready for use," concluded M. Crabifosse, almost out of breath.

"It is indeed most curious and interesting," declared John, who, to tell the truth, had not been particularly well amused, "and I am not sorry to

on the look-out continually when walking in the street, glancing to right, to left, before and behind him for the lurking shadows, and never able to discover any. But still he acted with great care and circumspection, for he saw how imprudent he would be did he not guard the secret of his business with the engraver in the Rue de Provence. So he thought it best to wait for the appointed day before going in search of his stamp, and he sent M. Crabifosse a letter to this effect, for fear he should wonder at his absence.

Nothing very interesting occurred to break the monotony of these few days. William, however little he allowed it to appear, felt a grudge against the girl who had acted in such a manner towards him; so, in spite of his longing to see her again—a feeling which he did not try to account for, drawing him instinctively towards her—he had the courage to show his displeasure by abstaining from a single visit to the Hotel

Bristol. He feared, too, that in a moment of weakness he might let out the secret he was so anxious to keep.

Miss Betty took little notice of a treatment which she felt she had well deserved, and assured herself that, had she been in his place, she would have done something much worse. Happily for her, she was not one to whom solitude was a burden, even in a foreign land. The little American took advantage of this philatelic calm to extend her walks into the remotest nooks and corners of Paris. She was particularly attracted by the great national museums, and spent whole afternoons in the Louvre, the Luxembourg, and at Cluny, lost in admiration of the number of masterpieces, both ancient and modern, that she found there.

The Stamp King, who also knew nothing of Paris or its wonders, spent his time too in exploring them. But, as this sort of thing seemed likely to go on indefinitely, and as, knowing nothing of John's projects, he had not his reasons for patience, he began to look around for some possible end to the ridiculous situation. First he thought of sending his valet to Prince Albrandi, but a moment's reflection convinced him that this would not do, and that his only chance of success was to go himself.

(*To be continued.*)

CORRESPONDENCE

Unused *v.* Used Stamps

Mr. Heginbottom's Protest

I SEE in my *G.S.W.* an article on the old, old vexed question of "Unused *v.* Used" (page 327), and although I think this subject-matter of discussion has been pretty thoroughly discussed in the philatelic Press, I feel bound to reply to this article, because, like so many past ones on this topic, it lays special stress on the favour of collecting unused only.

All the more do I feel bound to reply, because, curiously enough, it happens that quite recently in correspondence with a personal friend of mine (an enlightened collector, and one well known and highly esteemed in philatelic circles), he makes to me the somewhat startling remark that I am unable to join the front ranks of Philately because I only collect postally used stamps. He writes me as follows: "What a pity you have such a strong view on unused! "But for this you might be joining hands with the "front rank to-day; as it is, your method of collection "will always bar you doing so." Now, in reply to this, permit me to say that, in the first place, I have not the slightest wish to join the front ranks of Philately, or become a Great Mogul; and, in the second place, if, in order to attain to this great honour (?), I shall have to collect unused stamps, not only in single specimens

but in blocks, pairs, sheets, etc., then all the more do I repeat that it is my last wish to even endeavour to join the leading ranks. I fully admit that unused in some cases help Philately on more than used do, thus in cases of whole sheets of stamps in mint state, showing various types, etc. But the crux of my contention is that both classes are essential to true Philately. I fully admit unused, but I also admit that without used the former do not represent it, and it is this fact which many supporters of unused only don't admit.

Now it follows from my admission that both classes should be collected in order to form a complete philatelic collection of stamps, but here comes in the difficulty, namely, it would require a "Crœsus" to possess both unused as well as used stamps in their collections to approach anything like completeness; and in fact many earlier Colonials are unobtainable in mint state, even when one is willing to pay the money for them; and inasmuch as it is contended, I think, that a more complete collection of many countries can be made with used stamps than unused, does it not follow that to a collector of used only it is somewhat unfair to state that even if he happens to possess a complete or almost complete collection of stamps of a country, *ergo* he is for all that not able to enter into Philately's front ranks?

Mind you, I write entirely from non-personal

THE STAMP KING

By G. DE BEAUREGARD AND H. DE GORSSE

Translated from the French by EDITH C. PHILLIPS

CHAPTER XII (*continued*)

Showing how lost time is sometimes merely time gained

THEN, still in very bad humour, he tried little experiments. He observed that the Terminus Hotel had several exits—one leading into the Rue St. Lazare, another into the station, and a third into the Salle des Pas-Perdus. There were, then, three ways by which he might escape, and, with a little caution, rid himself of the exasperating watchfulness of his two spies. He tried these doors, one after the other; but from whichever one he issued, there, within a few steps, were M. Picquoiseau's two agents. They were not always the same ones, for extra men had been appointed to watch the three exits, but they were all very much alike, having a sort of family resemblance.

The unfortunate man took this good-humouredly at first, thinking he might be able to dispose of his "followers" on the way. With this idea he visited all the churches, museums, and large shops which he knew had several exits, and might have been seen at any of these places dodging in and out, doubling and turning in the hope of baffling his indomitable persecutors.

This lasted for two days and was just so much loss of time, and then William began to be really angry, for which he had, perhaps, some excuse. It cost him a great effort on several occasions to restrain himself from rushing upon the spies and giving them a good thrashing with his cane. Only what good would it have done? A crowd would have formed, and he would have had to appear before some police commissioner and give an explanation. When it came to that no doubt M. Picquoiseau's agents would find some difficulty in explaining why they were shadowing him with such indelicate persistence, but in all probability they would simply deny the fact altogether, in which case it would be William Keniss who would be convicted of unjustifiable assault. So to act in that way would be simple madness.

Then William considered whether it would be possible to buy off the spies, who, two by two, formed such an admirable escort. Such men could not possibly possess very strict consciences, and would certainly not refuse to be bought if the price were only high enough. But there was one grave danger in the way, even supposing the transaction were not seen by the director of the agency to which the six individuals belonged, and this was the fact that the director might have set a spy upon his spies, who would inform him of their treason, when the six faithless agents would be immediately replaced by six fresh ones, whom he would have to "buy" like the first. At this little game he risked losing not only money but time, which might be better employed.

Then, in exasperation, the idea of a disguise occurred to him. John was sent in search of a hairdresser in the neighbourhood, who was a specialist in this line, and who dressed him up in a wig and a grey beard, which, in conjunction with a pair of blue spectacles to hide the brightness of his eyes, and a long overcoat, for which he sent to a tailor in the Quartier Latin, and which completely covered his own elegant outfit, gave him the appearance of a venerable old savant or professor. Thus made up William Keniss thought himself unrecognisable, and was fully persuaded that he could pass without any suspicion under the eyes of the two wretches who were waiting for him at the door. But the poor fellow knew little of the men with whom he had to deal, nor of how they were trained to detect any possible deceit or fraud.

Scarcely had he taken a step outside before he discovered that the two spies, without a moment's hesitation, but with a little smile that was not habitual to them, were again on his track. So, to avoid looking more of a fool than he could help, the unhappy William hailed a fiacre and, followed at a little distance by another, drove for an hour through the streets of Paris before daring to return to his hotel. The next day and the day after, first in light whiskers and then in dark ones, the young American renewed the experiment. But each time, in spite of all his efforts and a carefully-thought-out costume, the detectives kept on the scent and stuck to him like leeches.

William Keniss was at last convinced that one of M. Picquoiseau's agents must have procured a situation in the Terminus Hotel, where he could keep a special watch on the corridor in which his rooms were, and give the others precise information of all his

THE DISGUISES

movements; for, however cleverly he might be disguised, he had only to turn his head as soon as he got into the street to perceive the two bloodhounds on his track. Then it occurred to the unhappy William, somewhat late in the day, that Miss Betty was being kept informed of all his acts and doings, and that she could not therefore be ignorant of the equally idiotic and futile efforts he was making to escape. We can indeed imagine Miss Betty's amusement when she received her three daily reports and read how her rival had appeared, now as a Russian prince, then as a private coachman, and later as an old Jew broker. The thought of it plunged William into the utmost confusion, and he determined to let events follow their natural course without committing himself to any fresh eccentricities.

But his anger was growing day by day, and would doubtless have exploded in some way before long, when the 12th of May, 1896, the date fixed by M. Crabifosse, and waited for impatiently by John, at length arrived.

"PERFECT!" EXCLAIMED JOHN

CHAPTER XIII

In which John and his stamp are both taken in the very act of flight

HAVING obtained permission to go out, John immediately repaired to the Rue de Provence, after carefully providing himself with five hundred francs, which constituted nearly all his worldly fortune. It was all ready, and M. Crabifosse was occupied in polishing the block of steel, on the other side of which was engraved in many fine lines the copy of the Brahmapootra stamp.

"You see I have kept my word," said the engraver. "Now you have only to see it printed ; but I cannot undertake to do that myself, not having sufficient choice of paper, ink, and a hundred other little details. We will go to M. Babuchon, the art printer, of 44, Rue de la Chaussée-d'Antin. I have sent to tell him what we want done and your instructions with regard to the gold tint, paper, perforation, gum, etc."

M. Babuchon was no less punctual than M. Crabifosse, for he was at work composing a special gold ink, of a soft yellow with a slightly grey tint, a sort of beautiful shot colour, which is called grey-gold, and obtained by a mixture of fine gold and iron. On a table close by were arranged twenty little squares of soft bluish white paper, thick and yet flexible. They were perforated exactly according to the outline in the photograph of the original stamp.

The block brought by M. Crabifosse was coated with the precious ink, and with the help of a small press a first impression was taken on one of the little squares of paper.

"Why, it is perfectly superb !" cried John, when the wet proof, laid carefully on a piece of glass, was handed to him for inspection.

"You are satisfied then, sir ?" asked M. Crabifosse and M. Babuchon at the same moment.

"I should think so, indeed !"

Several more proofs were then printed, so that he might choose the most perfect, and, as one of them was decidedly finer and clearer than the rest, M. Babuchon carefully dried it and then brushed over the other side with pure gum.

"I am sorry to be so slow," he said when he had quite finished, "but we have, unfortunately, no machinery here for drying the gum as they have in the Boulevard Brune. It is very remarkable. Have you ever seen it, sir ?"

"No," said John, his first experience leading him to take an interest in the matter in spite of himself.

"It is simple and ingenious," continued M. Babuchon. "The freshly-gummed sheets of stamps are placed on felt bands—with the gum upwards of course. These bands, moving over wheels, carry the sheets for more than two hundred yards under a number of little windmills, which turn very fast and keep the air in motion over the damp sheets, so causing rapid evaporation. In this way they are completely dried in less than half an hour, instead of the two days it would otherwise take."

"Not a bad idea," said John sententiously.

Then, while M. Babuchon held the chosen proof near a little gas stove to dry it as quickly as possible, John burnt all the others, one by one, in the flame ; after which, with a hammer which was lying close at hand, he so defaced the block as to make it quite unrecognisable.

"There, M. Crabifosse," said he, "that is proof for you that one copy of this stamp is all I want, and that I am not going to issue a series of forgeries."

"I am very much obliged to you," returned the engraver, feeling a little ashamed of his earlier scruples.

"Here you are, sir," said M. Babuchon, proudly handing John the square of paper, gilt, gummed, glazed, and dried.

John took it hastily and with joy indescribable.

"Are you satisfied with it?" asked M. Crabifosse again.

"I should be very hard to please if I were not," he replied. "Nobody could possibly believe the stamp was a forgery. I have had the original one, belonging to my master, Mr. William Keniss, in my hands and examined it closely, and I assure you I don't see one bit of difference between them. It is the same perforation, the same kind of paper, the same shade of gold, not to speak of the design, which is marvellously exact."

To admire it still more, John held the stamp in the hollow of his hand, without noticing that the window near which they were standing was open and forming a decided draught between that and a second open window. There was a very high wind that day, and from time to time great gusts blew into the room, one of which suddenly caught up the little piece of paper and whirled it into space, while John stupidly watched it mounting up, up, almost to the roofs of the houses. Then, more slowly, it began to descend, turning over and over till it reached the ground on the other side of the street close to a lamp-post.

"I can see it! I can see it!" cried John, who had been staring with open eyes and mouth and trembling body at the peregrinations of his stamp. And, hustling past M. Crabifosse and the printer, he rushed downstairs at the risk of breaking his neck. Now he was in the street. With a last bound he was close to the stamp and stooped to seize it. But at that very moment came a fresh gust of wind, caught up the stamp—which just grazed John's nose, as if to defy the poor fellow—and started it again on its zigzag course through the air, looking like a capricious and fantastic golden butterfly rambling adventurously about in the rays of the sun.

John, as we can easily imagine, set off in pursuit of it. With hair flowing in the wind and disordered array he rushed like a hurricane through the streets, first on one pavement and then on the other, overturning everything that came in his way. Here a stout lady, whom, with a shove of his elbow, he sent rolling into the middle of the road ; further on an old gentleman, whom he tripped up and left lying full length on the wood pavement ; then it was a dog, whose tail he crushed. In this way the stamp and John traversed the Rue de la Chaussée-d'Antin, the Rue Jubert, the Rue de la Victoire, and the Rue Caumartin, and emerged, the one aerially and the other terrestrially, on the Boulevard Hausmann, opposite Printemps. A dozen times during their course John just missed the stamp as it touched the ground, but each time, by an exasperating fatality, he was a second too late, and only succeeded in seizing a few specks of dust and in seeing the tormenting piece of paper reascending towards the sky.

(To be continued.)

SPECIAL CORRESPONDENCE

Notes from Mysore

BANGALORE, *May* 15*th*, 1905.

The Village Post Office

THE village post office in Southern India is fearfully and wonderfully made (generally *fearfully*) ; it is usually a mud hut, in the most squalid, over-populated, and plague-infected portion of a ditto-ditto village. In most cases it consists of two rooms ; one is used as an office, and the other as the home of the postmaster and his family (which usually varies between eight and twelve). The building is a glorified mud hut, and the glorification part consists of the signboard, which states that the building is the post office ; but as the inscription is in Tamil or Canarese, one has to take the statement on trust. The postmaster is usually a mild Hindu, who fattens on five rupees a month. His stock of stamps consists of a dozen or so of the values of 3 pies, $\frac{1}{2}$, 1, and 2 annas, a packet of envelopes, and a dozen packets of post cards. He is provided with a cash-box, which sometimes contains as much as a rupee.

Registration

The operation of registering a letter in one of these offices is a curious experience. In the first place it causes great excitement, since it is as rare as an earthquake. The mild Hindu takes the letter, turns it over a few times, and then looks at you with suspicion, as though you had murdered a baby and were sending away the proofs of your guilt. Then he calls out for a chair and the registration book, and for ten solid minutes he fills in things in various languages, spends another five minutes in changing the date-plug of the postmark, and then takes the money, and invariably finds he hasn't change ; so you wait while his friends collect the amount in the village, and if you are born under a lucky star, you may get into the "open" again in the course of an hour.

Testimonials

I had an amusing experience with one of these men a few days ago. I called at the post office and couldn't find anybody there, but after waiting for some time, an urchin clothed in a cummerbund and a smile informed me that the postmaster was preparing for my visit. The preparation consisted in shaving his head and putting on his "best bib and tucker," neither of which operations may be hurried with impunity, since you may cut the former and tear the latter. At last he appeared, sold me my eight annas' worth of stamps, and begged that I would give him a testimonial to the effect that he had "given me complete satisfaction in the execution of his duties." I asked to see his other "*chits*,"* and one of them was to the following effect : "X. Y. is, I believe, one of the quickest postmasters in India *when he chooses ;* I have known him for ten years, and during that time he has *not chosen.*"

Shades

Several of the home journals have recently noted shades in the case of the 2 and 8 annas stamps with the King's Head, but so far I have seen no mention of the extremely well-marked shades of the $2\frac{1}{2}$ annas. The early printings were in a very similar shade to that employed for the same value of the Queen's Head series—a pale, washy, and uneven smudgy colour. The next shade was richer and more evenly applied, and the current shade is a fine rich blue, perfectly clear, and producing an effect quite different from that of the first printing, which is unpleasing. The 3 pies, grey, is the only other sinner in the way of shades—three quite distinct ones may be found. All the high values are quite constant at present.

Rumours

The air of India is filled with rumours—all from more or less reliable sources. We are told that the remainders of the 2, 3, and 5 rupee stamps with the Queen's Head are to be recalled and surcharged 10 annas ; but as there do not appear to be many remainders (the stamps are sold out in many of the large offices), we will hope it is only a rumour. The unissued stamps will be with us shortly if accounts are true, and then there *may* be a deluge of fiscal postals ; so look out for unused $\frac{1}{2}$ and 1 anna Indian receipt stamps of all kinds !

A Rarity

Here is a simple little calculation. In 1904 several provisional telegraph stamps appeared ; they could not be purchased *entire* at any post office, and the remainders were recalled and burnt ; one or two copies may have leaked out. At any rate we may, for the sake

* Testimonials.

THE STAMP KING

By G. DE BEAUREGARD and H. DE GORSSE

Translated from the French by EDITH C. PHILLIPS

CHAPTER XIII (*continued*)

*In which John and his stamp are both taken in the very
act of flight*

BUT a strange murmur began to strike upon John's
ears as, worn out with his long run, he began visibly
to falter. At first he paid little attention to it, as it
was nearly drowned in the barking of all the dogs in
the neighbourhood, who had also joined in the chase ;
but as the cries drew nearer he began to wonder what
they meant, and listened carefully as he still ran on.

"Catch the thief ! A thief ! A thief ! Stop him !"
were the sounds he heard ; and, however surprised he
might be, he never for a moment doubted to whom
they referred. But the agile American had no time
just then to be offended, nor to stop and demand explanations from his pursuers, who were heaping such
insulting epithets upon him. For the stamp sped ever
onwards.

Suddenly there was a calm. The wind fell, and the
little piece of paper settled comfortably down at the
foot of a tree about five yards from John, who, though
his legs would hardly support him, made one last
formidable and prodigious effort, and threw himself
on hands and knees on the pavement beside it. This
time he had the stamp ; he held it in his hand !

Unfortunately, just as John seized it, two vigorous
hands caught his shoulders and compelled him to rise.

"Loose me ! Let me go !" he cried.

But the hands clasped him all the more firmly.
Struggling to free himself, John turned and recognised
M. Crabifosse and M. Babuchon. The engraver and
the printer, seeing him rush off without paying his
account, thought it was a swindler with whom they
had to deal, and immediately followed in pursuit. It
was they who had started the cries of "Thief ! Thief !
Stop him !" which had been taken up by the crowd.

"So, so, my good man !" said they. "This is how
you get off without paying bills in your country,
is it ?"

"Bother your bills for a moment !" cried John. "Let
me go ! Let me go, I say !"

"Pay us first, and we'll see about that afterwards."

"See about it afterwards ! I tell you you'd better
let me go at once, or else——"

"Or else what ?"

"I shall fight."

"*We* shall see about that, my friend."

"Shall you ? See that, then !" And so saying he
dealt each of his adversaries two vigorous blows with
his fist, thanks to which he found himself free ; then
he turned to take up the stamp from the foot of the
tree where it had fallen, only to discover that, while
he had been disputing with his two creditors, a whole
crowd of people had collected round them, all gesticulating and crying—

"Take him up ! Take him up !"

"Me ?" said John. "The first who touches me had
better beware !"

And he crossed his arms proudly and looked round
with a defiant air on the assembled crowd, and his
eyes blazed so that not one of them dared to put his
threat into execution. But both M. Crabifosse and
M. Babuchon continued to cry excitedly—

"He is a thief ! A cheat !"

At length two guardians of the peace arrived—last,

as usual—and, pushing aside the people who surrounded
John, came up to him, while one of them demanded—

"What's all this ? What's it about ?"

"Why, look here——" began the American. But a
volley of shouts interrupted him.

"Seize him !" the crowd still clamoured, without
even knowing the crime of which the poor fellow was
accused. John tried once more to explain, but with no
better success, for the cries became more and more
menacing. In the midst of the uproar, though, he
caught a few scraps of sentences :—

"He is a thief, and has just stolen six pairs of socks
from Printemps'," said one.

"No, indeed, he is not," returned another. "He is
an anarchist, and has just thrown a bomb in the Rue
des Pas-Perdus from the Gare Saint-Lazare."

Little groups were beginning to form farther away,
in which people spoke of a sensational crime, one man
averring that six people had just had their carotid
arteries severed, and murmurs were beginning to
swell demanding the lynching of the miserable as-
sassin. Poor John would have been torn in pieces
had not one of the policemen interfered to save
him from the rage of the mob, who were all the
more furious the less they knew about the matter.
The fact of everyone speaking at once was making
the two severe guardians of the public peace very
angry.

"It's no use trying to get anything out of them,"
said one. "You must just come with me to the police
station."

"I !" cried John.

"Yes, you, and no resistance, if you please, unless
you want to run the gauntlet when you get there."

"Run the gauntlet !"

"Now then, get along."

"Oh, I'll come ! But these two gentlemen must
come with us, as they are the cause of it all."

"*They* are the cause of it all, are they ?" returned
the second officer. "Very well ; let them follow us—
and quietly, if possible."

"Yes, yes, we will follow you," said M. Crabifosse
and M. Babuchon with one voice, for, being better
acquainted with the habits of the Parisian police, they
knew what running the gauntlet meant ; that is, a
volley of blows administered with fists, boots, sabres,
etc., by the whole assembled force. So they did not
wish for any nearer acquaintance with this kind of
amusement.

John and his two creditors then set off under the
protection of the officers, while, a few paces behind, a
large crowd, still gesticulating and shouting, formed
their escort.

Mr. Keniss' valet was greatly troubled at this adventure and heartily tired of it. As he left the spot
where the altercation with M. Crabifosse and M.
Babuchon had taken place, he cast one last glance at
the foot of the tree where his stamp had fallen, and,
misery of miseries, the beautiful gold stamp was no
longer there. Mechanically raising his eyes he saw it
gracefully borne along by a fresh gust of wind towards the Madeleine. So the beautiful project which
he had elaborated with so much care was destroyed at
a blow ! It was indeed trying to think he had brought
his fertile and powerful imagination to bear on a
matter that had ended in such a *fiasco*, after a week's
anxiety and vicissitudes !

JOHN RUSHED LIKE A HURRICANE THROUGH THE STREETS

"What an idiot I was," he thought, "to destroy the block and the other proofs! Now it will all have to be begun over again, even if I have the courage for it."

While John thus soliloquised, without troubling himself about the virtuous indignation that was poured upon him as he passed, the group of which he formed part arrived at the Poste de l'Opéra. An inspector happened to be there at the moment, who immediately demanded of his subordinates the reason of this triple arrest. The more intelligent of them was about to explain, but scarcely had he opened his mouth when John interrupted him, anxious to put an end to the ridiculous misapprehension of which he was the victim. He quickly recounted the story to the inspector, who could not help laughing heartily.

"Well, sirs," he said, "I suppose none of you wish this matter to go any farther?"

John, M. Crabifosse, and M. Babuchon looked at each other.

"No," they answered in turn.

"Then you have only to settle this little matter of money between you and then you are at liberty to go."

"But——" began M. Babuchon.

"Well?" said the inspector.

"M. John Cockburn favoured us with a few nasty blows just now."

"Oh, that alters the matter altogether! What have you to say to that, M. John Cockburn?"

"Only that I was provoked beyond endurance by the unjust suspicions they showered upon me and the way they were making me lose my stamp. But since they don't like it I take back the blows, and to settle the matter, as a sort of indemnity, I will pay them double if they wish it."

"Do you agree to that?" asked the inspector.

"Yes, yes," returned the printer and engraver in chorus, without even stopping to consult.

"Then you have only to pay it, M. John."

Which John did with an apparent good grace, however highly exasperated he might feel, and then left the office without any sign of farewell, and returned in a melancholy and thoughtful mood to the Terminus Hotel.

(To be continued.)

OUR COMPETITIONS

HERE are a few more selections from the many excellent papers sent in for our best Anecdote or Limerick competition:—

Stamped on the Back

AN amusing trick was played by Fred upon his brother-in-law, Bedford, in a bathing-machine. Bedford had rubbed down, and was about to resume his raiment, when Leslie gave him a slap on the back, which, of course, was a most natural action, and occasioned no surprise. But two or three days afterwards Bedford felt a strange sensation in the middle of his back, and, his wife being asked to look for the cause, found a postage stamp had been firmly stuck upon him midway between the shoulder-blades. "Why, where have you been?" she asked. "Been?" said he. "Why, to town, of course." "Then," she remarked, "you must have come back by post." The stamp was removed by the help of warm water, but Bedford will not soon forget Fred's slap on the back.

From *Recollections of Fred Leslie.*

A Valet's Philatelic Windfall

A FEW years ago there died in the city of Glasgow an old man, who lived in a large house along with his two old servants—a cook and a valet. When his will was read it was found that he had left £200 to the cook, but what was the surprise of all when it was discovered that he had only left an old writing-desk to the valet!

On opening the desk, the valet discovered it to be packed full of stamps. These he took to a philatelist, who offered him £500 for them, which he accepted. The philatelist, it is said, shortly afterwards sold them for £750. PERCY PRESTON.

A Penny to Pay

SOME years ago, the rural letter-carrier left three letters at a country house and sent a message to say that "there was a penny to pay for one of them." The lady examined the letters, and, finding they were properly stamped and no overcharge marked on them, told the letter-carrier he was mistaken. "Very likely, Miss," he said. "Master" (naming the post-master) "told me there was a penny to collect from someone, and I thought I might try and get it from you before I forgot all about it."

Limericks

> There once was a youth of Mauritius,
> With tendencies terribly vicious;
> He stole a rare stamp,
> This shocking young scamp—
> 'Twas the *twopenny P.O. Mauritius!*
> FRED EDMONDS.

> There was a young man of Mauritius,
> Whose "Post Office" gems were delicious:
> But they said, "We're afraid
> These are only 'Post Paid'"—
> Which made that young person feel vicious.
> REV. P. E. RAYNOR.

> Many brand-new sets from the East,
> All manner of men and of beasts;
> But are they the thing,
> Or are they to bring
> The dibs from the easily fleeced?
> ALFRED ERNEST MARTEN.

THE STAMP KING

By G. DE BEAUREGARD AND H. DE GORSSE

Translated from the French by EDITH C. PHILLIPS

VICTORIA MEETS JOHN

CHAPTER XIV

*Which clearly demonstrates that the false and the true
are occasionally very much alike*

WHEN Betty saw that William Keniss had no
intention of coming near her, she expressly
forbade Victoria to visit her friend John. This
was a great trouble to the excellent young person, who
was in deadly fear lest her beloved should forget her,
whenever she was compelled to spend even two days
without recalling herself to his memory. However,
she had no intention of disobeying her mistress, and
contented herself with prowling for long hours in the
neighbourhood of the Terminus Hotel in the hope of
catching a glimpse, even in the far distance, of him to
whom she was forbidden to speak. But she never
even saw so much as his nose, which caused a fit of
depression and sadness which she tried in vain to
conceal.

Miss Scott, as we have already heard, spent her time
in becoming better acquainted with Paris. But her
walks were no hindrance to her reflections, and, on
the very day on which John was such an unlucky
victim of the vagaries of the atmosphere, it occurred
to her how very careless she had been in not having
Mr. Keniss' valet shadowed also, and she determined
to repair the error without delay.

"Victoria," she said, "I want you to go to M.
Picquoiseau's for me; ask him for two fresh detectives,
and go with them yourself to the Terminus Hotel.
Wait there till John appears and point him out to
them, explaining that I wish for information concerning his movements, the same as those of his master.
Go at once."

Though the commission was a somewhat delicate
one, Victoria made no objection, for she would at least
see the friend whose long absence was torturing her.
As she took up her position in the Rue Saint-Lazare,
accompanied by the two spies, John arrived from the
Rue du Havre looking sullen and weary, for he had
just escaped out of the hands of the police, and felt as
much ashamed as a fox whose tricks had been discovered; he was furious too at having lost his forged
stamp.

He was not more than a few steps away when Victoria caught sight of him.

"There he is!" she exclaimed. "Do you see him?"
John took it all in, murmured "Ah! I am caught,
am I?" and passed on quickly and with dignity towards the hotel.

To see him there, so near, alone, free but disdainful,
was too much for the tender Victoria. She followed
him, and, in a voice trembling with emotion, asked—

"What! Mr. John, you will not even say 'Good
day'?"

"Leave me," he returned drily. "You are acting a
most shameful part."

Then Victoria, seeing she was discovered, began an
eloquent speech, which John answered with a very
forcible one. "It was abominable," he said, "to spy
on people and to penetrate into their secret life. It
was just like a woman's treachery to weave such plots
and to so basely betray the sacred laws of friendship!"

"But it is not I; it is Miss Betty," groaned Victoria
in deepest desolation.

"You are her accomplice."

"No, no, John, I swear I am not. I carry out her
orders, but I am not responsible for them, you know."

"Oh, very well," cried the fiery American. "If you are not responsible, you can just tell your mistress that she makes a great mistake if she thinks she can stop us in such a way as that from carrying out our plans."

"But then——"

"Do you suppose we mind being shadowed? We shall just stop in Paris and enjoy ourselves till Miss Scott is tired of her absurd little game."

"Miss Betty has plenty of perseverance——"

"Nevertheless she can't have us followed all our lives."

"I suppose not."

"Then we shall just wait patiently till she gives up spying upon us, and only then, you understand, shall we take steps to procure the Brahmapootra stamp."

At length, after interminable protestations from Victoria, John seemed to calm down a little.

stamping their feet on the pavement the other side of the street.

"Come, come," he cried; "look at me well so that you may know me again." And he smiled superbly and disdainfully to show that he had no intention of being their dupe, but meant to give them as much trouble as possible.

Victoria returned to the Hotel Bristol in a deep reverie, and the rest of the day passed without any further incident. The next day, Thursday, the 14th of May, after breakfast, Betty informed Victoria she would not need her that day as she intended visiting Versailles. No sooner had she started than the maid, turning over the leaves of the Paris *Guide*, hastily sought and found the address of the United States Legation, 63, Rue Pierre-Charron.

"They will tell me there what formalities Americans

A LAD CAME RUNNING UP TO THE GROUP

"Well, ungrateful man," said Victoria sweetly, "since I have given you so much trouble, I'll do my best to serve you now."

"Oh, I dare say!" said he sceptically.

"I will, indeed. And look here, as we shall be in Paris for some time yet, shall I arrange about our wedding?"

At these words John started back.

"You've chosen a nice time to speak of that," he cried.

But poor Victoria begged so earnestly that, tired out, he ended by saying—

"You can do whatever you please."

They parted with these words, she delighted at having received *carte blanche*, and he satisfied at having treated her harshly, and so made her ready to do anything he might wish in the future.

John continued on his way to the Terminus Hotel, but before entering he turned for the last time to the two spies, henceforth attached to his person, who were

have to go through when they want to get married in France," she thought.

So she called a fiacre and was driven there immediately. But the concierge, to whom she made known her wishes, returned banteringly—

"What! do you want people to work just as usual on fête days? It's all shut up, my dear." And, as Victoria opened her eyes very wide, he continued, "Don't you know it's Ascension Day? You must come again some other time."

Sadly discomfited, the good girl dismissed her fiacre and returned on foot through the Champs-Élysées, the sweetest dreams and the most melancholy thoughts striving in her mind for mastery. When she reached the corner of the Avenue Marigny her attention was attracted to a group of people, of all ages and conditions, in animated discussion round a young man, whom, to her surprise, she recognised as William Keniss. He was examining books and albums filled with stamps, which one and another handed to him in the hope that he would either buy some or give his opinion concerning doubtful copies. For Victoria had arrived at the Stamp Bourse, to which William had strolled out of curiosity.

It was not in this pretty, shady corner of the Champs-Élysées that the Stamp Bourse was originally held. The original one saw the light in the year 1860 in the garden of the Tuileries, at the foot of the statue of Diana.

Though the first postage stamps date from 1840, collectors had twenty years later only been heard of for some three or four years. But philately began to make rapid strides, and, in 1859, there were already three dealers established in Paris. From that time the number of philatelists rapidly increased, and the day came when they assembled in such numbers in the Tuileries Gardens that the police were obliged to interfere and beg them to remove to the Champs-Élysées, at the corner of the Avenue Gabriel and the Avenue Marigny, at which place their Bourse grew and developed until the year 1880. In that year a fresh interruption by the police took place. But the philatelists, usually so calm, were absolutely furious at having their habits and arrangements upset, and showed but little disposition to comply with the orders given them. Some among them had then, of course, to go to the police station and explain their conduct. Force was on the side of the law, and the little market was compelled to emigrate to the spot on which it was now discovered by Victoria.

At the beginning the "Stamp Bourse" was only attended by the pupils of the schools and colleges, who met thus to make exchanges among themselves without it costing them anything. The meetings then only took place on Sundays, but in 1887 Thursdays were added by general demand. Little by little the circle enlarged, and, instead of schoolboys only, all collectors were drawn to the Bourse in the hope of some godsend or advantageous bargain. But one rarely comes across a good thing on the Stamp Bourse, for it is caught up as soon as it appears by one of the buyers sent for that purpose by the big stamp dealers

of the capital. The Stamp King, however, to please the lads who offered him their merchandise, had bought a few at ridiculously high prices, so he was besieged on all sides by vendors, little and big, who took him for a beginner in philately, and shamelessly emulated each other in trying to take advantage of him.

" Is that you, Victoria ? " he said, a little piqued on beholding his friend's maid ; for it occurred to him that Miss Scott, not content with having him followed by two spies, had also set her faithful companion to watch him. " How did you come here, and what are you doing ? "

" I came by the merest chance," said Victoria. " I had just been out for a walk, and, returning along the Champs-Élysées, I saw this crowd and came to see what was going on ; so here I am."

The Stamp King had exchanged a few more careless words with Victoria, when suddenly there was a great disturbance in the Bourse.

" Look, look ! " cried a lad who came running between the groups.

" What is it ? " said another.

" A quite new stamp."

" Let us look at it ! "

" Do you know what it is ? "

" No. Don't you ? "

" No. I found it in the Rue Tronchet."

The little lad, for fear someone should steal his stamp, which had already passed through about a dozen different hands, hastened to repossess himself of it. William Keniss and Victoria, who had seen the boy run up, were standing close to him when he said, " It is certainly an Indian stamp," and with one accord they stopped talking, and as the boy, surrounded by several of his comrades, sat down on a bench a few yards away to consult a catalogue someone had lent him, they each drew near with an assumption of such perfect indifference that neither suspected the other of being drawn by a similar thought. But suddenly a cry escaped them both at the same moment— —

" The Brahmapootra stamp ! "

(To be continued.)

SPECIAL CORRESPONDENCE

Our Victorian Letter

MELBOURNE, *May 15th*, 1905.

A Find of New Zealands

VERY little has happened here in philatelic matters since I last wrote, the only thing of any importance being a find of a block of twenty-four unused 6d. New Zealand, 1864 issue, perforated. These, when discovered, had a thick coating of black dirt on the back of them, which the finder of the stamps proceeded to wash off, when he was agreeably surprised to find the stamps were watermark N Z.

The Famous " Hill " Collection

I had a peep at one of the volumes of the famous " Hill " Collection of Victorian stamps a few weeks back, and was surprised at the good things that were in it. Every stamp is a picked clean copy, lightly postmarked. The collection is practically complete, as it contains every known stamp that has been issued in Victoria, excepting one or two of the rarest watermarks, such as the 6d. Laureated, watermark double line 2, and 2d. Emblem, watermark 6. It is one of those good old collections that were formed in the early days, so few of which now remain in the colony, nearly all having left these shores for a permanent resting-place in the Old World. It is to be hoped

that Mr. Hill will not be tempted to part with it, as he will never again be able to get together such a fine lot of Victorian stamps. The collection contains several specimens of the same stamp, and abounds in shades, many of which are seldom met with. I saw many things in it I coveted, such as a used pair of " Too Late " stamps, a half-page of the various errors of transfer of the lithographed 2d., Queen on Throne, and a fine lot of the 2d., half-length, fine background and border, in a very rich colour.

The Tasmanian 1½d. Provisional

I am informed that the object of issuing the 1½d. stamp in Tasmania was for use on pictorial post cards when posted to the Old World. If one each of the 1d. and ½d. pictorial issue were used on the cards, very little room would be left for the address, so to get over the difficulty a smaller stamp was selected and surcharged 1½d. to meet the rate of postage on the cards.

Mr. Hausburg's Visit

Amongst the visitors to Melbourne last month was Mr. L. L. R. Hausburg, a prominent English philatelist and member of the London Philatelic Society. I had a long chat with him on philatelic matters, and found that he had given much study to the stamps of the Australian colonies. I was enabled to learn much valuable information from him, especially regarding

THE STAMP KING

By G. DE BEAUREGARD AND H. DE GORSSE

Translated from the French by EDITH C. PHILLIPS

THE LAD HESITATED

CHAPTER XIV (*continued*)

*Which clearly demonstrates that the false and the true
are occasionally very much alike*

BOTH had instantly recognised the famous stamp of
the Maharajah in the little paper which the lad, to
facilitate his researches, had placed on his knee and
was holding there with the tip of one finger. So they
stared at each other in absolute stupefaction for a few
seconds without a word.

Victoria was the first to break the silence.

"I will give you fifty francs for that stamp," she
said to its possessor, who was still turning over the
pages of the catalogue.

"Fifty francs!" cried he, starting up in surprise at
the exorbitant and unexpected offer.

"Yes, indeed!" said Victoria. "And I'll pay you
straight away."

The lad hesitated a second and his eye sought that
of William Keniss, who was looking on at the scene
with an imperturbable smile. The little fellow then
looked at Victoria, who was trembling with anxiety to
conclude the bargain.

"Well, will you let me have it?" she said.

"No," he returned resolutely.

"Why not?"

"Because I believe it is worth more than fifty francs."

All the people in the Stamp Bourse now began to
assemble round these three actors to hear what was
going on.

"Well, then," said Victoria, "ir you won't let me
have it for fifty francs I offer you sixty."

"No."

"Seventy!"

"No."

"Eighty!"

"No!"

"Ninety!"

"No!"

Great drops of perspiration rolled down Victoria's
cheeks. The lad was sure to think that if anyone
offered him a hundred francs for his stamp it must be
worth a lot more, and would certainly ask an exaggerated price for it. Now Victoria had only a
somewhat modest sum with her, and felt desperately
that she would not be able to bid very high, and that,
even could she do so, there was William Keniss, whose
pocket-book was sure to be stuffed full of bank-notes,
and who at the last moment, when she could go no
further, would step in, in his usual calm way, and
make a decisive bid.

So Victoria determined on a bold stroke.

"A hundred and fifty francs!" hoping that the lad,
dazzled by the enormous sum, would immediately
close with the offer. So her confusion can well be
imagined when the little man of the world only replied again with an ironical smile—

"No."

She lost all hope from that moment and merely went
on bidding mechanically—"A hundred and sixty! A

hundred and seventy! A hundred and ninety! Two hundred!"

Here she was compelled to stop, for that was about all the money she had with her, and, changing her tactics, she began in a honeyed tone—

"Look here, my child, what do you want for your stamp? Fix the price yourself and I am ready to pay it. Now then, how much?"

The little merchant lost no time in reflection.

"Five hundred francs!" he replied.

"So be it!" said Victoria quickly. "I accept your price of five hundred francs. Just come with me to the Hotel Bristol, in the Place Vendôme, and I will give you that sum in exchange for the stamp."

"Very well, madam, I am at your service."

The young philatelist was just rising to follow Victoria, when William Keniss struck in.

"Madam," said he, "you say you will give five hundred francs for that stamp. Well, I offer six hundred."

"Seven hundred!"

"Eight hundred!"

"Nine hundred!"

"A thousand!"

"A thousand!" cried the little fellow, his eyes shining covetously.

During this time the circle of curious onlookers had become considerably augmented. They now began pushing and jostling each other, so as to see and hear better.

"Let him have it! let him have it!" cried all the boy's little comrades.

But at the same moment an unknown voice rose from the midst of the group—

"Don't give it to him unless he pays for it at once. A hundred sous in the hand are better than a hundred francs in the bush!"

William Keniss and Victoria both looked round, but failed to discover the orator to whom they owed this anonymous and disagreeable intervention.

"The dishonest creature! The insolent fellow!" they cried in chorus.

The lad evidently appreciated the depth of the argument, for, turning to Victoria, he asked—

"Let's see, madam, how much could you give me, money down?"

Victoria, unable to hide her hopelessness, hesitated a few seconds before replying.

"Two hundred francs."

"And you, sir?"

"A thousand, to which price the auction had just amounted, as I do not wish you to lose anything by your new method of sale."

"A thousand!" pronounced the little merchant with comic solemnity. "Going!—going! Will no one bid any higher?—gone!"

William Keniss took a bank-note out of his pocket-book and gave it to the exulting young auctioneer, who handed him his stamp in exchange. Then, as he walked off, he said ironically to Victoria, "*Au revoir!*" and left her trembling with rage.

When he was about a hundred yards from the place where he had just bought his stamp he stopped to examine the precious bit of paper. He had not done this before, greatly as he doubted its authenticity, because he wished Victoria to believe he had won the duel in which he was engaged with Miss Betty.

It did not take William Keniss long to discover that he had purchased a vulgar forgery, so conversant was he with every detail of the real stamp. But the Stamp King never for a moment thought of going back in search of the little fellow who had sold a simple forgery at so high a price. On the one hand, he reflected that the price had not been asked but offered, and on the other, that the merchant, not knowing even to what country the stamp belonged, had not guaranteed its authenticity.

"My good John," said he to his valet as he re-entered his rooms in the Terminus Hotel, "I have just bought something for you."

"You are too kind, sir."

"Look!" And William Keniss held out the false stamp to John, who could not repress a cry as he recognised the one which he himself had made.

"Wherever did you find it, sir?" he asked.

"At the Stamp Bourse." And he recounted the adventure through which he had just passed.

"It is surprising!—surprising!" John repeated over and over again, playing his part like a first-rate actor.

"Yes, I admit it is an odd thing."

"But are you quite certain, sir, that the stamp is false?"

"Oh, yes, rather! How in the world can you ask me that, you, who are such an authority on the subject of forgeries? Why, my dear John, look at it well. It seems to me there's not a shadow of a doubt."

"Yes, sir, that is so."

"Well, then, I make you a present of the stamp. It will do splendidly for your collection of forgeries."

"I don't know how to thank you, sir."

"Don't thank me; thank chance, to whom you owe the present."

"Then I'm very grateful to chance."

And, slipping into his watch-case the false stamp, which he quite thought he had lost for ever, and

JOHN PUTS THE STAMP INTO HIS WATCH-CASE

which he was very happy to recover, John muttered under his breath, without being heard by William Keniss—

"And now, Miss Scott, we two have to settle this little matter."

(*To be continued.*)

THE YOUNG COLLECTOR'S PACKET.

Mr. Pettifer added that philatelists were conversant with every means of printing and producing stamps, they had a knowledge of stamp matters which did not altogether come within the functions of postal authorities, and that the services of stamp collectors, more especially of the Sydney Philatelic Club, were always at the disposal of the Postmaster-General. Philatelists wished finality in regard to this matter, and hoped that the Postmaster-General would take every means of carrying their wishes into effect.

Mr. Smyth referred to the chaotic state of affairs which at present exists, and while not concerned in postal administration, commented on the want of uniformity which at present is the case, there being values of stamps in some States which are not in others. He said that stamp collectors desired to be a help rather than a hindrance to the postal authorities, and that while better work might be produced abroad, he would prefer to see as much as possible done in this country, even if it were not up to the standard of excellence which might be desired. He added that the use of State stamps at present is misleading, and that many people abroad hardly know there is such a nation as the Australian Commonwealth.

Mr. Smith : I am very pleased in having an opportunity of meeting representatives of your Society, and I have no doubt that the information which has and can be given will be of value, and will help us in dealing with the question. This is no new matter. It has already been considered by other governments, and is under the consideration of the present Government, but there are certain financial difficulties in the way. I realise the importance of the subject and the great convenience it would be to have a stamp that could be utilised in any part of Australia, and you can rest assured that the matter is receiving every consideration. There are no two opinions as to the necessity for a uniform stamp being issued as early as possible ; the only difficulty is as to the best way of bringing it about.—*The Australian Philatelist.*

THE STAMP KING

By G. DE BEAUREGARD AND H. DE GORSSE

Translated from the French by EDITH C. PHILLIPS

CHAPTER XV

How John is on the verge of discovering that he is hoist with his own petard

JOHN rose at daybreak next morning. He had not been able to close his eyes all night, and now, as the light began to steal through the curtains of his room, he could not stay a minute longer in bed. Then he reflected on the means he must adopt to cause his false Brahmapootra stamp to fall, in the simplest manner possible, into Miss Betty's hands, and to make her, when once she had it in her possession, start off immediately for New York. So he went down to the hotel office to learn the date of the departure of the next steamer.

"To-morrow, Saturday," they told him.

There was not a moment to lose. If Miss Betty was to go by this, she must catch the steamer train that very evening at the Gare Saint-Lazare. On the other hand, it would not do to hurry her too much for fear of suggesting dangerous suspicions to the little American.

"The transatlantic train starts at ten o'clock this evening," thought John. "I will not go to the Hotel Bristol till towards the dinner-hour. I will tell Victoria a nice little story in as few words as possible, and she will immediately go and repeat it to her mistress, who, if she does not wish to miss the boat—and, after what she will have heard, she will be very anxious not to miss it—will only just have time to strap up her trunks and rush to the station without losing a moment."

This decision once taken, John felt more at his ease. He helped his master to dress, and then, when he had gone out, strolled off for a walk himself, for it was a magnificent spring morning. The first persons whom John saw in the street were the two spies, who had kept watch on him since the evening before, thanks to the good Victoria. He had no difficulty in recognising them, and immediately greeted them with an amicable " Good morning," accompanied by an ironical smile. M. Picquoiseau's agents, taken by surprise, pretended not to have seen him and turned away their heads, while John profited by this momentary inattention to jump into an omnibus, " Gare Saint-Lazare—Place Saint-Michel," which was passing within in two steps of him ; and as the heavy vehicle carried him away, he cared not in what direction, the astute American could see the two individuals still standing there, but glancing hopelessly from right to left, no doubt asking themselves if the "client" whom they had been set to shadow had flown away or dropped down into one of the city sewers. John had outwitted the two Argus-eyed ones, but he thought it prudent not to leave the omnibus in which he had taken shelter until it arrived at the Place de l'Opéra, where he descended, well assured that for that day at least he had disposed of the followers with whom Miss Betty Scott, in order to paralyse his efforts, had endowed his noble person.

Then he entered a restaurant for some lunch, and, this duty accomplished, he took a fiacre and drove to the Jardin d'Acclimatation, which he had not yet seen, and which he particularly wished to see before his departure from Paris. There he spent a charming afternoon. The parrots, monkeys, stags, antelopes, elephants, gazelles, kangaroos, zebras, camels, dromedaries, giraffes—all the animals represented there, in fact, whether by one specimen or by many, received a visit from him in turn ; and so the time passed without John observing its rapid flight. However, it occurred to him at last to look at his watch.

"Good gracious !" he cried. "Five minutes to six ; I have only just time to drive to the Hotel Bristol !"

And he set off at once, rejoicing in his well-spent day, and more delighted still at the thought of the superb trick he was about to play on his friend Victoria. She, on her part, had been very careful not to tell Miss Betty what had happened the evening before on the Stamp Bourse, for fear she should receive a scolding for not having managed the business better.

It was exactly twenty minutes to seven when he arrived at the hotel in the Place Vendôme where his master's rival was staying. In the vestibule he was met by the worthy M. Pavilly.

"Monsieur wishes——?" said he.

"To see Miss Victoria Crockett, Miss Scott's maid. I must speak to her at once."

"She has just this minute come in. You will find her in their rooms on the first floor."

John mounted the stairs, four steps at a time, and soon found himself in Miss Scott's apartments, the door of which was opened by Victoria herself.

"Oh, is it you, John?" she cried at sight of her friend. "How good of you to come to see me! You can come in ; I am quite alone."

"Miss Scott is not in then?"

"No, she has not come back yet. She spends the whole day exploring the neighbourhood of Paris, and sometimes doesn't get back till quite late."

"Oh, bother it!"

"Do you mind?"

"Just a little."

"Why?"

"Look here!—But I must tell you first of all this is a very serious matter."

"Oh, dear! You do frighten me! Has Mr. Keniss ——?"

"Mr. Keniss has nothing to do with the matter. It is entirely between you and me."

"Do explain yourself."

"Guess, first, what has brought me here."

JOHN LOWERED HIS VOICE

"How can I possibly guess? I am not a thought-reader."

"Well, I will tell you then. It is remorse."

"Remorse?"

"Yes ; for the way in which I spoke to you yesterday at the Terminus Hotel."

"Oh! Then you admit you were a little too hasty?"

"Indeed I do, and I regret it deeply. But don't let us say anything more about that. Tell me, Victoria, you would like us to get married?"

"How can you ask such a thing?"

"I am right, then, in saying you would like it to be as soon as possible?"

"Oh, yes! At once ; immediately."

"Oh, no! That is too soon. It's no good thinking of that."

"So much the worse."

"The only thing we can do is to fix the date of the ceremony as early as possible."

"But how can we?"

"Ah, that is my secret! I will tell you, however, for I want to make you forget how I parted from you yesterday." And John, lowering his voice and looking round as if he feared to be overheard, continued, "You are quite sure Miss Betty has not returned?"

"Quite ; because this is the only door she could come in by. But why all this mystery?"

"Because I have a most grave revelation to make."

Frightened at the very mysterious tone which her friend John had assumed during the last few minutes, the prudent Victoria drew back a step or two in spite of herself.

"Have you assassinated someone?" she cried.

"Oh, no! calm yourself! not yet!"

"Not yet!"

There was silence for a few seconds before John continued in a very low voice—

"I know how you missed getting that forged Brahmapootra stamp yesterday. For it was bad, as bad as could be, and my master was had for his two hundred dollars. But my time has not been wasted, for Miss Betty set her spies upon me a little too late. In fact, I have the real, true, and authentic stamp myself, and Mr. Keniss knows nothing about it."

"What! what!" cried Victoria.

"Yes, my dear, I have it, and here is the proof." And he opened his watch-case and exhibited the stamp which his master had given him.

"But," said Victoria a little defiantly, "how do you prove it is the right one?"

"Oh, there is quite a history attached to it, but it would take too long to tell you."

"But then——"

"It is enough for you to know that, profiting by my freedom of action and without saying anything to Mr. Keniss, I had undertaken researches on my own account. By an unlooked-for chance I just happened to get on the right scent. I was passing along the Place de l'Opéra the other day when an old gentleman suddenly fell under a carriage in front of me. I threw myself upon him and dragged him up, happily unhurt. 'Who are you?' he asked, after thanking me. 'John Cockburn,' I returned modestly. 'Very good. Here is my card ; come and see me to-morrow morning at the Grand Hotel, where I am staying, and I shall be happy to show my gratitude by doing anything in my power for you.' I took the card and read the name, and what was my stupefaction, joy, and delight to discover that I had just saved the life of the chief cook of the Maharajah of Brahmapootra!"

"Get along with you."

"It's quite true, Victoria. The next morning I hurried off to the Grand Hotel without saying anything of the adventure to Mr. Keniss, and was introduced, with all the honours due to my rank, to the Indian whose carcass I had had the unlooked-for honour of preserving. 'In what way can I recompense you?' said he. 'Give me a stamp that belongs to your master, and that I want badly for my collection,' replied I. 'I will see if I can get it for you,' said he. 'The Maharajah will arrive in two days' time, so you can come again three days hence, and if he has the stamp I will ask him for it, and as he cannot refuse his cook anything he will be sure to give it me, and I will hand it on to you in payment of the debt of gratitude I owe you.' So three days afterwards I returned to the Grand Hotel and came into possession of the stamp that Miss Betty Scott and Mr. William Keniss are both so anxiously seeking, and which they might search for to the end of their days if I didn't make up my mind to give it to one or the other of the two rivals."

(To be continued.)

THE STAMP KING

By G. DE BEAUREGARD AND H. DE GORSSE

Translated from the French by EDITH C. PHILLIPS

VICTORIA HELD UP THE STAMP TRIUMPHANTLY

CHAPTER XV (*continued*)

How John is on the verge of discovering that he is hoist with his own petard

JOHN paused for want of breath. He had been telling the most absurd tale, knowing how often it happens that the greater the falsehood the better it passes, and he was not much surprised to see how little astonishment there was in Victoria's questioning gaze.

"But why didn't you give the stamp to your master?" she asked.

"Well, I didn't like to—on your account. I felt sure you would never forgive me, and as we're going to marry each other, that wouldn't do, would it? So I have brought it to you to give to Miss Betty—only Mr. William must not know anything about it."

"How kind and generous you are!"

"Never mind compliments, for time presses. There is a steamer which starts from Havre to-morrow morning, and you had better persuade Miss Scott to go by it. In fact, she *must* start for New York at once, for if she stays a day longer in Paris Mr. Keniss may discover my treason, and that wouldn't be pleasant for me, you know."

"Yes, I see what you are afraid of, and I wouldn't have you get into trouble on any account after doing my mistress such a service. So I promise you I will persuade her to go this very evening."

"I can depend on you for that?"

"Yes, indeed you can."

But John saw that Victoria was not altogether pleased at the idea of setting off immediately, so he began again in a peremptory tone—

"Yes, no doubt our wedding will have to be put off

a bit longer, but I promise you to hurry the matter up as soon as we come home, and it cannot be long before we do, as my master has no further reason for staying here. Moreover, you promised the other day to do whatever I asked you to, and here is your opportunity, so make the most of it."

At that moment the bell rang.

"That is Miss Betty!" cried Victoria. "Go into that room and stay there till I've let her in. She mustn't find you here, for you would have to go into the whole matter, and it would take too long."

"You are right. Good-bye, Victoria, till we meet again in New York."

"Oh dear, that is true! We shall not see each other again till we are in New York!"

"And then we will get married."

So Victoria hid her lover in the room she had indicated, and left him laughing in his sleeve at the trick he had just played upon her, until, after a few seconds, he heard the entrance door shut again, after which he warily gained the ante-room and hurried away without making his presence known to Miss Betty Scott. In fact, he was not sorry to escape an explanation with the young lady, who would certainly not be contented with the bare outline of the history he had just recounted to Victoria. But hearing it from Victoria she would probably believe it all, thinking that her maid had not understood all he said, or that she was repeating it incorrectly.

The matter turned out just as John had foreseen it would. Scarcely had Betty entered the sitting-room before Victoria began—

"I have something for you, Miss Betty."

"Something for me?"

"Yes, Miss Betty; can you guess what it is?"

"A letter, perhaps?"

"No, miss."

"A telegram?"

"No, Miss Betty."

"How can I possibly guess, then?"

"It is the stamp—the famous stamp! Look here!" And Victoria opened her hand, in which the precious little piece of paper was firmly enclosed. Then she seized it between the thumb and first finger of the other hand, like a butterfly whose wings one is afraid

HE SAW THE TRAIN DISAPPEAR

of spoiling, and showed it triumphantly to her mistress

' The Brahmapootra stamp!" exclaimed the latter, taking it from her. "Am I dreaming? But no, no! It is the stamp itself. Where did you find it? Who gave it you? But it must be a forgery, I think. Speak, Victoria, speak!"

And Victoria, able at last to get in a word, began a confused story, in which John and Mr. Keniss and the Maharajah's cook were all mixed up together. She spoke of the necessity of keeping the secret, and of a prompt departure the very next morning by the *Bretagne*. In fact, she spoke with so much energy and conviction that Betty, vanquished little by little, ended by saying—

"Certainly, certainly, we must start at once." And, without seeking further enlightenment, she rang all the bells, called up the hotel people, and had her trunks strapped up in the twinkling of an eye. The little American had that very day received some money from her banker in New York, which enabled her to make such a rapid departure. But if she had been so easily persuaded, it was because she was determined not only to win her wager, but to win it brilliantly, and without giving any one at the Philatelic Club a chance of thinking there had been any compromise between her and her rival, and for this it was necessary that she should not go back in the same steamer with him.

Miss Scott could not control her delight, and laughed aloud as she thought of the discomfiture of William Keniss when he heard of the precipitate departure—and with the stamp!—of his lucky adversary, through the telegram she would have the wicked pleasure of sending him from Havre, at the very moment of going on board the steamer. The two women hurriedly dined, and, an hour later, the great omnibus carried them to the Gare Saint-Lazare, in time to catch the express which would land them in the morning at Havre, to cross by the *Bretagne*.

As for John, he had remained on sentry-duty in the Place Vendôme to judge of the success of his plot, and it would be impossible to depict his joy when he saw the luggage brought out and the two women getting into the omnibus. He ran behind it all the way to the station, and, hearing his two spies trotting heavily after him, said gaily—

"It is my turn to spy this time. Miss Scott never anticipated such a pursuit as this."

The crafty fellow followed them right into the station, and, as soon as he had seen the train disappear into the night, carrying away our two travellers, he returned to find Mr. Keniss, who was much astonished at his radiant visage and at the burst of laughter with which he entered.

"Well, what is it now?" asked the young American.

"Oh, sir, it is really too amusing!"

"What is?"

"The way I have just paid out Miss Betty and Victoria. It is too comical!"

And John subsided into a chair, too overcome with delight to utter another word. But Mr. Keniss, perplexed at the strange behaviour of his valet, insisted on an explanation. So John, in short sentences, constantly interrupted by bursts of laughter, told the whole story of his prowess, while William listened in freezing silence.

"And you have done that?" he said sternly, when John assured him that he had, with his own eyes, seen the two women get into the train for Havre.

"Why, yes, sir," said the valet, his ardour cooling a little.

"Then you are a nice fellow! A liar and a cheat!"

John, who had expected a very different reception after such a service rendered, was mute with astonishment.

"My luggage and my coat, at once!" said Mr. Keniss in a ringing voice. "We must go by the very next train, and if we do not arrive in time to repair your infamy, I shall dismiss you for the villain that you are!"

THE STAMP KING

By G. DE BEAUREGARD AND H. DE GORSSE

Translated from the French by EDITH C. PHILLIPS

BETTY SETTLED HERSELF IN A ROCKING-CHAIR

CHAPTER XVI.

What a woman wills——

THE cables were loosed, the gangways raised. The tugs attached to the *Bretagne* were pulling at the monster with all their force. Great jets of steam issued from the funnels, and the siren uttered from time to time its sonorous bellow. The boat was thus drawn through the flood-gate which separates the basin of the Eure from the outer port. On the quays, from the custom-house to the semaphore, the on-lookers were gathered, those who happened to be passing at the time stopping to assist at the always imposing spectacle of a steamer leaving port.

On the deck of the *Bretagne* the numerous passengers, in their turn, were contemplating the magnificent scene which was unfolding before their eyes—the crowd of people, and the houses on the quays, behind which rose the towers and steeples of Havre, the hills of Ingouville, and the cliffs of Saint-Adresse. Boats all hastened out of their way; whistles were blown, and cries and shouts exchanged, giving an impression of incessant movement and intense and laborious life, as the steamer slowly made her way through the outer port.

Betty settled herself in a rocking-chair among the groups of passengers in the stern, and Victoria was busy arranging the cushions comfortably for her young mistress.

"Are you all right now, Miss Betty?" she asked.

Meeting with no response, and accustomed to such silence, which showed the girl's deep preoccupation, Victoria troubled her no further. But curiosity, aided by her tender regard for Miss Betty, caused her to keep an eye on her while appearing to take no notice. The girl reclined comfortably in her chair with a far-away gaze, which seemed to take no interest in the scene before her, so absorbing to her fellow-passengers. It was evidently no rash supposition of Victoria's, that her mistress was lost in thoughts of a sober rather than of a diverting character.

"Are you there, Victoria?" she demanded suddenly.

"Yes, Miss Betty," returned the maid, who was standing behind her mistress and now leaned over her to hear what she had to say.

"Look here," said Betty, "I have reflected deeply on what you told me about that stamp."

A passing shiver shook Victoria's meagre frame as Betty continued—

"Yes, I have thought and thought, and can make nothing of it."

"But it is very simple, Miss Betty. As I told you——"

"I know, I know," interrupted Miss Scott. "I have all your story by heart, and, to tell the truth, it seems to me most suspicious."

"Oh, Miss Betty!"

"You can say what you like, but it is no less true that the way in which the stamp has fallen into your hands, its being in Paris at all, the circumstances, the strange chance—in fact, everything connected with the matter, is wonderful in the extreme."

Victoria began to be seriously alarmed as she saw Betty's determination to clear up the matter, and dispose of the suspicions which were all the more alarming because they had come so late.

"In any case," she ventured to say, "it's no use troubling about it now. We have got it, and that is the chief thing."

"I do not think so," said Betty. "Now let us proceed in order. Begin your story again at the very beginning and repeat it every word."

The unhappy Victoria's anxiety was at its height. And there was no means of escaping this inquisition, which threatened to be minute and to last during all the seven days' crossing. It was necessary, however, to enter into the spirit of it to prevent the growth of Miss Betty's ill-timed desire to know everything.

"You remember, Miss Betty, that I told you——?" began Victoria.

At this moment, as the boat passed the breakwater of the north jetty, exclamations were heard among the passengers.

"Look! Look! What is that? It must be a madman!"

Shouts and protestations arose from the quay; a violent movement was seen among the crowd, and in the midst of the disturbance two men appeared, rushing breathlessly forward, thrusting the people out of their way, breaking up the groups, pushing and knocking back all who opposed them. Every one on board the *Bretagne* followed the mad course of the two desperadoes, who dashed towards the jetty, at the very moment the boat moved slowly out of the port. They pushed into the front rank against the parapet, and one of them waved his handkerchief and shouted frantically.

"What in the world can he want?" every one wondered, but decided finally that he must be a husband, lover, brother, or friend anxious to exchange a last adieu with one of the passengers. Betty, interested at length, and thinking she would have plenty of time later on for the cross-examination of Victoria, left her chair and drew near the side of the boat.

"Am I dreaming?" she cried, grasping the hand of her maid, who had followed her.

"John and Mr. Keniss!" cried Victoria, overwhelmed with amazement.

"This is astounding!" cried Betty. And, in recognition of what she took for a delicate attention on William's part, she drew out a cambric handkerchief and waved it, crying, in clear, crystal tones—

"Good-bye! We shall meet again soon."

William, for it was indeed he, saw her, and leaned over the parapet as if to get a little nearer, and as the boat passed close by him he cried in a loud voice—

"It is a forgery! A forgery!"

The little American was not long in comprehending the import of these few words. White with anger, and forgetting her usual calmness of demeanour, she fell back into her chair, while the *Bretagne*, which was now out of the channel, plunged into the open sea. But she was not the woman to waste her time in useless despair.

"Victoria!" she cried, suddenly jumping up.

"Yes, Miss Betty," replied the poor girl in a trembling voice, for she quite anticipated violence.

"Go this instant and fetch me the stamp, a magnifying-glass, and the photograph of the original."

The maid disappeared at once in the direction of her mistress's cabin, while the girl muttered to herself—

"Oh, this is too hard! it really is too hard!"

When Victoria returned she took from her hands the little articles she had brought, and, armed with the magnifying-glass, immediately set herself to examine in turn the photograph of the true stamp which she had received from M. Moulineau and the copy which had come into her hands the evening before. The examination lasted several minutes, during which Victoria awaited the result with the greatest anxiety.

"It is indeed a forgery!" cried Miss Betty, with a crushing glance at her maid.

"Is it possible?" murmured Victoria, scarcely knowing what she was saying.

"Look at it yourself!"

"But I don't understand it, Miss Betty."

Taking no notice of the remark, the young girl forced the resisting Victoria to examine the forgery.

"See here," she said, "towards the left, this flower, whose right petal is stiffer in this copy than in the original. And this Hindoo character in the middle, the upper part of which is a little longer than it should be. And this hair in the Maharajah's beard, which stands out at least the fiftieth of a millimetre too much. And this little arabesque, the curve of which is less pronounced in the forged stamp than in the original. For the stamp is forged, you wretched girl! absolutely bad! as bad as ever it could be! And if at this moment I am covered with shame and ridicule, it is to you and to my miserable credulity that I owe it!"

"Oh dear! oh dear!" moaned Victoria.

"It is high time to lament!" continued Betty, with growing anger. "Ah! the suspicions which I had just now were not without foundation. I must get to the root of the matter this instant. Once for all, tell me the truth or—you leave me."

The girl hesitated, in spite of her anger, before uttering this terrible threat. To dismiss Victoria! To destroy in one minute the remembrance of thirty years' service and devotion! To upset the life and break up all the hopes of a poor creature without any other worldly support; too young still to give up all hope of happiness, but too old to begin life over again!

Poor, unhappy Victoria, at the very thought of such a thing being possible, lost control of herself and burst into tears, powerless to answer a word to Miss Betty's inquiry. Nothing more was needed to melt the warm heart of the young girl, who, feeling almost ashamed of her words, seized the hand of her faithful attendant and said with repentant tenderness—

"Come, my dear friend, do not grieve. Of course I do not mean what I said just now. Send you away! I am horrified at the very thought of it, and only yielded to a moment's passion, for which you must forgive me." And with a charming grace she took Victoria in her arms and embraced her before the eyes of the surprised passengers, who continued their promenade on the deck with a smile of amusement.

But if Betty had a kind heart, she had, none the less, a stubborn will. So she soon returned to her absorbing thought and began again, though in a friendly voice this time, while Victoria wiped away the tears which still filled her eyes.

"Now tell me the truth quickly, since you no longer bear me any ill-will, for time presses."

A little surprised at this last remark, since they had a whole week's leisure before them in which to talk, Victoria, frequently interrupted by little sobs, like the tail-end of a tempest, went over, point by point, and with perfect candour, the account of her interview with John, and the circumstances under which the forged stamp had come into her possession. She omitted nothing which was blameworthy in her conduct, even dwelt with complacence on her occasional duplicity, and accused herself without the least evasion.

"There, that is all there is to tell," she concluded. "I have been to blame, I know, but I only had your interest at heart, Miss Betty, so do please forgive me."

Then, in a few words of affectionate reproach, Betty pointed out to her how imprudent she had been. Mr. Keniss would be quite right to blame such conduct severely. Actions such as these should be rigorously avoided by honourable people, and, even had the stamp been perfectly authentic, nothing could justify the manner in which it had been procured. But evidently Mr. Keniss knew what to think of it, or he would not have hastened to Havre.

"Now," concluded Betty, "besides that it would be most humiliating and painful for me to return to New York with a forged stamp, I must immediately repair the involuntary wrong I have done my kind rival. So go and get our luggage ready and we will be back at Havre in an hour."

"In an hour!"

"Certainly. Be as quick as you can."

Within herself Victoria, who had begun to recover from her recent despair, reflected sadly—"Back at Havre this evening! Another mad idea. Oh, dear me! What will happen next?"

However, as the time was not propitious for speaking her mind, she went off to Miss Betty's cabin to carry out her orders.

The boat was going now at full speed, ploughing through the green water and leaving a long track of foam, which was visible right to the entrance of the port. The jetties and houses of Havre were every moment becoming smaller, their size diminished by

you, so please be good enough to let me have the means."

"I can only repeat, mademoiselle, that it is not in my power to give you this satisfaction," said the captain. "You do not wish to take the *Bretagne* back, I suppose?" he added, with a touch of irony.

"Of course not."

"Well, then?"

"Sir, I desire you to have me taken back in one of your boats."

The captain smiled with a gesture of kindly protestation.

"Alas! mademoiselle, I have no right to dispose of my boats in that way, but never have I so regretted the formal rules by which I am bound."

"I will buy it from you."

"I am no more able to sell than to lend."

THE BOAT WAS GOING NOW AT FULL SPEED

the distance. For a few moments Miss Betty remained thoughtful, as if undecided how to act; then, suddenly making up her mind, she accosted one of the officers on board and informed him she wished to speak to the captain immediately.

"You are just in time, for here he is," returned the officer.

Having cleared the channel, the captain, in his frock-coat and gold-laced cap, was just descending from the foot-bridge to take a turn on the deck. Miss Betty ran to him and began abruptly—

"If you please, I must return to land this very moment."

The captain, thinking he could not possibly have heard aright, saluted her with perfect courtesy and an inquiring, "I beg your pardon, mademoiselle?"

"I said I must go back to Havre this very instant."

There was no possibility of a mistake this time, and the captain, astonished at such a whim, replied—

"But surely, mademoiselle, you are not ignorant of the fact that that is impossible?"

"Impossible!" said Betty disdainfully. "Surely you, who go to America so often, ought to know that, if the word has become French, it has not yet, thank goodness, become American. It must be done, I tell

"Not if I pay a big price?" asked Miss Betty, who, being an American, was inclined to believe that money would put everything right.

"Whatever price you offered, mademoiselle, it would be my painful duty to refuse."

"Two thousand dollars? Three thousand?"

"No, mademoiselle, do not continue. All the riches in the world could not tempt me to forget my duty."

"At any rate, you cannot compel me to remain on the steamer when peremptory reasons call me back to France," objected Betty.

"But, mademoiselle, you knew these reasons before you came on board, and no one, so far as I know, compelled you to come."

"Pardon me, sir. The reasons were only made known to me as we left the port. I was informed from the jetty that my stamp——"

"I pray you to believe, mademoiselle, that I have no wish to pry into your intimate concerns. Whatever they may be I am, and I shall continue to be, powerless to help you; to my great grief, believe me."

"This is arbitrary! You will carry me away against my will!" cried Betty, stamping her little foot on the shining deck.

(To be continued.)

THE STAMP KING

By G. DE BEAUREGARD AND H. DE GORSSE

Translated from the French by EDITH C. PHILLIPS

CHAPTER XVI (*continued*)

What a woman wills——

A FEW promenaders, drawn by curiosity, had gathered round them and had not lost a word of the discussion, which they found very diverting in its originality and unexpectedness. They saw the captain reflect for a minute, as if seeking some means of giving his exacting passenger a little help.

"Indeed, mademoiselle," he said at length, "it grieves me deeply that such a misfortune should happen to you, but there is only one thing I can do to prove it——"

"Oh, what is that? Tell me quickly."

"Do not expect too much. It has nothing to do with taking you back. But if you wish to send instructions to France immediately concerning the subject which troubles you, without awaiting your arrival in New York, which means a week's delay, I can telegraph."

"Telegraph!" said Betty in astonishment.

"Certainly, mademoiselle. The passengers have the right of corresponding, by signals, with the semaphores, while the steamer is in sight of the coast, and the semaphore sends the telegram on in the ordinary form. For a good half-hour yet we can be seen by the semaphore at La Hève. After that time I can promise nothing on account of the haze and the distance."

"I am much obliged to you," said Miss Betty, who could not refrain from a little dryness. And, without contending any further, she leaned on her elbows on the side of the steamer, feeling furious in her helplessness.

"Telegraph!" she mused. "What would be the good of that? To whom? For what? That could not justify me in the eyes of William Keniss, or give me any information concerning the real stamp."

Several of those who had heard this extraordinary conversation came up to the captain and began to make merry over the exorbitant desires of the young girl. But one of them left this group and drew nearer to her.

"Will you pardon me, mademoiselle, if I speak to you without having the honour of your acquaintance?" he said.

"What do you want with me, sir?" she returned severely enough, thinking perhaps that this might be a second Sir Oscar.

"Nothing but what may be to your advantage, mademoiselle," said the new-comer. "I think I understood that you have a great desire to return to land?"

"That is quite true."

"Would it be early enough for you if you were to arrive in Paris to-morrow morning?"

"What! Have you any means to suggest?" asked the girl with a quick flash of hope.

"Perhaps."

"Oh, do tell me quickly! You are killing me with suspense."

"Well, the captain offered to send a telegram for you. Why not telegraph to the Tug Company at Cherbourg?"

"I do not see how that would help me."

"The captain refuses to let you have one of his boats, but he could not refuse to put you on board one sent to meet you."

Betty listened breathlessly, but without, as yet, comprehending the idea.

"I will explain," continued the unknown. "Give the Tug Company an order to send one of their steamers to cross the line of route of the *Bretagne*. We shall be off Cherbourg in about four hours, so you will just have time."

"Oh, thank you." And Miss Betty, who knew how to act on sudden resolutions, ran to the captain, and, surrounded as he was by a numerous group, without concerning herself as to whether they listened or not, said—

"I will accept the offer you made me just now."

"Very good, mademoiselle; kindly write down what you wish me to say."

On a leaf torn from her memorandum book she wrote rapidly these few words :—

"TUG COMPANY,
"CHERBOURG.

"Send immediately, at any cost, quick steamer to meet *Bretagne* about to pass off Cherbourg *en route* for New York. Urgent.

"BETTY SCOTT."

Then she handed the paper to the captain, who, after reading it, shook his head.

"It would be quite useless, mademoiselle, for I could not allow you to go on board."

"Oh, indeed! Why not, if you please?"

"Because to do that I must stop the boat, and my time is limited, except for circumstances over which I have no control. Moreover, you are on the list of my passengers, and I am equally responsible for you, if you will forgive my saying so."

"I will absolve you from that responsibility."

"It is not in your power, mademoiselle."

These perpetual objections irritated the girl to a degree.

"Then you refuse to send my message?" she cried.

"By no means. I simply felt that I ought to point out the uselessness of it."

"Never mind that. Send it."

"I will do so at once. But let it be well understood that I have given you due warning." And the captain looked round on his auditors as if to appeal to them as witnesses, and went off to give his orders to the officer in charge of the signals. The flag was soon hoisted on the mizzen-mast to warn the signalman at the semaphore that there was a communication to receive, and, almost immediately, the glasses directed towards the cliffs of La Hève saw the red and white flag which showed that their signal was seen.

The passengers, interested in these manœuvres, now kept their eyes fixed on the vessel's mast. Along the rope, which mounted and descended with marvellous rapidity, carrying to the masthead the signals which served to interpret the words of the telegram, they saw in succession all the flags used for corresponding at a distance—the red, the yellow and blue, the white with the red cross of St. Andrew, the red with the yellow cross, the white chequered with blue, the blue quartered with yellow, the red and white, and many others.

Sometimes one was hoisted alone, sometimes several together, forming innumerable combinations. Then, when this came to an end, the semaphore hoisted a

MISS BETTY RAN TO THE CAPTAIN

white pennant with a red circle, to show that the message was understood and all was well. It was high time, for the steamer, thanks to her speed, was already at a great distance; and the cliffs, following the example of the town, were being gradually swallowed up in the fine May mist which spread over the sea and glanced in the sun like a silken veil. The news of the adventure soon went the round of the ship, and in every corner groups were forming to discuss the young girl's chances of success or failure.

"I say her perseverance will meet with its reward," said one of the daring little American's fellow-passengers.

"And I, that she will have all the trouble and expense for nothing," returned another.

"We cannot tell as yet," added a third vaguely, evidently with no intention of compromising himself.

In fact, Miss Scott's caprice had become the event of the day, and the *dénouement* was impatiently awaited. There were even some among the passengers who, of their own free-will, went to the captain and pointed out that there would be little inconvenience in stopping for a few seconds; that it would not cause them to be more than fifteen or twenty minutes behind time, and that it would be a humane act not to refuse the American lady a boon which she so ardently desired. The captain replied evasively to each of them, careful, while still going his own way, not to offend anybody.

As for Betty, all her efforts could not succeed in hiding her impatience. Her mind rushed towards the unknown, the uncertain, the improbable. A dozen questions at once forced themselves upon her, questions which it was impossible to answer, and which combined to throw her into an intolerable state of nervous excitement. Would her plot succeed? How would the captain behave at the last moment? And, above all, would her telegram arrive at Cherbourg in time?

It was this last subject which caused her the greatest apprehension. Would the Tug Company, at sight of her name and without any guarantee or payment in advance, start off one of their steamers? And if so, would this steamer arrive at a favourable moment on the route of the *Bretagne*, or might it not possibly happen that, without perceiving it, she would allow the liner to pass in the distance towards the open sea? And many other questions equally insoluble, equally fenced with difficulties and obstacles, rendered Miss Scott, as we have said, so nervously anxious that it was almost impossible for her to keep still.

Victoria, her preparations completed, made herself as small as possible at her side, not daring to ask anything or to risk the least observation. She was simply resigned—convinced in her heart that this second crossing would be no less eventful than the first, and that some serious step was contemplated, to judge by her mistress's looks and a few scraps of conversation overheard here and there.

(*To be continued.*)

THE STAMP MARKET

By AN ODD LOT

I APPEND a few prices of notable stamps at recent auctions :—

Messrs. Glendining & Co.'s Sale,
June 15th and 16th, 1905.

	£	s.	d.
Great Britain, 1881, 1d., lilac, printed on both sides *	2	4	0
Ditto, proof of the Mulready wrapper without the word "Postage" at foot	1	7	0
Switzerland, Zurich, 4 r., with vertical lines	9	2	6
British Central Africa, 1896, wmk. CC, £10, black and orange-red, mint	19	0	0
British East Africa, July, 1895, 5 a., with double surcharge	3	0	0
North Borneo, 1886, 5 c. on 8 c. (Gibbons' 21a), mint	4	12	6
St. Helena, 1864–74, 4d., carmine (Gibbons' 15), but perforated 14 × 12½, mint, a rare uncatalogued variety	0	14	0
Barbados, 1852, vertical half of 1d., used as a ½d., on portion of original	0	11	0
Ditto, 1878, 1d. on half 5s.	5	7	6
Ditto, 1892, 4d., brown, surcharged HALF-PENNY in black and in red (Gibbons' 106)	8	0	0
British Honduras, 1866, 6 c. on 10 c., inverted surcharge (Gibbons' 45)	4	15	0
Falkland Islands, ½d. on half 1d., double surcharge	1	2	0
Mexico, 1861, medio real, brown, with Gothic surcharge, mint	1	9	0
Virgin Islands, 1899, 4d., error PENCE, mint	4	0	0

	£	s.	d.
New South Wales, 1871–83, 6d., perf. 12 × 10, mint, surcharged O.S. in red, an uncatalogued variety	0	19	0
New Zealand, 1862, 2d., slate-blue (Gibbons' 45)	1	11	0
Ditto, 1863–6, 1s., deep green, unused and fine	1	1	0
Queensland, 1879–81, error "O," 1d., scarlet *	1	2	0
Tasmania, 1864–9, 1d., carmine, compound perf. (Gibbons' 71a) *	4	4	0
Tonga, 1891, 1d., rose, four Stars (Gibbons' 15b) *	2	4	0
Victoria, 1861, 1s., green, mint	3	17	6
Ditto, ditto, 1d., green, no wmk., imperf.	2	18	0

Messrs. Puttick and Simpson's Sale,
June 27th and 28th, 1905.

	£	s.	d.
Bulgaria, 1882, 5 stotinki, rose, error, mint	9	0	0
Finland, 1866, 10 penni, purple-brown, error	5	5	0
France, 1870–3, 20 c., blue, a *tête-bêche* pair, mint state	2	4	0
Great Britain, 1858–79, 1d., red, Plate 225, in mint state *	1	16	0
Ditto, 1860, 1½d., lilac-rose on bleuté, a fine block of four, in mint state *	4	10	0
Ditto, 1876, 4d., deep vermilion, Plate 16	70	0	0
Ditto, I.R. Official, 1902, 5s., carmine	13	0	0
Ditto, O.W. Official, 1896, ½d., vermilion, an imperf. pair, showing portions of six overprints	1	16	0
Ditto, Govt. Parcels, 1883–6, 9d., green, imperf., mint	1	2	0

* Unused.

THE STAMP KING

By G. DE BEAUREGARD AND H. DE GORSSE

Translated from the French by EDITH C. PHILLIPS

THE LITTLE VESSEL WAS ADVANCING

CHAPTER XVII

*In which Miss Betty engages in war with
man and the elements*

BETS were already made involving large sums of money. Some held the opinion that the steamer would not even come to the rendezvous, others that it would be there punctually, while many simply waited for whatever might happen.

For some time now there had been visible in outline on the horizon the coasts of Cotentin, the towers of La Hogue, and the point of Barfleur, from which the liner must set off direct for New York. As they drew rapidly nearer, this point could be more and more clearly seen, with its lighthouse and low cliffs, and at length, when the *Bretagne* was exactly opposite the cape, a turn of the helm caused her to incline slightly to port, and by the curve of the track in her wake it could be clearly seen that the steamer had abandoned her west-north-west course for one bearing west-south-west.

The cape doubled, the land quickly disappeared, enveloped in the light mist, as the vessel steamed towards Cherbourg, while her port side was soon occupied by a long row of passengers armed with glasses and optical instruments of all kinds. The captain, again stationed on the bridge, turned his powerful glass in the direction of Cherbourg, while Miss Betty, becoming more and more nervous, paced the deck without daring to look for fear of being too soon disillusioned.

"There she is!" cried one of the passengers, who was keeping watch through a particularly long telescope. There was no need to be more explicit, for everyone immediately understood that he referred to the steamer so anxiously expected.

"Really!" cried Betty, immediately pushing aside two of the spectators so that she might see for herself.

A small black spot might now be clearly seen in front of the liner, surmounted by a thin streak of smoke, which spot, growing larger by degrees, took the form of a small steamer rapidly approaching to meet the liner's route. When she was at least two miles off she hoisted signals, which removed all doubt. The colour of her funnel showed, moreover, that she belonged to the Cherbourg Tug Company, and her manœuvres proved her intention of coming up with the *Bretagne*.

Now she almost disappeared between two waves, then suddenly rose to the very summit of another, for the force of the ocean, no longer restrained by the peninsula of Cotentin, began to be pretty severely felt. When Betty had assured herself that it really was the steamer she had sent for she called to the captain, who was still on the bridge, beseeching him to stop the vessel and allow her to disembark. But the captain leaned over the balustrade and replied politely but firmly—

"Mademoiselle, it grieves me to tell you, once for all, that it is absolutely impossible."

"I appeal to you to grant my request, and I call upon all the passengers to witness your abuse of your powers."

"I can only do my duty," returned the captain, with a roughness he was unable to repress.

The passengers, who had gathered round so as to lose nothing of the discussion, here showed their disapproval of the captain's behaviour, which was undoubtedly in accordance with the rules, but neither conciliating nor kind; murmurs, mingled with protestations and even with menaces, began to be heard. The time occupied in exchanging these few words had permitted the little steamboat to approach, and it was now scarcely a cable's length distant.

"You still refuse?" cried Miss Betty, trembling.

The captain's only answer was to order an increase of pressure, that the boat's speed might be accelerated. Immediately the groaning of the screw was heard as it turned faster and more heavily. The boat creaked dismally as if overcome by the prodigious effort, and the steam, escaping from every valve, drowned the cries of the indignant passengers.

"You have brought it upon yourself," cried the girl, but her voice was lost in the tumult. And at the words, with the rapidity of lightning, she broke through the circle of passengers, jumped on a chair, climbed over the side of the boat, and threw herself into the sea, while Victoria uttered a cry of hopeless

THE YOUNG AMERICAN
SWAM WITH DIFFICULTY

despair. One of the witnesses of this mad act was just able to seize the hem of Miss Betty's dress, but the piece of stuff tore off, and the unhappy girl disappeared in the masses of white foam which enveloped the boat.

"Stop!" thundered the captain. "Man overboard!"

Immediately, in the midst of the cries of terrified women and of menacing shouts and distracted clamour, the sailors ran to their lifebuoys, while the screw, reversing rapidly to stop the course of the steamer, left foaming eddies upon her track.

The men on the tug, who had also been spectators of the scene, threw all their buoys in the direction in which the girl had fallen. Then followed a moment of deep anxiety. Dead silence reigned, or was only broken by the desperate cries of Victoria, who was

with great difficulty held back from following her mistress.

At last the streaming head of Miss Betty emerged from a wave close to the tug. The little American, encumbered by her clothes, was only able to swim with difficulty. However, thanks to her energy and her good physical training, she was just able to reach one of the buoys, to which she clung, and was gently drawn by the rope attached to it to the side of the steamer, on to the deck of which the young girl, in a fainting condition, was hoisted, to the great relief of the passengers on board the *Bretagne*.

"Miss Betty! Miss Betty! I must go to Miss Betty!" cried Victoria at the top of her voice and in the wildest excitement. And as she continued to vow that she would drown herself if they tried to keep her on board, and as the course of the steamer was now stopped and the passengers interceded with the captain more earnestly than ever on the maid's behalf, he gave way and signalled to the little steamer to approach.

But this she could not do without encountering grave difficulties, the roughness of the sea rendering it almost impossible. And even when the tug got near enough for the luggage of the two women, their portmanteaux and bags, to be lowered into it, there was the still more difficult task of transhipping Victoria. Now the caprice of the waves would cause the little tug to graze the side of the liner, then they would carry her several fathoms away, dragging her down, tossing her up again and rolling her in every direction, while the huge and immovable *Bretagne* scarcely trembled in their grasp.

The impatient Victoria was suspended in a kind of improvised swing, one end of the rope being passed round the pulley of one of the ship's cranes and held by four strong men, who only waited a propitious moment to allow their burden to descend on to the moving deck of the little steamer.

This, after the recent tragedy, was comedy irresistible. Balanced like a living pendulum and suspended over the greenish abyss, Victoria seemed little at her ease. Once a wave, higher than the rest, caught her feet, and the sudden cold, mingled a little with fear, drew from her a terrified cry. But the scene was so amusing, and there was so little real danger in the poor girl's position, that shouts of laughter were heard on every side, especially when it became evident that her chief concern lay in the proper arrangement of her petticoats.

Suddenly the tug, uplifted by a wave, came nearly to the level of the steamer, seeing which the sailors who held the rope let it slip. But the movement was not carried out with sufficient promptitude, and the little boat, descending at an even quicker rate, sank into the hollow of the next wave, so that the unfortunate Victoria had a fall of several feet, and would have risked at least the breaking of a limb had not the sailors on the tug hastened to catch her in their arms. For a moment the passengers feared there had been an accident, but they were soon reassured by seeing her rise intact and hasten to Miss Betty, who, lying at full length on the deck of the steamer, was just recovering consciousness.

Then, as the *Bretagne* took up her interrupted course, the enthusiasm of all on board at such a manifestation of will and courage broke forth, and the sound of prolonged applause reached the little steamer as she ploughed her way on the return journey to Cherbourg.

"You here, my dear friend?" said Betty tenderly as she opened her eyes and recognised Victoria kneeling beside her.

"Yes, Miss Betty, and very happy at seeing you out of danger."

"It is all the same to me. I will pay whatever is necessary, but I must be there. It means five hundred francs extra for you."

"Five hundred francs!" It was more than enough to set the engines going. The pilot rushed to his men, and, stimulating their zeal by promising to share with them the offered prize, gave a number of orders, which were executed with startling rapidity, and the tug, bounding from wave to wave, was urged forward

THEY LET DOWN THE IMPATIENT VICTORIA BY A ROPE

"Yes, we have had a lucky escape, and I am surprised to find myself alive after my plunge into the waves. But you—how did you come here? Have they really let you come on board the tug?"

"Yes, indeed, Miss Betty."

"Then all's well that ends well," concluded the courageous girl. But other cares returned, and she called the pilot and said—

"My friend, I wish to catch the six twenty-four train from Cherbourg to Paris."

"Oh, madame," said the good man, who was still a little upset at this strange way of procuring passengers, "it is five o'clock now, and I don't know if——"

at full speed. Betty and Victoria, meanwhile, took refuge in the narrow cabin, and sought in their trunks, almost broken open by their fall, the means of making themselves presentable. Six o'clock struck as the little vessel entered the trading dock at Cherbourg. Betty, more than ever on the alert, jumped on to the quay, paid the considerable sum due for her voyage, fulfilled her promise with regard to the reward, and, followed by Victoria, hastened to the station, where, sinking on to the cushions in the express, she said to her faithful companion—

"And now we have succeeded so admirably, let us sleep till we get to Paris."

(To be continued.)

THE STRAND POSTAGE STAMP ALBUM.

Well arranged, reliable, and thoroughly correct. Seventh edition. 100 Postage Stamps, all genuine and different, and of a catalogue value of over 8s., are presented with each Strand Album. The book, which is printed on an unusually good quality paper, is bound in a new and specially designed cover. The size is a new and convenient one, viz. 9½ inches by 7½ inches. Sufficient guards have been inserted so that when the Album is full the covers shall be level with each other, and not bulged, as is often the case in imperfectly constructed books. 300 pages, post-free, 2s. 11d.; abroad, 3s. 4d.

Stanley Gibbons, Ltd., 391, Strand, London, W.C.

THE STAMP KING

By G. DE BEAUREGARD AND H. DE GORSSE

Translated from the French by EDITH C. PHILLIPS

HE SAW THAT THE COMMANDER WAS OCCUPIED IN SEARCHING THE PORTMANTEAUS

CHAPTER XVIII

Wherein William congratulates himself on having found a very cheerful travelling companion

WILLIAM, having done all in his power to prevent Miss Betty's departure, returned in a melancholy mood to the station, in order to take the train back to Paris. He was very unhappy at not having succeeded in warning his friend, and a very little more would have been needed to make him dismiss the too officious John Cockburn; but the latter pleaded his cause so well, urging that his only desire had been to render his master assistance, that he felt bound to relent and forgive him.

An hour later the Stamp King and his valet were comfortably settled in their compartment. So many unexpected things had happened since the evening before that neither of them had the least desire to talk. With faces turned to the windows, and a far-off look at the landscape through which they were passing, each fell into a deep reverie; William Keniss especially, who travelled again in thought over this same journey from Havre to Paris, which he had made not many days before with the most charming and delightful companion. How angry she must be with him at that very moment, storming against him, perhaps, for having deceived her in so unworthy, though involuntary, a manner. And would she ever forgive him, when he had explained that the only one to blame in the whole matter was John?

But little by little the young American put these dismal thoughts to flight. He even experienced a certain pleasure in his freedom, and had so far regained his tranquillity by the time he had arrived at the Terminus Hotel that he quickly changed his clothes in order to dine and go to the Opera afterwards.

"You can do what you like this evening," he said to John before going out. "I shall probably not be back till late, but in any case you need not trouble about me."

"Very good, sir."

"I must tell you definitely, though, that we leave Paris to-morrow."

"And where do we go, sir, if there is no harm in my asking?"

"To Italy."

"Italy!"

"Certainly. Now that, thanks to you, Miss Betty is on her way to America and cannot return in less than a fortnight, even if a fresh voyage has any temptation for her, I need take no further precautions. In any case I shall arrive at Naples before she does."

"Oh, then it is to Naples we are going?"

"Yes, my friend, to Naples. Though I do not know why I tell you that after the proof you have just given me of your discretion."

"But I have no one to make a fool of myself with now, sir."

"No, Victoria is no longer here. Know then, my dear John, that the Brahmapootra stamp is at Naples, in Prince Albrandi's collection."

"Prince Albrandi?"

"A great philatelist."

"As great philatelists, I know you, sir, Miss Scott, Monsieur de Rothschild, who has just bought the Duke of York's collection for 1,500,000 francs, the Emperor of Russia, and Monsieur Ferrari; but Prince Al—, Al—! What do you call him, sir?"

"Albrandi."

"Prince Albrandi I don't know at all."

"Your ignorance is easily explained, as this gentleman has only been collecting a short time."

"Oh, is that it?"

Thereupon William Keniss left the hotel, and as it was about dinner-time, directed his steps to one of the great restaurants on the Boulevards.

He was already longing for the morrow, that he might set off. And yet there was no hurry, as he had now the whole week before him in which to go to Naples, conclude the purchase of the stamp, and return. A week! It was certainly enough. It was even too much! For William Keniss had now but one desire—that the bargain which he hoped to make with Prince Albrandi might be concluded early enough to enable him to catch the next steamer for New York, at Havre, on the following Saturday. In fact, he was in a great hurry to see Miss Betty, to explain all that had passed, and how ashamed he was of the unworthy and revolting conduct of his valet.

But for this purpose it was necessary that the young lady should not start off again for France immediately on landing at New York—of which act she was quite capable.

"I can easily prevent that," thought William. "I have only to send her a cablegram from Naples as soon as I have the stamp."

So William Keniss finished his dinner without his thoughts straying for a moment from his charming rival. Then, not knowing what to do with himself till midnight, he sauntered towards the Opera, where *Faust* was being played that evening.

He had not taken his seat many minutes before the neighbouring one on his right was occupied by a gentleman who looked the acme of elegance. He could not have been more than thirty-five, with a slender figure above the medium height, bristly hair, and heavy moustache curled up at the ends. His dress-coat was irreproachable, and a white camellia of unusual size graced his button-hole. One would say at a glance that he was an aristocrat, a member probably of one of the crack clubs. In passing before William Keniss the unknown bowed gracefully and begged his pardon for disturbing him in a foreign accent, which the Stamp King immediately recognised as Italian.

But the curtain had just risen on the study of Doctor Faustus, who was soon singing his great song, "A moi les plaisirs," followed by the frantic applause of the entire house. William's neighbour was especially exuberant, though from his appearance one would not have expected it.

"Bravo! Bravo!" he shouted over and over again, raising his hands above his head to clap, while the unfortunate auditors near him were beginning to cry "Hush!" Upon this the unknown relapsed into silence until the end of the scene; but when the curtain fell his enthusiasm broke out again, and he made more noise than all the others put together.

"Who can this fellow be?" thought William Keniss.

The Stamp King then rose, with the idea of getting a little fresh air outside. But his neighbour politely stopped him.

"Excuse me for the liberty I take, sir," said he, "but are you aware that there is no interval?"

"No, I was not aware of it. Thank you."

"There is no need for thanks. One owes these little services to strangers, for I take it from your accent that you are not French."

"No, I am an American."

"An American? And may I ask to whom I have the honour of speaking?"

"I am William Keniss, of New York."

"William Keniss!" the unknown could not refrain from ejaculating.

"Can it be, then, that you know me?"

"No, indeed," replied the stranger hastily. "But permit me, in return, to introduce myself—Commander Luigi Spartivento."

"Italian, I presume?"

"Yes, sir, Italian."

"Then it is a very lucky accident that has placed me at your side this evening. I am starting for Italy to-morrow, and I trust you will be good enough to give me a little information about the country."

"Not only can I do that, but, up to a certain point, I can pilot you there, for I also go to-morrow evening by the 8.55 express."

"Indeed!"

"But to what part are you going, may I ask?"

"To Naples."

"To Naples!" How fortunate that I should have met you. That is exactly where I am going."

Commander Luigi Spartivento and William Keniss were interrupted at this moment by the bell, announcing that the curtain was about to rise.

"Don't let us talk any more," said the commander. "This is the Kermesse scene, and it is admirable."

"I see you love music," returned William.

"I do more than love it. I adore it and idolise it."

In fact, several times during the course of the act Commander Spartivento—who, perhaps, affected a little too much the air of being music-mad to be so in reality—manifested his enthusiasm with so much exuberance that the rest of the audience, peaceful citizens though they were, began to show symptoms of annoyance. One of them even made use of the following interval to carry his grievance to a superintendent, who, in the most courteous fashion, begged the noble Italian to put the soft pedal on his too evident admiration of Gounod's immortal work and the excellent artistes who were interpreting it.

"What! What!" cried the commander. "I may not even applaud if it pleases me? Where is the manager? I will take my complaint to him."

"Be calm, I beseech you," said William in annoyance, for a crowd of about fifty persons had already gathered round them in the corridor.

"No, I will not be calm till I have made my complaint. Where is the manager?"

At this moment electric bells rang on all sides to recall the spectators to their seats. William Keniss took advantage of the opportunity to take his new friend by the arm and lead him back, very much against his will, and literally foaming with rage.

"*Diavolo!*" he cried, staring with arrogant insolence at the surrounding spectators. "If I only knew which of these imbeciles it was who complained of me I would cut off his ears!"

"Commander! Commander!" William kept repeating with increasing annoyance. And he tried to draw Luigi Spartivento from thoughts of vengeance to admiration of the Opera House.

"Instead of exciting yourself like this," he said, "just look how splendidly the boxes are decorated."

The Opera House was indeed a magnificent spectacle. For from floor to ceiling all the ladies were in light evening dresses, with bare shoulders and covered with diamonds—a marvellous expanse of varied colours, a fairy flash of scintillating gems.

Spartivento, in his fury, would not look, but continued to crush the orchestra with his wrathful glances. William Keniss could not help comparing him to a great lion in a rage, which brought a discreet smile to the thin lips of the irascible commander.

"Oh, no!" he said. "If they think to keep me from applauding or from hissing they are very much mistaken!"

"What! Are you going to hiss?" cried William, who began to fear that his neighbour would commit some still more trying eccentricities.

"Yes," he said resolutely. "I shall hiss to show the clowns they cannot mock with impunity Commander Luigi Spartivento."

"But they will turn you out."

"It's all the same to me."

"But not to me, my dear Commander, not to me. They have seen us talking together and they will think——"

"Yes, that is true. They might even be capable of turning you out at the same time as your humble servant. So, as I don't wish to cause you annoyance the first time we meet, I will exchange my seat for that one at the end of the row, which, I have noticed, has been empty all the evening."

"As you please," said William, laughing in spite of himself at the anger of his new friend, towards whom he could not feel any ill-will, so eager had he been to offer his services as guide to Italy.

"The curtain is going to rise, so I will leave you.

Whether anything happens or not we shall meet at the exit."

"Agreed."

So the commander took the seat he had pointed out to William, and the curtain rose upon Marguerite's garden. The house had become silent as if by enchantment, so that the dropping of a pin might be heard. It seemed as if word had been given to the spectators to hold their breath, lest they should disturb the strain of pure, sweet melody sung by Siebel and Marguerite at the commencement of this act.

(To be continued.)

POST OFFICE ANNUAL REPORT

THE Fifty-first Annual Report of the Postmaster-General for the year ended 31st March, 1905, has just been published as a Parliamentary Blue Book. We print *in extenso* the portion relating to stamps and postal packets :—

Statistics of Postal Packets

It is estimated that the number of postal packets delivered in the United Kingdom during the year 1904–5 was as follows :—

	Number.	Increase per Cent.	Average No. for each Person.
Letters . . .	2,624,600,000	1·0	61·2
Post cards . .	734,500,000	19·7	17·1
*Halfpenny packets .	843,700,000	2·8	19·7
Newspapers . .	170,400,000	2·6	4·2
Parcels . . .	97,200,000	3·0	2·3
Total . .	4,479,400,000	4·2	104·4

Letters and Post Cards

The increase in the number of the letters, although greater than that of last year ('7 per cent.), is still slight compared with that shown in former years; and there is again a decrease ('5 per cent.) in the letters delivered in London. This is no doubt to be largely attributed to the still increasing use of pictorial post cards, which has contributed to bring about an increase of 19·7 per cent. in the number of post cards passing through the post. Private post cards are now estimated to number no less than 81 per cent. of the total number posted.

Registered Letters and Parcels

The number of letters registered in the United Kingdom during the year 1904–5 was 18,504,690, a decrease of 2·8 per cent. on the figures for 1903–4; whilst the number of parcels registered was 1,041,521, a decrease of ·2 per cent. on the previous year. The decrease is believed to be principally due to the continued depression in the cheap jewellery trade.

Express Delivery Services

The total number of express services was 1,403,053, as compared with 1,290,833 last year. The increase, 8·7 per cent., though considerable, is less than that of previous years.

In London there were 916,740 express services, 1,446,085 articles being delivered in this manner, including 552,035 letters sent out for delivery in advance of the postman.

Undelivered Postal Packets

The following are the numbers of undelivered packets dealt with during the year :—

Description.	Number.	Increase (+) or Decrease (−) as compared with previous year.	
		Number.	Per Cent.
Letters . . .	10,743,447	− 404,834	− 3·63
Post cards . .	2,386,124	+ 140,797	+ 6·27
*Halfpenny packets .	12,559,049	+ 131,368	+ 1·06
Newspapers . .	622,731	− 10,448	− 1·65
Parcels . . .	257,389	+ 3,874	+ 1·53
Total . .	26,568,740	− 130,243	− ·52

* Including also foreign Book Packets, etc., over 2 oz. in weight, prepaid at the halfpenny rate.

Undelivered Letters

The decrease in the number of undelivered letters is believed to be partly due to a diminution in the number of foreign lottery circulars posted in this country, and furnishes therefore double cause for satisfaction.

Registered and Property Letters

The number of registered letters and letters containing property sent through the post with insufficient addresses was 315,965. These letters contained £17,830 in cash and bank notes, and £622,123 in bills, cheques, money orders, postal orders, and stamps. One packet contained jewellery whose value exceeded £2,000. The number of letters containing valuable contents posted with no address at all was 4,507, the contents including £157 in cash and bank notes, and £9,412 in various forms of remittances. It was found possible to restore the greater number of these letters to the senders.

Although the number of insufficiently addressed letters was smaller than in the previous year, the total value of the contents thus jeopardised by the carelessness of the public was greater by more than £4,000.

There was a slight increase in the number of articles found loose in the post during the year. These included £1,171 in cash and £12,058 in cheques and other forms of remittance.

Home Mail Services: Use of Motors

I have been able to make considerable extensions in the use of motor vans for the conveyance of mails; and I am glad also to be able to report a substantial advance in the reliability of the services already

THE STAMP KING

By G. DE BEAUREGARD AND H. DE GORSSE

Translated from the French by EDITH C. PHILLIPS

CHAPTER XVIII (*continued*)

Wherein William congratulates himself on having found a very cheerful travelling companion

THE commander also was motionless and silent. What was he waiting for, that he did not begin the little manifestation he had promised his friend William Keniss? Simply that there might be a man on the scene, for, not forgetting the respect due to women even when one is in a rage, he would not hiss either Siebel, Marguerite, or Dame Marthe, but Faust or Mephistopheles. For this reason Spartivento waited a few minutes with quiet resignation before showing the people how very little notice he took of the reprimand they had just brought upon him.

At length Faust commenced the beautiful air—

"Salut, demeure chaste et pure!"

and at the same moment the commander put a key to his lips and broke in upon it with a shrill whistle. The singer stopped short, and, one after another, the orchestra followed in confusion. The nearer spectators rose and shook their fists, while those in the boxes and upper galleries leaned over to see as much as they could at the risk of tumbling head-first into the stalls.

"Turn him out!" was the cry. "Turn him out!" Spartivento, in defiance, thrust his hat on his head and whistled his loudest.

"Turn him out! turn him out!" sounded on all sides.

The situation began to look dangerous for the commander, who sat with smiling serenity in the midst of the storm, when two of the municipal guard appeared at one of the doors, and, in spite of his protestations, marched him out *manu militari*, to the enthusiastic applause of the spectators, who were delighted to get rid of one who had interfered with their enjoyment from the beginning. Now, Spartivento disposed of, the garden scene might go on without interruption. William Keniss, who had not left his seat, was highly amused, and congratulated himself on having made the acquaintance of so lively a person.

"He is so original that he will make a most amusing travelling companion," thought he.

So the Stamp King took advantage of the interval to go in search of his new friend, whom he found marching tranquilly backwards and forwards at the top of the Opera stairs.

"Well, how did it go off?" he asked.

"Perfectly," returned the commander. "They contented themselves with escorting me to the door. Will you come and have a cocktail with me?"

"Most willingly."

So Commander Luigi Spartivento and William Keniss went and settled themselves on the terrace at a café to become better acquainted with each other, and towards one o'clock in the morning, having conversed on a thousand subjects—America, Italy, and what not—they parted with a hearty grasp of the hand like old acquaintances, arranging to meet the next evening at the Gare de Lyon.

William woke in the morning at about ten o'clock. Through the windows of his room, facing the south, entered the rays of the beautiful May sun, which, in the balmy atmosphere of Paris, seems to clothe itself in a soft mist and to lavish its gentle beams more generously than elsewhere. John came and opened the windows and admitted the delicious morning perfumes. Down below, in the Place du Havre, were a number of conveyances heaped up with flowers, spreading all around the reflection of their colours and the charm of their scent. Piles of fruit and fresh vegetables—perhaps also the Parisian dames, as they passed with little bunches of flowers in their dresses—perfumed the atmosphere, and gave to the air that voluptuous scent which is known nowhere else but between Meudon and Saint-Mandé.

William dressed in a contented frame of mind. Life itself was happiness, as it should be to a man who has slept well after a pleasant evening, possesses a good digestion, sees the sun shine, has a healthy appetite, youth, and money, and is on the point of reaching a desired goal at the end of an enchanting journey.

"I shall not want you to-day," he said to John when he was ready. "It is such a lovely day that I shall just wander about. I must remind you, though, that we start this evening for Naples. Pack up our luggage, forget nothing, pay the account, and be in the waiting-room at the Gare de Lyon at eight o'clock to the minute." William then went down, had a magnificent carnation arranged in his button-hole by one of the flower girls, and sauntered about for a few minutes.

"Holloa!" said he suddenly. "Eleven o'clock, and our places are not secured for the journey!"

He made inquiries, and returned almost to the point from which he had started on being told he would find the offices of the Lyon Company in the Rue Saint-Lazare; and soon catching sight of the magnificent entrance leading to them he entered the great hall.

"Why, it is Monsieur Keniss!" said a voice.

William turned his head and perceived Luigi Spartivento, who rose from his seat and came forward with outstretched hand.

"Good morning, Commander," said William, well pleased at the meeting. "To what happy chance——?"

"I have come for the same purpose as yourself, probably, to book my seat for Naples."

"That is exactly it. Shall we travel together?"

"With pleasure."

"What shall we take?"

"A coupé seems to me——"

"Oh, no," interrupted William, with a disdainful gesture. "Besides the fact that three cannot lie down comfortably——"

"A sleeping compartment, then?"

"That's better, but you never feel at home in them; and I have a horror of changing trains a dozen times. Would you not prefer a saloon carriage that would take us all the way?"

"You would have to engage one all to yourself," said the commander, by whom the question of economy could not be entirely neglected.

"That is my intention," laughed William. And, after a moment's reflection, he continued with true American frankness, "You need only trouble about your own seat, my dear Captain, for whether I travel alone or no I should none the less take the saloon and the six places."

This arrangement seemed to please Spartivento, as he agreed at once. But he evidently wished his new friend to make as cheap a bargain as possible, as he said—

"In any case, as the carriages are arranged in two distinct compartments, each containing three beds and every convenience, and capable of being united or separated at will by a door which can be locked, if anyone wants to take the one compartment it would be quite useless to reserve it at your own expense."

"I quite agree with you there," returned William. "So long as I can go to bed, dress, and not change carriages before arriving at Naples, I ask no more."

With these words they repaired to the booking-office of the Rue Saint-Lazare, and William stated what they wanted.

"A small saloon carriage to go as far as Naples, which I will take entirely at my own expense, unless you have someone willing to take the second compartment."

"Very good, sir," said the clerk, plunging into the ready-reckoner to calculate the price of such accommodation.

While this was going on, Spartivento, overcome by a sudden scruple, said in a low voice to his extravagant companion—

"This is really unconscionable on my part—I am wrong in accepting your kind offer."

"What in the world do you see unconscionable in that, my dear Commander? It happens that I engage a saloon for my own special use, and I ask you to take a place in it, which place you pay for. So you don't even owe me any thanks."

The commander appeared to yield against his will, and William's conscience congratulated him on the little service he was able to render to a man of extensive acquaintance in high Neapolitan circles, as he believed, and consequently one who would be able to help him most efficaciously.

"It will be six hundred and nineteen francs ninety to Modena," said the clerk, looking up. "For the Italian part of the journey you must pay the difference at the frontier. There is a deposit of fifty francs to pay now."

William drew out a pink and blue note and gave it in exchange for a receipt, on producing which and paying the remainder of the sum he would be put in possession of his saloon that evening. This accomplished, he went out again with Luigi Spartivento into the Rue Saint-Lazare

"What are you going to do this morning?" asked the commander in a friendly tone.

"I'm quite free, and have nothing to do but walk about till it is time to start."

"In that case will you do me the favour of taking luncheon with me?"

William, who was glad to begin at once the enjoyment of such agreeable company, accepted with pleasure. So Spartivento called a fiacre and they started off to lunch in the Bois de Boulogne.

The commander was an astounding talker, well-informed on all points—on deep questions of science or politics as well as Parisian gossip, having seen much, learned much, and retained much. With that southern loquacity so alluring in some people, he talked and talked and gesticulated, interspersing witticisms and amusing sayings with the most interesting conversation. He related his travels, detailed his adventures, and told of the illustrious friendships that his birth and culture had procured him in the four corners of Europe. William, completely fascinated, had no wish to interrupt, being ready to profit by such marvellous tact and the kindness which offered it with so much good-will.

Luncheon with such a congenial spirit, under the cool vault of the trees, with a view of carriages passing without intermission, and the joyous warbling of birds in the branches, was, as might have been expected, a gay meal. When they rose from the table, having become intimate, thanks to their long chat

and still more to the champagne, they returned to Paris and called at several shops, mutually counselling each other concerning their little purchases, and finally sat down to dine together in the neighbourhood of the Opera House. Friendship was finally cemented by a bottle of old Mesigny, which William, being host this time, had up from the restaurant vaults.

But time fled; the pneumatic clocks showed that it was already past seven, and time to think of going to the station.

"Have you any luggage to take?" asked William.

"No, my dear fellow. The omnibus of the Hotel Continental, where I have been staying, will convey it all to the station."

"All right then."

As eight o'clock struck they entered, inseparable from henceforth, the waiting-room of the Gare de Lyon, where John, faithful guardian of portmanteaus and rugs, had already arrived. William immediately went to pay the balance of the hire of his saloon, and was somewhat surprised when the clerk said—

"It will only be half, sir; that is, three hundred and ten francs. Two other travellers have turned up and taken the second compartment."

"And they go all the way to Naples?"

"Yes, sir."

"Very good." And returning to Spartivento he said, "Do you know we are going to have some companions after all?"

"So much the better. It will cost you the less."

They made their way to the train, and were very much astonished to find that the travellers who had taken half their saloon were already settled there, with the door shut, the blinds drawn down, and the lights extinguished.

"Well, these people must be fond of mystery," said the commander.

Without troubling any more about them they settled themselves down, arranged their beds, and slept, while the train steamed off at full speed towards Modena and Italy.

THE STAMP KING

By G. DE BEAUREGARD AND H. DE GORSSE

Translated from the French by EDITH C. PHILLIPS

THE TRAIN SPED ALONG WITH INCREASING VELOCITY

CHAPTER XIX

Wherein Betty proves to William that all roads lead to Rome, even that by way of New York.

SOFTLY couched, and rocked by the vibration of the train, William and the commander did not wake till late the next morning. They were in the station of Saint-Jean-de-Maurienne, and the clocks pointed almost to the hour of nine. John, who, in his position of confidential valet, companion, or we might almost say, friend, had been allowed to profit by the third bed in the half-saloon engaged by William, continued to snore conscientiously, with his nose buried in the pillows. But at a shake from his master he sat up, stupidly wondering if the world had come to an end.

"Come, come, you lazy fellow!" said William. "Are you not ashamed of yourself? It is nine o'clock! Hot water, quick! Arrange my brushes in the dressing-room, let down the shutter, and clean our boots."

John got up quickly to obey his master's orders and opened one of the windows, letting a ray of light penetrate into the carriage together with an exquisite breath of morning air.

"Ah!" said the commander, drawing a long breath, "it is most lovely weather."

The train was now passing through wild valleys, outlined with high mountains, and by the noise the engine made, puffing out its grey smoke with great effort, it was easy to perceive that they were continually mounting higher and higher, and that it needed all its strength to drag the heavy train of carriages up to Mount Cenis.

"No news of our neighbours?" asked Spartivento.

"Faith! no," said William, "and, to judge from their precautions, they seem anxious to keep in hiding."

"Oh, well, it's all the same to me. I am not curious, but I should like to just see their faces."

"You will soon have that satisfaction," said William. "They are evidently in the same case as we, and must get out at Modena, because of the douane in the first place, and, in the second, to pay for their half of the saloon on the Italian frontier."

"Apropos of which," said the commander, apparently searching for his pocket-book, "I must pay you my share. Have you change for a thousand-franc note?"

"Oh, leave it, leave it, my dear fellow; we can settle all that at Naples."

"As you please." And Spartivento made no further effort, but went on dressing, talking of one thing and another until the train stopped in a large station and they heard a voice shouting, "Modena! All luggage to be examined." Upon which they both jumped out with the satisfaction of people who are at length able to stretch their legs after a long period of inaction. But, instead of going straight over to the douane, they took up a position opposite the next compartment, with the evident intention of seeing something of their invisible neighbours.

Suddenly a cry of stupefaction escaped William's lips, while the commander, turning livid, precipitately retreated into the compartment he had just left.

"Good morning, Mr. Keniss," cried a little mocking voice. "You did not expect me, I see."

And Betty, fresh, bright, and smiling, jumped out on to the platform, followed by Victoria. John, who was descending too, and whom the commander had just knocked down in his haste to regain his place, nearly fell over again with surprise at the sight of Victoria, whose engaging smile could scarcely convince him that it was not a supernatural apparition.

"You! you!" cried William, who also thought himself the victim of a hallucination.

The astonishment of the two men was so complete, and their expression so naively discomfited, that Betty and Victoria could contain themselves no longer, but burst into a roar of laughter.

"To the douane, ladies and gentlemen, if you please," said a big Italian official, bearing down upon them.

He had to repeat his invitation before William could move a step. He remained petrified, and though an American, and consequently little accustomed to be surprised at anything, he tried in vain to gather together his thoughts and account for the presence of his charming rival.

"After all," he said, as they gained the douane,

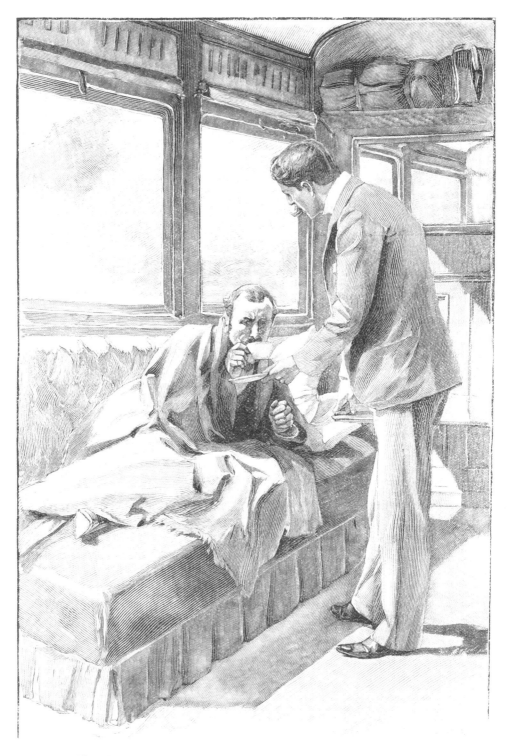

WILLIAM PREVAILED UPON THE COMMANDER TO DRINK THE BOILING PHYSIC

"you will have to tell me by what unheard-of chance
——"

"You shall have all explanations in good time,"
said Betty, laughing. "But had you not someone
with you?"

"Why, of course," said William, looking all about.
"Commander Luigi has disappeared!"

"Luigi, did you say?"

"Yes, Commander Luigi Spartivento."

Betty gave vent to an indifferent "Oh!" and inquired no further. But William, being puzzled, returned to the carriage, and, standing on the footboard,
perceived the commander busily occupied in rummaging over all the portmanteaus.

"What in the world are you doing there?" asked
William Keniss. "Are you not coming?"

"No—no—excuse me," returned the noble Italian,
visibly taken aback, "I stayed to take care of our
smaller luggage and open it for the officer who comes
through the carriages."

"As you like. I will go and superintend the opening of our boxes."

"Good; and then we meet again."

While they exchanged these few words Betty had
hastily whispered in her maid's ear—

"Remain near the compartment and notice particularly what this companion of Mr. Keniss is about."

So Victoria planted herself before the door and
stayed there, which appeared to so embarrass the
commander that he retired into the lavatory.

But the boxes had now been all examined, and
William and Betty, having paid for the remainder of
their journey, returned to their respective carriages.
Then, the signal being given, the train began to
wind up the ascent which led, by a number of zigzag
turns, to the Mount Cenis tunnel—so called from the
neighbourhood of the peak and the name of the old
route.

"Can you imagine such a meeting?" said William,
entering, to find the commander washing his hands.
But as he appeared more upset than desirous of
listening to confidences, William ended by being
quite anxious about him.

"Are you in pain?" he asked.

"Yes, just a little, thanks."

"What is it, my dear fellow?"

"Nothing—it will go away—only a little sickness
—I will lie down for a bit."

And, rolling himself in his rug, Spartivento threw
himself on the bed, smothering his head with a silk
handkerchief, though the day was getting very warm.

William, full of solicitude, covered up his feet and
lavished a hundred delicate attentions upon him, asking every few minutes—

"Do you feel better now?"

"Yes, yes; leave me alone. I shall be all right
soon," was the commander's invariable reply.

With prolonged whistling and formidable rumbling
the train now entered the tunnel. As the entrance
on the French side is at an altitude of 3800 feet, while
on the Italian side it emerges at a height of 4160 feet,
and there is consequently an ascent of 360 feet to be
made, that is, about one in a hundred, the trains
coming from Modena do not travel very fast, the
expresses occupying nearly forty minutes in passing
through the tunnel, during which it is impossible to
converse for the noise.

So William sat down and waited tranquilly for the
end of this short night, thinking all the while of his
astounding meeting with Betty. He was giving his
mind to this rather than admiring the work of the
immense subterranean passage, seven and three-
quarter miles in length, the making of which had
occupied nine years—from 1861 to 1870—at a cost of
seventy-five million francs, and had necessitated the
employment of two thousand French and Italian workmen, assisted by gigantic boring machines worked by
compressed air. He did not doubt that the enterprise

was one of the grandest and most daring of modern
times, leaving far behind the justly celebrated works
of the Romans, but he was more occupied in wondering if he was to see all his vexatious complications
come to life again, and whether the inexplicable
presence of Betty on his track was going to upset his
plans altogether.

At length, after an interminable three-quarters of
an hour, they emerged once more into the light.
The sun shone again, and the train passed more
quickly down the Alpine slopes towards the picturesque Piedmont valleys.

"How do you feel now, old fellow?" asked
William, bending over the commander.

"Still very uncomfortable," murmured Spartivento.

"Wait a minute. I have something with me that
will do you good, and I will make you an infusion.
John, put some water to boil."

The commander groaned, doubtless to indicate that
he could have done without such foresight, then he
plunged his head again among the rugs and remained
motionless. While William, in his character of nurse,
was busying himself over his infusion, two or three
discreet little taps were heard on the door of communication between the two compartments.

"Don't open it! Don't open it!" cried the commander, sitting up and seeming to regain all his
energy in the fear of seeing Betty or Victoria come in.

"Why not?" asked William, astonished. "I know
these people very well, and can understand the impatience of one of them so much the better as I
should myself have gone to their compartment as
soon as we got out of the tunnel."

However, judging that the presence of a stranger
might be disagreeable to the commander and aggra-
vate his sufferings, William raised the grey cloth
curtain, and half opening the door, said—

"Excuse me, Miss Betty. I will be with you in
one minute."

John had now prepared a large cup of the beverage,
and William forced the commander, in spite of his
resistance, to swallow it nearly boiling.

"But it burns me atrociously," groaned Spartivento,
turning very red.

"Come, come," returned the improvised doctor.
"It must be drunk hot to have any effect." And he
hurried him all he could, being anxious, to tell the
truth, to rejoin Miss Betty and have an explanation
from her.

"Here I am at last!" he cried, entering the second
part of the saloon, inhabited by Miss Betty. "And
now, I beseech you, let me know——"

"And they say women are curious," returned Betty,
still laughing at William's surprise, in which she
thought she could recognise a little vexation.

"Come, surely one has a right to be a little bewildered."

"Oh, well, I will have pity on you." And Miss
Betty, with charming ease of manner and little laughs
to emphasise the amusing parts of her story, gave
her adventures in detail, minute by minute and hour
by hour, from the moment the train left the jetty at
Havre.

"How dauntless, how foolish, how mad you were!"
cried William at each fresh incident in the extraordinary tale.

"No," said Betty, "I wanted to get back, that's all."

"Ah! you are not a competitor to be despised
when you have once made up your mind."

"That is necessary, my friend."

Then she recounted her return to Cherbourg, her
sleep in the express, and her awakening in that very
Gare Saint-Lazare where they had arrived together
but a short time before, and her return to the Hotel
Bristol at four o'clock in the morning.

"And, finally, I may tell you, that if I have found
you again, it is thanks to the faithful bloodhound who
never left you."

THE STAMP KING

By G. DE BEAUREGARD AND H. DE GORSSE

Translated from the French by EDITH C. PHILLIPS

CHAPTER XIX (*continued*)

Wherein Betty proves to William that all roads lead to Rome, even that by way of New York.

" I KNEW you were having me spied upon," said William.

"Oh, what an ugly word!" returned Betty. " I simply took an interest in your proceedings. So I was informed that you had taken places for the P.L.M.—a whole saloon, if you please—and that alone showed me you were going to Naples—a place I don't know, but which is very celebrated, and which I shall be delighted to see. Of course I don't ask you what you are going to do there ; it is as much to your interest to keep it a secret as it is to mine to discover it. But you, Mr. Keniss, who are so touchy as to other people's acts, it seems to me that your stamp——"

"Oh, Miss Betty!" And William, greatly distressed, poured forth reasons, excuses, and justifications, all telling against John, so many and so well, that Betty said, as she offered him her hand—

"Bah ! I know perfectly well that it is no fault of yours. You are far too honourable and courteous, and such a suspicion never once entered my mind."

Whether sincere or diplomatic—and can one ever know how to take a woman's word?—it produced its effect, for William was moved, and, seizing her little hand, carried it to his lips, retaining it in his own rather longer than a man who is indifferent is wont to do.

They arrived at Turin, and, while the train stopped a few minutes under the magnificent arch and sumptuous arcades which give this station the aspect rather of a cathedral or palace than a railway station, John, quite out of breath, entered the compartment occupied by Betty, William, and Victoria.

"Oh, sir, do come at once. I think that gentleman who came with you is really very ill."

"What is the matter with him?"

"He is mad. While I was busy in the dressing-room he carried off all the bags and ran away. But I saw him as he was just going out of the station, and I caught him and brought him back by force into the carriage."

"Hear ! hear !" said Betty mysteriously.

"You will excuse me if I go and see him?" asked William.

"Go and help the poor man, by all means."

The Stamp King left his neighbour, and found Commander Luigi had thrown himself again on his bed, under heaps of rugs and in the midst of the scattered baggage.

"I hear you are feeling worse."

An indistinct rattling sound came from among the pillows and cushions, and at first William could make nothing of this strange invalid. Then the commander, having risked a glance and perceived that his companion had returned alone, raised his head, perspiring, red, and suffocating.

"Why, my dear friend, you are being smothered down there !" cried William.

"Oh, no, I'm all right. It's the infusion."

"How do you feel? Where is the pain?"

"All over, and in no place in particular. It is very bad."

The commander's eyes never left the door which separated the two compartments of the saloon. Once the handle moved at the shaking of the train as it started, and he plunged again into the midst of the rugs, and for a quarter of an hour could not be persuaded to show the tip of his nose.

"What can I do for you? Is there anything that would relieve you?" persisted William.

A stifled voice, deadened by the thick coverings as by a gag, replied—

"Nothing, nothing. Do be quiet. Leave me alone."

The poor man seemed so feeble and depressed that his friend thought it would be more charitable to leave him in peace, as sleep would have a more salutary effect upon him than all the medicine in the world. But he stayed near, so as to be ready to assist him in case of need, and thus the journey proceeded till they arrived at Genoa, enlivened by the beauty of the scenery and the splendour of the blue Mediterranean, which came into sight as they left the Apennines. But from time to time he paid a short visit to Miss Betty.

"Well, what news?" the girl would ask.

"Still very weak. I can't make out what is the matter."

After passing Genoa evening fell, and finally, when night blotted out the lovely panorama of indented coast and sapphire sea, William went to pay a last, good-night visit to his neighbour.

"Is he better now?" asked Miss Betty for the hundredth time.

"He does not seem to improve at all, but has alternate stages of frenzy and prostration which quite alarm me. I tried to persuade him just to glance at this fascinating Gulf of Genoa, but even that could not rouse him from his stupor."

"He must indeed be very ill," observed Betty with a smile.

"I had thought of doing him a kindness by asking you to go and see him, as he was not able to come to you. I explained that I knew you very well and that you would not mind coming——"

"And then?" asked Betty, looking puzzled.

"Oh, then he was just terrible. He jumped up like a madman, with staring eyes, crying, "No, no, no one ! Don't bring anyone ! Don't bring her !" "

"One would think I was not much in sympathy with him," returned the little American gaily. Then she drew from her bag a little box, which she opened, and took out the pin found in her trunk a few days earlier, on her first arrival at the Hotel Bristol.

"When you dress to-morrow morning," she said, "put this pin in your tie. I found it by accident in Paris, and I think I cannot make a better use of it than by giving it to you."

This was uttered with such charming grace, and with an air so free and yet so full of reserve, that William took the gold serpent twining round the malachite and overwhelmed her with thanks, declaring he would never wear any other.

"You will tell me what the—the—what do you call him ?——"

"Commander?"

"Yes, what the commander thinks of it. I feel sure he will admire it. But be sure and not show it to anyone before to-morrow."

A sudden thought occurred to William.

"You are so kind to me," he said, "and I am

ashamed that you should have been beforehand with me; but I will not wait any longer before offering you a diamond, which came into my hands in a no less remarkable way in London, and which I meant for you."

While speaking he was searching in his pockets, especially the one in which he felt sure he had put the Maharajah's diamond, but, to his great surprise, however much he searched he could find nothing.

"It is very strange," he murmured; "I was so sure of having kept it about me." And he felt and felt with growing anxiety.

"I must have buried it at the bottom of a bag without thinking," he ejaculated. "I will look for it to-morrow by daylight."

Betty, noticing how disconcerted he was at the failure of his research, tried to comfort him.

"No doubt you have packed it with your other things. I thank you none the less, and consider the gracious act accomplished."

William then retired into his compartment, shut the door and drew the bolts, which appeared to give the commander great relief.

"Ah, that is better!" he said, stretching himself.

"Indeed! I am very glad to hear you are feeling better. Will you come and see Miss Scott?"

"No, no!" returned Spartivento hastily. "We must not disturb her now. It is too late."

The commander walked up and down the carpet laid across the saloon, stretching, yawning, and shaking himself, as a man who is thankful at relinquishing an uncomfortable position.

"While I think of it," said William, but without attaching any importance to the matter, "why did you leave the train at Turin in such a hurry, carrying off the portmanteaus with you?"

"Do you know I actually thought we had come to the end of our journey," returned the commander. "My ideas were so confused, and my head in such a muddle, that I felt sure I heard them cry, 'Naples! Naples! All change.'"

William, being very tired, went immediately to bed, reassured now as to his companion's health, while the express continued on its route towards Rome.

CHAPTER XX

How William, though Betty's creditor, is about to become her debtor.

TOWARDS half-past six in the morning they arrived in Rome. As there was only a short stop there before the train left for Naples, William and Betty, anxious though they both were to take a peep at the Eternal City, had but just time to glance at S. Maria degli Angeli and S. Maria Maggiore, and only at the exterior of these, and then were obliged to return hastily to the station.

During their absence John and Victoria had been walking up and down the platform talking of their own little affairs.

"Well, Mr. Cockburn, goodness only knows where we are going!" said Victoria.

"But I know too," said John with a patronising air.

"Yes, yes, to Naples; but after that?"

"That is a secret."

"Oh!" returned the girl with dignity, "I don't ask you to tell me. And yet it interests me, for our marriage suffers by it. What delays there are!" she added with a sigh. "Doesn't the time seem long to you?"

"Oh, yes, certainly," returned John negligently.

"Then when do you think we shall be able to marry?"

"You are always asking me that. I will think about it."

"You always say that." And Victoria continued her melancholy complaints as they walked along under the great glass roof by the side of the train, now ready to start.

The commander, who was watching them from the saloon, whence he had not yet issued, chose a moment when their backs were turned, seized all the small baggage, jumped out, and ran to one of the doors leading out of the station.

"Your ticket," demanded the man in charge.

"I'll give it you in a minute. Can't you see my hands are full?"

"I can't let you go out without your ticket."

The discussion was growing warm, when William and Betty suddenly appeared at the same door, coming into the station. Quick as lightning the commander turned on his heels and rushed back to the saloon, climbed in, and threw himself again among his rugs. Betty, who had had a good view of him, began to laugh, and William, always full of solicitude for his companion, was troubled to see that his strange illness had returned after his partial recovery the evening before.

"It just shows what a feverish state he is in," he said. "I sincerely hope the poor man will arrive home without any mishap."

But in his haste the commander had let fall one of his own bags, which, as it rolled along the pavement, opened, and scattered some of its contents. William, coming after him, stooped to put them back again, and what was his surprise to see, among the combs and tooth-brushes strewn on the ground, a shining object, which he immediately recognised as the diamond he had bought in London from the Maharajah of Brahmapootra

"Well," said he, "how in the world could this diamond get into the commander's bag?"

"Apparently the commander must have put it there," returned Betty.

"He is mad," concluded the Stamp King, "or he must be the most absent-minded of men."

At these words Betty made a little impatient gesture, which passed unnoticed. Then she returned to her compartment, and William, after presenting her with the diamond, regained his.

(To be continued.)

THE STAMP KING

By G. DE BEAUREGARD AND H. DE GORSSE

Translated from the French by EDITH C. PHILLIPS

JOHN AND VICTORIA WALKED UP AND DOWN THE PLATFORM

CHAPTER XX (*continued*)

How William, though Betty's creditor, is about to become her debtor.

THE doors were shut, the signal for departure given, and the train began to move. Two heads immediately appeared at the two doors of the saloon.

"John! John!" cried William.

"Victoria!" cried Betty.

The engaged couple, who, lost in talk, had not noticed the movement of the train, turned quickly and caught hold of the brass handles.

"Stand back! stand back!" shouted the porters. "It is too late."

But all attempts to pull them back were in vain; so tight was their hold on the handles that they would not let go, and, the doors opening, they were able to return to their respective compartments in the midst of the maledictions of the officials, since the train was now going at a good rate. The reprimands they received for their carelessness can be easily imagined. But all's well that ends well, so William returned to the commander.

"You are still feeling ill then?" said he.

"Yes, very ill," groaned the commander, half rising. But at the moment he caught sight of William leaning over him, and in his tie the gold serpent given him by Miss Betty. It was as if he were suddenly hypnotised; his staring eyes seemed unable to detach themselves from the shining jewel.

"What is the matter? What are you looking at?" asked the young American.

"Where—where did you get that pin?"

"Miss Scott, our neighbour here, gave it me."

"I am lost!" stammered the commander, unconscious that he spoke aloud, and in despair he rolled himself again in his rugs.

"Come, come!" said William in a paternal voice, "the crisis is nearly over. We are close to Naples, and you will soon be at home."

Then the Stamp King, his anxiety growing greater than ever, went to see Miss Betty and ask her advice.

"I do beseech you to come and look at this poor commander," said he. "He is so ill that I fear for his reason. I can't understand it at all. The sight of your pin upsets him so, that it would be well if you could reassure him yourself. Your presence would be sure to do him good."

"Very well," said Miss Betty, rising. "I will come."

William half opened the door of communication and said to Spartivento—

"Miss Scott is coming to see you, old fellow."

"No, no!" cried the enigmatic Italian in accents of the profoundest terror. But William had shut the door to give the commander time to prepare for the young lady's visit.

They had passed Velletri, and, running through the mountains, came to Segni, Anagni, the town of Innocent III and Boniface VIII, Ferentino, set upon a height with a belt of Cyclopean walls, then Frasinone, magnificently situated, and Aquin, the country of Juvenal and the great St. Thomas.

At length, as the express wound round Mount Cassin, crowned by its famous Benedictine monastery, William deemed that the commander would have had time to compose himself, and stood back to let Miss Betty pass first into the neighbouring compartment. But scarcely had the girl opened the door when she fell back with an exclamation of horror and indignation.

"What *is* the matter?" asked William.

"The matter!" exclaimed Betty, not knowing whether she ought to laugh or be angry. "See for yourself."

William, on entering, had no difficulty in discovering the cause of Miss Betty's startled exclamation. For, in the middle of the compartment, Spartivento, in his shirt and without coat or trousers, was staring wildly at him. Ridiculous as the position was, William had

again with a good enough grace. William thought it would be as well not to leave his companion, for he was now convinced that the Italian sun had revived some old infirmity, causing him to fear the presence of a stranger. So he thought he had better try to distract his attention.

"Look," said he, pointing to a smoke in the distance, "there is Vesuvius."

Spartivento threw one careless glance, like a man who knows the country better than his companion, and sat down, with bowed head and preoccupied, though calmer, air.

The train now crossed the Volturno, stopped a few minutes at Capua, then at Caserta, whose immense castle, the summer residence of the ancient Neapolitan kings, appeared in outline on the left, below its

HE HURRIED TO THE EXIT

no inclination to laugh, fearing that this series of extravagant actions would end in an access of mad fury. So he spoke to him with the utmost gentleness.

"You will catch cold, my dear fellow. It is warm enough, I know, but in a carriage one is always exposed to sudden chills, which are very prejudicial to health. Come, dress yourself again————"

"But suppose the young lady comes back?" questioned the commander.

"That is all the more reason for it. You must make yourself look more respectable."

"But I don't want her to come back."

"She came with the kindest intentions," returned William still more affectionately. "She wanted to help you."

"No, no! I don't want to see her!" cried Spartivento, elevating his voice.

"Very well, you shall not see her. Cheer up and put your clothes on again," said William, handing them to him, and the commander, coaxed by the assurance that his solitude should be respected, dressed

enchanting gardens. Now they ran through the magnificent plains of Campania—plains so fertile and rich that they yield three harvests every year. But the commander appeared too weak to take any interest in the country. Yet when he perceived that the express was passing along the last slopes of Vesuvius he suddenly revived, rolled up his rug, and put on his dust-coat and hat.

"Ah, that is better!" said William, thinking that drawing so near home had completely calmed his fellow-passenger.

"Yes, I feel quite well again now," returned the commander, smiling.

"So much the better! So much the better!"

As William was gathering his things together, Spartivento, watching him out of the corner of his eye, said—

"You will do me the favour of staying with me, my dear Mr. Keniss?"

In vain William protested. As they entered the station at Naples he was compelled to yield and

SPARTIVENTO STARED WILDLY AT WILLIAM

promise to spend two days at least with the commander, at which he appeared greatly pleased. Looking out of the window Spartivento saw a magnificent footman, to whom he beckoned. The footman hastened to the carriage, and, before the train had even stopped, had taken possession of the two travellers' luggage, handed him by his master, who then jumped quickly out, crying to William—

"You get our trunks out, and I will wait for you outside with my carriage." Then he disappeared so completely that it would be impossible to say in which direction.

William got out and went to the door of the neighbouring compartment to lend Miss Betty a hand.

"Do you know, I am going to stay with the commander," he said.

"Where is he? Where is he?" asked Betty eagerly.

"Does he interest you to that extent?"

"Where is he, I say? You have not let him go?"

"Why, how excited you are about it!" returned the young man laughingly. "Calm yourself, for it is all right. He is waiting for me outside with his carriage."

"Catch him again, quick! Your portmanteau! Your bags!"

"Yes, but—— This is infectious!"

And William mechanically put his hand in his pocket. His pocket-book had disappeared! So had his watch and his purse.

"How very strange!" said he, looking stupefied.

"Run! Oh, do run!" besought Betty. "You might perhaps catch him yet."

A crowd of thoughts and suspicions flashed into William's brain; suspicions and thoughts which were to be but too soon confirmed. He ran to the courtyard. Nothing! No carriage! No footman! No commander! Precipitately he returned to the luggage—searched the waiting-rooms, the douane, the passages. Nothing! No one!

(*To be continued.*)

PHILATELIC SOCIETIES

The Junior Philatelic Society

President : Fred J. Melville.
Secretary : H. F. Johnson, 4, Portland Place North, Clapham Road, S.W.
Meetings : Exeter Hall, Strand, W.C.
Annual Subscription : 1s. 6d.

AT the monthly meeting of the General Committee for September on Thursday, September 7th, the following fourteen new members were elected :—

S. W. Wheatley, Newcastle, Staffs; Bertram McGowan, Dumfries; Stewart Kirkpatrick, King William's Town, South Africa; Miss Enid A. Brodie, Birmingham; C. F. Wills, London; S. H. Haynes, Kingston-on-Thames; J. Escoline, Morecambe; Dr. M. Piper-Rietzmann, London; Max Wertheim, London; L. J. Ayre, Barry; Thomas Sweeney, London; Ernest C. Hodgett, Southern Nigeria; G.

Allan Brockman, London; and J. Glassen, Johannesburg.

As the new season commences in October, prospective new members should make application at once to the Hon. Secretary, H. F. Johnson, 4, Portland Place North, Clapham Road, London, S.W.

Dundee Philatelic Society

DEAR SIR,—I am trying to start a Philatelic Society for Dundee and district. Will you kindly intimate in the *Weekly* that inquiries will be welcomed by

Yours sincerely,

G. H. WHITAKER

(Member Sheffield Philatelic Society).

9, BELLEFIELD AVENUE, DUNDEE,
September 9th.

THE STAMP KING

By G. DE BEAUREGARD AND H. DE GORSSE

Translated from the French by EDITH C. PHILLIPS

CHAPTER XX (*continued*)

*How William, though Betty's creditor, is about to
become her debtor.*

WHEN William at length returned to Betty,
breathless, furious, and discomfited, he found
her laughing heartily.

"Well, and did you find the commander's carriage?"
asked she.

"Oh, you do well to spend your time laughing!"
returned William. "There is no carriage there. I
have been robbed!"

"Then you acknowledge it, imprudent man! It
seems to me, too, that I have seen that head somewhere before."

"What! you knew him, and you never told me?"

"Pardon me," said Betty, who had the greatest
difficulty to keep from laughing. "I knew no Luigi
Spartivento. I only knew Sir Oscar Tilbury."

"What!" cried William, quite beside himself.
"That was——"

"Yes, my friend, Sir Oscar himself, of whom I
have spoken to you, and whom I am quite sure I
recognize now from the way he has of arranging
meetings with people at the different towns he
comes to."

"Well, what shall I do? I haven't a cent left.
Not even enough to stamp a letter or prove my
identity. But that servant who was waiting for him?"

"You are simple! These people, these cosmopolitan thieves, have all sorts of accomplices. I know
all about them, having paid dearly enough for the
knowledge. But come, I offer you the use of my
carriage, which will only be a hired one, but which
has the one good quality of being in existence. Will
you come——?"

"But——" objected William hesitatingly.

"Bah! One must yield to circumstances. I am
only showing you a little ordinary politeness, and you
have no choice in the matter. Come and dine with
me, anyhow, and we shall see what will happen afterwards."

There was nothing for it but resignation. William
and John followed Betty and Victoria into a large
landau which they happened to find disengaged, and
which conducted them by way of the quays, the
Strada S. Lucia, the Piazza del Municipio, S. Ferdinand
and the Plebiscito and the Villa Nazionale, to the
Grand Hotel.

While John and Victoria superintended the arrival
of the luggage in the hall of the hotel, William and
Betty entered the salon to rest a moment; for, though
it was not yet the middle of May, the heat was already
quite Neapolitan, and a burning sun was shining in a
sky of regal blue.

"Let us say little, but to the point," said William,
who had begun to form a resolution concerning his
misadventure.

"I am all attention, my dear sir," returned Betty.

"You know my position, and you have assisted in
despoiling me. I have no idea, therefore, of being
proud or of trying to hide the state of affairs from
you. On the other hand, you will probably admit
that I shall before long be again in a solvent position,
so, without any false pride, I can ask you to lend me a
hundred pounds while I am waiting for my banker to
telegraph me some funds?"

"Quite impossible!" returned the girl, with comic
emphasis.

"Impossible?" And William, whose thoughts had
been miles away from any idea of such a refusal,
turned very red at the humiliation.

"Oh, don't be alarmed," said Betty, seeing his
trouble. "I have the hundred pounds and plenty
more; thanks to you partly, my dear friend, for
without your generosity in Paris——"

"Well then——?" asked William, comforted a
little by the kind remembrance.

"Well then—I shall behave as if I hadn't them.
And yet you cannot doubt my desire to be agreeable
to you."

"I am afraid I must doubt it," said William drily.

"No, my dear Mr. Keniss, you will not. But as it
would be unkind of me not to give you my real
motive, please remember that, since at present you
are my prisoner and it is in my power to prevent
your escaping to carry out the schemes that brought
you to Naples, I should be very foolish to give you,
or even lend you, the key of the fortress in the form
of bank-notes. Run up accounts in my name, as
many as you please, and I promise to pay them—
when I know what I want to know; but, as regards
ready money, don't expect it, for you will not have
one cent."

William took the matter very well when it was
presented in this light, seeing that it meant no loss
of dignity.

"So, so," he said gaily, "this is merely a little
stratagem of war?"

"Exactly."

"Very well, so be it. I will go and pawn the
precious pin you gave me, and which frightened our
mutual thief so. I shall get the cost of a telegram
for it."

"Oh! a souvenir from me!" cried Betty, bursting
into a laugh as she looked at William's tie; to which
he put up his hand to take the pin—but the pin was
no longer there.

"What, has that also disappeared?" he cried.

"Faith," observed Betty, "the commander wished
to recover his own."

"His own? What can you mean?"

"Yes; he let it fall into my trunk when he was
rummaging it during our voyage. Now do you
understand how I knew he was the thief; why I
wanted him to see you wearing it, and why he was so
overcome at the sight?"

"But you might have told me—have shown me
how blind I was."

"But you ought not to have let the good gentleman
escape. So much the worse for you!"

The two young people had only the consolation of
laughing over their various relations with the too
seductive traveller, and of determining to do impossible things to bring him to justice.

"After all this, let us be serious," said William.
"I suppose you don't wish me to stop at this hotel,
where you are staying yourself?"

"Why not?"

"Because you are a young lady and I am a young
man, and it would not be quite the proper thing."

"Are we not Americans, and so free to do as we
please?" asked Betty, astonished at the scruple.

"Certainly, but we are not in America."

"Never mind. It is to my interest that you stay here, so pray resign yourself to it."

"Very good, Miss Betty. I obey."

The girl looked at the clock.

"Three o'clock," said she. "We have still some time before us. Will you accompany me for a drive in the town at four?"

"Most willingly."

"Then I will meet you here in an hour's time."

William and Betty then retired to their respective apartments, followed, the one by John and the other by Victoria.

"We are in a very delicate position here," said William to his servant when they were alone. "I know you for a chatterbox and a glutton, so I recommend the greatest discretion in your dealings with Miss Scott and Victoria, who will not fail to get all they can out of you. Don't accept anything from them, and don't tell them a word about our plans."

"Don't you fear, sir; I'll be dumb."

At this same moment Betty was saying to Victoria—

"We have our adversaries in our power, and we must profit by the circumstance in getting to know exactly what they have come here for. I will see if I can make Mr. Keniss speak, and you must try what you can do with John."

"Very well, miss; I will do my best."

Punctually at four o'clock William and Betty entered an elegant victoria, drawn by two Sardinian horses, whose harness, studded with silver nails, shone in the sun like carbuncles. They drove first past the magnificent gardens stretching before the Grand Hotel, and known as the Villa Nazionale. Then along Via Carracciolo, having, on the one side, the panorama of the blue sea, the old Castello del' Ova and the distant mountains of Sorrento, covered with a golden mist, and, on the other, the palms and rare trees of the park, which soften the severe outline of the Castle of S. Elmo.

Turning round the Pizzofalcone they gained the Toledo, the central artery of Naples, where an animated bustle was beginning after the midday siesta.

"What a noise! What busy people! What excitement!" cried Betty.

"If any one had told me a week ago that I should be here to-day, and, moreover, without any notion of what I have come for——"

William's only reply was a smile, but a minute later he remarked—

"I must not forget to enter my complaint against the commander."

The driver, being informed of this desire, turned towards the Palace of San Giacomo, the Town Hall, where are the offices of the Naples police. At his request William was introduced to the head of the police himself, M. Petto, a man of mature age, good-looking, and the best of company. Betty made one of the party, and the two Americans gave a graphic account of their unfortunate adventures with their brilliant but elusive adversary.

"Will you describe him to me?" said the chief, smiling.

This was a matter of no small difficulty to the two prosecutors. To William he had presented a turned-up brown moustache, closely cropped hair and dull complexion; to Betty a light, drooping moustache and bright coloured cheeks. On one point they were agreed—the colour of his eyes, which was a beautiful reddish brown with fawn-coloured rays emanating from the pupils.

"Very good," said the chief. "I shall find him before long, as he cannot be far away."

Delighted at this assurance, William and Betty thanked the obliging functionary as heartily as if they were already in possession of their money and papers, got into their carriage again, and returned to the Toledo to continue their drive; the driver, who could gabble a few English words, pointing out the objects of special interest.

"That," said he, "is the Royal Palace, with marble statues of the principal kings who have governed the country; a little further back is the San Carlo Theatre; opposite, the Umberto Gallery; yonder is the Bellini Theatre—the Gallery of the Prince of Naples—the Museo Nazionale."

And their drive continued through the Via Salvator Rosa and the wide Corso Vittorio Emanuele, which winds round the heights of S. Elmo, and whence you can catch, in places, incomparable views of the town and the bay.

"What an astonishing country!" said Betty. "What light! What a sun! What colours! It's enough to make one blind or mad."

"Yes, it is grand!" said William, yielding to the beauty of the scene.

Betty, knowing well how enthusiastic feelings, such as admiration, often lead to confidences, felt she might risk a leading question.

"Of course you are still looking for the famous stamp!" she said. "And it is no less evident that it is to be found at Naples, since you have come here. Is it not so?"

"Perhaps," said William enigmatically.

"You might just as well tell me at once," insisted Betty, "as I have warned you I shall not leave you till I know all about it."

"Who knows but what I may find means to escape you yet?"

"Thanks; you are very kind."

"I can assure you," said William, with a little irony in his tone, "I have no more wish to be disagreeable than you have. We are engaged in warfare and must each attend to his own tactics. You keep me a prisoner; what could be more excusable than an attempt to escape?"

"I shall follow you everywhere."

"Then it is superfluous to tell you beforehand the places to which I intend going, as you will soon see for yourself."

"You are not very gallant."

"I will become so again, Miss Betty, when you again become generous. Good deeds lead to good ones, the same as bad to bad."

"Your silence is a revenge then?"

"It amounts to pretty much the same thing. You refuse to lend me a hundred pounds; I refuse to tell you a secret. What could be more just and natural?"

"I have not refused them. I have simply imposed a delay."

"I will not act otherwise by you, Miss Betty. You shall have my secret, but at the right time."

A deep silence followed. The carriage, doubling round, had turned to the right into the Mergellina and commenced the ascent towards Pausilippe by the Strada Nuova.

"Look," said the driver, pointing to the imposing ruins, "that is the Palace of Donna Anna."

On their right rose the slopes of the hill, covered with orange trees and Italian pines; on the left, lovely gardens filled with flowers unrolled their lawns and beds away to the transparent blue waves of the sea.

At a turn in the Strada Nuova they came upon a magnificent edifice in the style of a castle of the time of Louis XIV. All around it were large shady groups of carob trees, citrons, and oaks. A profusion of flowers was growing everywhere on turf, which was continually being watered by the gardeners, while clear streams issued with silvery babbling out of a number of pink marble fountains. A large terrace with onyx balustrade ran along the front of the building, from which a magnificent view of the bay might be obtained.

"How splendid!" said Betty. "Whose house is this?"

"Ah!" said the driver. "That belongs to a man who has eaten up all his patrimony and will not be here much longer, for he must be nearly at the end of his resources."

"And his name?" asked William.

"Prince Albrandi."

The young American gave a start at the name, but fortunately it passed unnoticed by Betty. Then it was here, in this palace, that the long-looked-for second copy of the stamp was to be found! And he was only a few yards away! Almost near enough to touch it!

William's first thought was to jump out of the carriage and rush off to the Prince. But what could he say, and how explain this sudden freak to Betty? Much better wait till morning. So, contenting himself with remarking carefully the situation of the place, an easily recognizable one, the Stamp King, for whom the drive had now lost much of its interest, in spite of the attractions of the hour and the beautiful scenery, proposed that they should return to the hotel. Betty was of the same mind, glad to return home herself to form in solitude some decisive plan, since her rival had no intention of letting her into his secrets. So she gave the order, and the two travellers were speedily being driven back towards the Villa Nazionale.

An extraordinary and unexpected scene was there awaiting them.

(To be continued.)

SPECIAL CORRESPONDENCE

News from Finland

HELSINGFORS, *3rd September*, 1905

Current Stamps of Finland : Different Printings

IT seems to be still unknown in philatelic circles, especially to all young collectors, that the type of postage stamp now in use in Finland is issued in two quite different printings. In 1901 a provisional printing was executed by the private printing firm of F. Tilgmann and Co. Since 1902 the postage stamps have been made by the Stamp-printing Works, which is a government institution. The following was the cause of a provisional printing. According to the order issued by the Russian Minister of the Interior, the new stamps of Russian pattern were to be introduced on 14th January, 1901 ; the use of the old Finnish stamps was forbidden from that day. As a pattern for making the new type, one piece of every stamp was supplied from St. Petersburg to the Finnish authorities, and the original plates and illustrations were to be procured by them.

At first the authorities wished to order them in Finland, and the firm of F. Tilgmann and Co., printers, Helsingfors, accepted the order. In December, 1900, the ordered plates and clichés were supplied by the said firm ; but on being tried they were found to be quite useless, and therefore they were all rejected.

Fresh illustrations were ordered at once from Herr H. Berthold, in Berlin ; but owing to the shortness of time, they could not be supplied by 14th January.

Therefore it was necessary to provide a provisional issue by means of lithography, and Tilgmann, of Helsingfors, received the order to supply the required stamps by 14th January. This firm supplied stamps in the following numbers :—

2 p.	.	.	.	590,000.
5 p.	.	.	.	3,088,000.
10 p.	.	.	.	1,194,000.
20 p.	.	.	.	3,365,000.
1 mark	.	.	.	156,000.

At the same time the said firm received an order to print a small provisional issue of the 10 mark stamp in ordinary printing from clichés made by the firm itself and approved of by the government authorities. Of this 10 mark stamp 13,500 were issued.

All the stamps printed by Tilgmann and Co. were on chalked paper. The gumming and perforating took place in the Stamp-printing Works by means of the same machines as were used later in the case of the stamps printed by the government authorities.

In the summer of 1901 the new clichés were supplied by Herr Berthold, of Berlin, and approved of, and from them the various Finnish stamps have been made by the authorities themselves.

Thus there exist two issues of these stamps—one being a provisional issue made by a private printing firm, and the other the ordinary regular issue.

I append a list of the stamps of both issues, with a note of the chief points of difference in the stamps referred to.

speculative postal issues.

Again, What's a Junior?

I HAVE been plied with questions as to when a stamp collector ceases to be a "junior," and I am quietly amused over the problem.

"Anywhere this side the grave," is evidently the solution of the Junior Philatelic Society.

But you know the admission of antiquities to membership has plenty of precedents. There are, for instance, well-known junior clubs and political and trading concerns which are not by any means confined to the little kiddies.

However, I am told that the Executive Committee of the forthcoming International Philatelic Exhibition, after many sleepless nights, have shortened the life of the philatelic junior to the span of twenty-one years.

Am I Eligible?

THIS is another poser that I am faced with. Why I should be appealed to is indefatigable Hon. Sec. of the Juniors. But I believe I shall have to undertake to see their stamps, their birth certificates, and—their teeth, and fix up a regular hour per week for doing the business.

Southampton Philatelic Row

As my readers are aware, the premier Philatelic Society of London moved from the purlieus of the Strand to Southampton Row last season.

This season the Herts Society moves to the same building.

And now the dealers have commenced to migrate into the self-same road, the first to flit thither being Mr. Nissen. Pemberton and Co. are just around the corner, and no doubt as soon as Kingsway is properly opened up to Southampton Row the others will pack up their traps for location in "more commodious" new premises in this popular new thoroughfare. Where the carcass is, there will the ——

Still, I have my doubts, for some wicked ones say certain bones are not worth picking.

THE STAMP KING

By G. DE BEAUREGARD AND H. DE GORSSE

Translated from the French by EDITH C. PHILLIPS

CHAPTER XXI

Wherein it appears that the well of truth ought to be full of wine!

JOHN and Victoria, having watched the carriage containing their respective master and mistress disappear in the distance, concluded that they had some little time at their disposal. So they went for a walk in the shady part of the Villa Nazionale, talking all the time.

"All the same," said Miss Betty's maid, "you have not been nice, or even honest, in this matter of the forged stamp."

"Oh, bah! A mere trifle!"

"Trifle! Trifle! And yet you deceived Miss Betty, deceived me, and put Mr. William Keniss in a very ugly position."

"Don't say any more about that, if you please," said John, visibly annoyed.

"Well, look here now!" continued Victoria, in a tone of friendly reproach. "Ah, naughty man, you are fortunate in having some one to care for you in spite of everything. But it is only fair that you should make me forget your infamous fraud by giving me one great proof of affection."

"If I can I will—willingly."

"I know you can, and you really owe it me, for you have behaved like a——"

"Come, come to the point."

"Very well, I will. You sinned through the stamp; you must expiate your fault by means of the stamp. You have led me into error with the forgery; it is only just you should tell me where the real one is."

"Never!" cried John with a tragic gesture. "Mr. Keniss is kind enough to honour me with absolute confidence, and I shall always do my best to deserve it. Yes, I do know where the stamp is, but you may as well understand, my dear, that you will never learn it from me. I would be torn to pieces rather than betray such a secret."

This was said in so pompous and peremptory a tone that Victoria was intimidated and insisted no further, for fear of intensifying the check to her diplomacy.

"At least you will not mind going about with me a bit?" she said. "Goodness knows when we shall get another hour's freedom, and I should rather like to see this celebrated town of Naples."

"As much of that as ever you like."

"See Naples and die," murmured the elderly spinster sentimentally, the saying appearing to her poetic in the highest degree.

"Many thanks," laughed the good old fellow John "in that case I should prefer to postpone my visit till a little later!"

"They say that because Naples is such a marvellous city," said Victoria, returning to the practical; "but you go on living all the same after having seen it."

"Oh, then I don't mind."

"Wait, I am going to call a fiacre." And Victoria had already advanced to the Chiaja, which runs by the side of the park, when John hastily called her back.

"No, no," cried he. "No fiacre!"

"Why?" asked Victoria. "It is only a lira and a half, and I can easily pay that."

But John, calling to mind his master's recent injunctions, energetically refused to hire a carriage for which he could not pay himself. In this case also Victoria had her trouble for nothing, and she was forced to console herself by saying in a melancholy tone—

"Then I suppose we must walk." So they sauntered through the Strada S. Caterina and the Chiaja towards S. Ferdinand.

The heat was overpowering, although the sun was on the decline and it was half-past four o'clock. All along the streets the green window-shutters were

followed them with true Neapolitan obstinacy, crying, with varied expression, "Signor! Picciola carrozzella! Signor!" But all in vain. John drew himself up more proudly at each of these invitations, which pierced Victoria's heart.

Suddenly, not far from the church of Santa Chiara, after walking up a sunny ascent, the maid stopped short.

"There! I can't do one bit more!"

And with her already damp handkerchief she wiped her dripping forehead, where her false curls were hanging in lamentable disarray.

"In mercy, Mr. Cockburn, let us go into this café. I am dying with thirst."

The temptation this time was very strong, for John's own throat felt like the Sahara. But he hardened his heart and refused once more.

"No," said he, "I cannot accept anything to drink."

"Well, you needn't drink anything, but come in,

THE HEAT WAS OVERPOWERING

closed; the white walls were sparkling and dazzling. The shops could scarcely be seen, being hidden behind large linen awnings, and with curtains covering the doors to keep out the flies. The two pedestrians advanced slowly over the burning flagstones with which the streets were paved. They breathed heavily and perspired as if they were walking in a furnace. So Victoria, who was not very vigorous, and John, who was inclined to corpulency, gave a discouraged "Oh!" at almost every step, and as it was uphill all the way they began to despair of ever reaching their destination.

"How wrong it was of you to insist on coming on foot," groaned the poor girl.

"Can't help it," replied John heroically. "Duty before everything."

But, in spite of all, worn out, and in a bath of perspiration, they at length reached the Palazzo Reale, whence, after a rapid glance round, they penetrated into the little cross streets between the Municipio and the Hotel des Postes. Several drivers, seeing them dragging painfully along in this trying atmosphere,

for pity's sake. You look on while I drink; that's understood. I'm too thirsty for anything."

After all, John reflected that he had no right to abandon his companion in this unknown place any more than to prevent her quenching her thirst.

"Come then," said he.

And he followed the girl into a little *trattoria*, determined on watching her drink her wine without faltering.

Victoria had, to commence with, great difficulty in making herself understood. The host, a crabbed Sicilian, exerted himself to utter interminable phrases in an extraordinary dialect, asking her, apparently, what she would have. Despairing of making him understand exactly what she wished for, she at length replied with a confident "Yes" to one of his unintelligible questions, upon which he disappeared through a trap-door into the cellar of the establishment, and, returning quickly, deposited on a rickety table a huge bottle holding six litres of the wine of Ravello, and two glasses. Scarcely had it appeared before the bottle was covered with dew, showing the coolness of the wine it contained, which had also a most appetizing golden tint.

Seeing that his customers were not in the habit of handling so large a flask, the Sicilian took charge of it and filled the two glasses to the brim with what looked like liquid gold, and the glasses themselves were soon covered with a most inviting moisture.

Victoria seized hers eagerly and emptied it at one draught, while John stoically refrained from even looking at his.

"Oh, what nectar! I never tasted anything so exquisite in all my life."

Then, perceiving the Tantalus condition of her companion, she had pity on him.

"Come, Mr. Cockburn, give in and take a glass."

"No," said the unhappy man in a hollow voice.

"I swear, on the faith of Victoria, no one shall know it."

John's eyes sparkled. After one supreme moment of hesitation he put out his hand and seized the tantalizing glass, murmuring—

"You are sure you won't tell?"

"I have sworn it."

Then, as in a frenzy, he swallowed the wine, and then a second glass and a third, the whole disappearing like three drops of water on a sandbank. His cheeks flushed, and the effects of the triple bumper soon manifested themselves in gaiety and talkativeness.

"So, so," he began, "you want to know where the stamp is to be found, do you, Miss Victoria?"

"Isn't it very natural?"

"You are all curiosity, but, though you have treated me to very good wine, I am not going to tell you."

"As you please," said Victoria calmly. "I asked and you can't tell me; so much the worse; but I can do without knowing."

"Naturally, as you will have to do without. But, on my word, I must have some more of this wine. The proof of its goodness is that it makes one thirsty."

No sooner said than done. A fourth glass rapidly followed the other three. John now began to sing, to drum on the table, and to smile at Victoria.

"Well, suppose I did tell you where it is?"

"Where what is?" asked Victoria naively.

"Why, the stamp, my dear girl, the stamp! The famous stamp!"

"Oh, I don't care about it, as it might get you into trouble," said the maid, with a preoccupied air.

"Trouble? After all, I am free to say what I please, am I not? By Jove! I am thirsty!" In proof of which statement a fifth glass of wine disappeared down John's throat.

While carefully abstaining from pressing him, Victoria watched him drink, and the idea occurred to her of profiting by a circumstance she had not been purposely guilty of bringing about. By the heightened colour and increasing talkativeness of her guest she knew that the wine was exercising its usual influence, and as she was aware that people cannot stand contradiction when they have been drinking, she resolved to try it without delay.

"No, Master John," she said, "I don't wish you to tell me about the Brahmapootra stamp. I don't wish it, you understand? It wouldn't be honest."

"Not honest? Who says I am not honest? I am honest, I tell you, very honest!—Well, well; how thirsty I am!"

Upon which John tossed off a sixth glass.

"Did you maintain that I was not honest?" he began again, with a hiccough.

"No, no, Master John; certainly not."

"Yes, you did; you said so. Well, to show you how honest I am, I'll just tell you where that miserable stamp is."

"No, I don't wish to know, Mr. John. It's very wrong of you."

"Oh! very wrong, is it? Well, it's at——"

Accompanying his speech with a too comprehensive gesture he had knocked over the bottle, which fell on the ground and smashed noisily, while the wine, with which it was still three-parts full, ran all about. Nothing more was needed to interrupt John's revelation and send him off into a hearty fit of laughter.

But the host came up to them, and with a furious air jabbered a number of invectives, pointing to the floor, which was inundated by the odorous contents of the huge flask. This brought John's gaiety to its height, which still more exasperated the angry Sicilian. He was advancing to seize his careless and laughing customer when Victoria slipped a piece of gold into his hand, the sight of which caused a smile to spread over his wrathful visage.

"*Grazzie! Grazzie!*" repeated the delighted owner of the shop, who would willingly have offered all his biggest bottles for people to break at the same price.

Then Victoria rose and took John's arm, and he allowed her to draw him into the street, laughing all the time. She pushed him into one of the carriages which had followed them and was conscientiously waiting outside.

"To the Grand Hotel," she said to the driver.

At first John, being a little stunned at this brusque treatment, sat quietly in the carriage. But suddenly, awakened by the bright daylight and the jolting of the vehicle, he jumped up, at the risk of losing his equilibrium, and began shouting—

"Yes, yes, I will tell you where that extraordinary stamp is!"

Really frightened this time, Victoria tried her best to make him sit down, saying not now for the pleasure of contradicting him, but in the effort to calm him and prevent a dangerous fall or compromising row—

"No, my friend, my dear friend, don't say any more about it, I beseech you, but sit down."

Already a few saunterers, attracted by John's curious behaviour, as he stood up gesticulating like a madman, had stopped and watched him pass, shrugging their shoulders with a smile.

"Listen, all of you," he shouted, "and learn where this stamp is, the only one in all the world!"

"For goodness' sake be quiet!" implored Victoria.

"Quiet? Never! It would be infamous! I must speak at last, for the good of humanity. Run, run, all of you, and come and hear the good news!" And he beckoned all round to call those who were passing by to the carriage door. A few urchins ran up and excited him still more by their cries, while Victoria, quite put out of countenance, covered her face with her hands.

"Run, run!" John continued to shout at the top of his voice. And the group, which the strange equipage drew after it, grew larger every moment. Men, women, and dogs followed pell-mell, laughing or barking according to their kind, in a tumult which seemed highly to amuse the improvised orator.

At length, when he thought he had a sufficient audience, he placed himself in a commanding attitude and cried in a stentorian voice, "Albrandi has got it! Albrandi!" To which a hundred voices answered with a great shout, "*Evviva il Principe Albrandi!*"

It was a deafening clatter. John, flushed as if about to fall down in an apoplectic fit, continued to cry, "Albrandi has got it! Albrandi!" And the crowd, continually reinforced by stragglers, replied with laughter and shouts, "Albrandi! Albrandi!"

THE STAMP KING

By G. DE BEAUREGARD AND H. DE GORSSE

Translated from the French by EDITH C. PHILLIPS

CHAPTER XXI (continued)

Wherein it appears that the well of truth ought to be full of wine!

WHEN the wave emerged in the Villa Nazionale a number of carriages, driving there at the fashionable hour, were compelled hastily to draw on one side, to the great fear of the ladies within, who thought it a rising of the populace.

The overwhelmed police officers tried in vain to stem the torrent and approach the carriage where John was continuing his sensational cries. It took more than a quarter of an hour for the ridiculous procession to reach the hotel, with a large reinforcement of noisy shouts. The trams from Pausilippe were interrupted; two trains from Pouzzoles, lying to at Torretta, waited for the road to become passable; landaus, victorias, fiacres, entangled in inextricable confusion, in vain sought an opportunity of finding their way out. People climbed the carob trees, palms, and lamp-posts and any other posts of observation they could find. And the one word, clamoured by thousands of voices, echoed to the outermost ranks of the crowd, who repeated it confidently, "Albrandi! Albrandi!"

Just as the fiacre, not without difficulty, drew near the hotel, the landau containing William and Betty also arrived there.

"Why, whatever is the matter? A riot?" cried William, jumping out.

Then, for the first time, he distinguished the name "Albrandi" among the shouts and caught sight of John, still standing in his carriage, whence he refused to descend, and repeating obstinately—

"Albrandi has got it! Albrandi!"

"Wretch!" he exclaimed, without any clear idea of what had happened. And, throwing himself on his valet, he caught him by the throat, nearly threw him to the ground, and forced him, with great strides, to enter the hotel, to the great amusement of the waiters, who had rushed up to see what was the matter. Betty also approached the fiacre, from which Victoria, more dead than alive with fear and shame, had no strength to move.

"What does this mean?" she asked. "Who is this Albrandi, and what has he got?"

"The stamp, Miss Betty."

She could say no more, for her voice died away and she fell full length on the flag-stones. Two of the servants took her up in a dead faint and carried her into the hotel, where Betty followed them.

But a crowd having the effect of drawing together a still greater crowd, the mass which encumbered the streets became alarming. All communication was cut off, carriages stopped, pedestrians trodden under foot, flower borders and grass plots invaded. From all sides rushed up reporters in quest of news, stopping each other to ask what it all meant. But no one, as we can well understand, could explain the matter exactly.

So in all the groups there were endless, hot discussions, the noise of which resounded throughout the neighbouring streets. The crowd chattered and jabbered without in the least knowing what about. They were agreed on one point only—that something extraordinary had happened "at Prince Albrandi's palace."

At last the police were compelled to call in the military. And, while the disorder was at its height, trumpets began to sound at the other end of the town. Nothing more was needed to dissolve the enormous crowd, who melted, like a cloud of dust, into the adjacent streets, and soon left the place clear.

But as the soldiers passed under the window of the Grand Hotel, along the street, cleared as if by magic, a window on the third floor was opened, and the disordered head of John suddenly emerged and launched for the last time into the calm evening air the four magic words, "Albrandi has got it! All Brandy! Ha! ha! ha!"

CHAPTER XXII

Wherein it is shown how William and Betty, having reached their object, despair of ever attaining it.

WHEN William and Betty met in the dining-room of the Grand Hotel they were in very different moods. The young girl was scarcely able to hide, under an amiable smile, the joy she felt in the unexpected discovery of the precious secret. William was wondering whether John had really told all, or whether the name of Albrandi had simply escaped him in a moment of exuberance without any comment. But neither of them allowed these thoughts to escape them as they exchanged their impressions of Naples during dinner. But, in speaking of their drive in the afternoon, no mention was made of the sumptuous dwelling of the Prince or of the disturbance in the Villa Nazionale; and their silence on these subjects was the more remarkable as they were the two special events of the day.

William's uneasiness increased, for he concluded, logically enough, that, as Betty asked nothing about it, it was evident she was already enlightened. But Miss Scott remained impenetrable, and the unfortunate William rose from the table no better informed than when he sat down. The one important thing for him now was to execute once more, with Prince Albrandi, the manœuvre which had succeeded so well with M. Moulineau—that is, to see him alone and before Miss Betty. And, as the little American must at least have dangerous suspicions touching this name of Albrandi, shouted in her ears a hundred times, it was necessary to act without any delay.

THE HOST JABBERED A NUMBER OF INVECTIVES

So William, feeling all the more disquieted because John was still in no condition to answer questions or give him any exact information on the state of affairs, resolved to go at once to the Prince's house. He profited by the confusion arising, when the guests were leaving the table, to glide into the crowd and gain the vestibule and the outer door. But Betty had not lost sight of him, and was close behind him as he descended the first step.

"You are going out?" she asked.

"Oh, are you there?" said the young man, turning round with a disappointed expression.

"Yes, I ran after you. You sneak off just like a common commander."

William felt highly displeased, and scarcely took the trouble to hide it.

"Yes," continued Betty, "I know I am a great nuisance, but I warned you. I can't possibly let you go out alone, especially without any money. Just think, if anything happened to you——"

(To be continued.)

SPECIAL CORRESPONDENCE

Our Constantinople Letter

CONSTANTINOPLE, 8 *September*, 1905

The New Turkish Stamps

By my letter of this day I give you some news as to the new stamps of Turkey and of the foreign post offices in the Levant.

The new stamps of Turkey appeared on 1 September, the anniversary of the accession to the throne of H.M. the Sultan; this new set consists of eighteen stamps:—

Postage stamps: 5, 10, 20 paras, 1, 2, 2½, 5, 10, 25, and 50 piastres.

Newspaper stamps: 5, 10, 20 paras, 1, 2, and 5 piastres.

Unpaid Letter stamps: 1 and 2 piastres.

It will be seen that this time there are two new values, 2½ and 10 piastres, which were not included in the former issues and which have been created specially for the packets sent by parcel post, as these values were being needed continually in that branch; as to the Unpaid Letter stamps, the 10 and 20 paras have been withdrawn in this issue, but they are needed, as it seems, and they will be also created soon.

The 1901 Series, perf. 12½

An interesting thing happened during the last ten days of August. As the result of a formal order issued by the Turkish Government, the new stamps could not be issued before 1 September, the date of the anniversary referred to. As some of the values of the old stamps were lacking, one was obliged to get printed a certain number of the old types; but as the perforating machine used in the old types had been put out of use as the result of being used so much, the stamps were perforated by the machine used in making the new issue of stamps, and the same perforation was used, that is, 12½ instead of 13½. Only 100 sheets were printed (100 stamps) of the 5 paras, violet, but in a *very* dark violet, in all 10,000 stamps; 50 sheets of the 20 paras, red instead of the pink, in all 5000 pieces; and 25 sheets of the 5 piastres, violet-pink, printed in a bright red-violet, in all 2500 pieces. These stamps were used only about ten days by the Post Office of Stamboul alone, and I think they will be in very great demand, especially unused, as nobody had time to lay in a stock of them, and they are no longer in circulation in Turkey.

The New British Levant Stamps

The British Post Offices in the Levant have issued also new stamps by surcharging the word "Levant" on all the stamps of the mother country, that is, ½d., 1d., 1½d., 2d., 2½d., 3d., 4d., 5d., 6d., and up to the 1s.; thus at this moment one can use indifferently on letters posted at these offices either the old stamps surcharged in "piastres" and "paras," or the new issue of stamps

surcharged "Levant." The stamps of 2½d. and 5d. were surcharged already respectively "40 paras" and "80 paras." When this stock is exhausted they will be used again, but they will bear the surcharges of "1 piastre" and "2 piastres" instead of the former surcharges.

The Demand for Higher Values

On the other hand, as the highest value used in the British post offices was the 2s. 6d. surcharged "12 piastres," and as often the leading banks and offices in sending away title deeds, share scrip, etc., were obliged to pay from £4 to £5 for the postage of such a letter, it resulted in the Post Office being compelled to cover the whole envelope with the 2s. 6d. stamps, and this was inconvenient both to the sender and to the Post Office. Upon a request being made to the Postmaster-General in London, it was decided to surcharge also the 5s., pink, with the surcharge "24 piastres," for use in the British offices in the Levant. Hence the reason for the rearrangement now of the list of postage stamps in use at the British offices, a list which I gave in my last letter:—

Stamps surcharged "Levant": ½d., 1d., 2d., 2½d., 3d., 4d., 5d., 6d., 1s.

Stamps surcharged in paras and piastres without the word "Levant": 40 paras on 2½d., 80 paras on 5d., 4 piastres on 10d., 12 piastres on 2s. 6d., and 24 piastres on 5s.

First Supply of British "Levant" Stamps Sold Out

This new issue surcharged "Levant" was such a success that at the end of three weeks the first supply of several hundred pounds' worth received by our post office was completely exhausted, and another large supply had to be ordered by telegram as the result of the orders which came in.

German Levant Stamps

Although the German stamps with "Reichspost" have been superseded for more than two years in Germany, and replaced by stamps bearing the inscription "Deutsches Reich," the "Reichspost" stamps continue to be used in the German offices in the Levant surcharged in paras and piastres. Recently the postal authorities published a notice to say that towards the end of this month fresh stamps will be used which will bear the same surcharges, but on the stamps of the type "Deutsches Reich" instead of "Reichspost." The stamps of the old type will be exchanged for the new ones at all the German post offices in the Levant until 1 January, 1906.

Russian Levant Stamps

A new value will be issued soon in these offices, namely, that of "5 paras" on the 1 kopeck, orange.

THE STAMP KING

By G. DE BEAUREGARD AND H. DE GORSSE

Translated from the French by EDITH C. PHILLIPS

CHAPTER XXII (continued)

Wherein it is shown how William and Betty, having reached their object, despair of ever attaining it

WE can easily believe that Betty also had had an idea of rushing off to the Prince's palace ; but as she never doubted her rival would go himself, it was even more important to prevent his doing so by constant watchfulness, and to wait patiently for a time when she should be free to pay her own visit without fear of interruption.

"What a delightful evening !" she exclaimed. "Do you care for a walk ? "

"If you like," said William, trying to make the best of it.

So they started on foot towards the town again and walked for a long time, talking all the while of insignificant matters. But when the hour was past at which they could decently call upon the Prince they confessed to feeling very tired, and, returning to the hotel, retired to their rooms, not without mysteriously impressing, the one on John and the other on Victoria, the fact that each wished to be called at six o'clock the next morning. This was done.

William, while dressing, had opened his window, which commanded a view of the bay, and breathed the morning air, rejoicing already in the prospect of a speedy triumph.

"Perhaps it is a little early to pay a visit to the Prince," he reflected. "But, though these Neapolitans are indolent, they don't stand on ceremony, and he will receive me in his bedroom. And besides, I have no choice."

One thing troubled him a little, however. John, now quite sober, confessed that he had indeed revealed to Victoria the fact that the Maharajah's stamp was to be found with Prince Albrandi.

The young American finished dressing all the quicker on receipt of this news, took his hat and gloves, and left his room just as the clock struck seven. But scarcely had he taken a dozen steps along the corridor before an exclamation of disappointment escaped him—

"What, you again ! "

"Gracious goodness ! Yes."

It was Betty, Betty herself, who, called at the aforesaid hour by Victoria, had also risen in haste, and was now feeling thoroughly discomfited at the fact that her rival had had the same idea as herself. For a moment they remained looking at each other without knowing what to say or how to account for their early morning energy. Then, overcome by the absurdity of the mystery with which they were surrounding the object of their attempted visits, a secret which was no longer a secret, Betty burst out laughing and said—

"Since we cannot manage this business alone, shall we go together to Prince Albrandi ? "

William was at first little pleased at obtaining this clear proof of the truth of John's confession. But if he was inclined to be pessimistic, it seldom lasted long, on account of his energy and excellent disposition.

"Upon my word," he said, almost cheerfully, " I really think it would be about the best thing we could do."

"Really ? Wouldn't it annoy you ? "

"No more than any other unavoidable event."

"Well, in that case, it's very good of us to have got up at such an unseasonable hour. Shall we wait till twelve o'clock ? "

"That is the time for the siesta."

"Ten o'clock, then ? "

"Very good."

"Good-bye for the present."

"Good-bye." And each returned to their respective rooms to try and snatch a few moments more sleep, well enough pleased, if the truth were known, at being able to speak and act openly in the matter. At about a quarter to ten John handed his master a closed envelope, seemingly stuffed with papers.

"Victoria has just given me this for you, sir," said he.

William immediately opened the envelope and drew out a card and twenty delightful thousand-franc notes. They came from Betty, who had no longer any interest in keeping her rival without money.

The card was thus inscribed—

"Betty Scott, delighted at losing a creditor and preserving a friend, begs Mr. William Keniss to accept the enclosed and to remember that, according to the terms of his agreement, he must from this moment again become gallant."

"What an extraordinary girl ! " murmured the young man. "What a generous nature ! What fearlessness ! And how well she knows how to add a charming grace to all her actions ! "

And he slipped the notes into his pocket, and then the card itself, which he could not resist first carrying to his lips.

We can imagine his earnest thanks and tender gratitude when, a quarter of an hour later, he met his lovely rival in the drawing-room. He also gave her a detailed account of his visit to the Maharajah, having no longer any interest in keeping it from her. Betty laughed heartily, gave him her little hand to kiss without affectation, and then said—

"My dear competitor, I think it is quite time we started on our quest. But whose fine equipage can this be ? " she added, glancing through the window.

William looked, and, being equally struck by it himself, said—

"We shall get a nearer view as we go out."

They had just reached the hall as a tall, very bronzed gentleman, with black moustache, long, hooked nose, and big hands covered with yellow gloves, came in and furiously accosted the manager, who was standing near.

"Sir," he cried, " I have just heard that there was a scandalous demonstration in front of this hotel yesterday, in which, it appears, my name was largely implicated."

The manager, who, no doubt, was well acquainted with the new arrival, bowed profusely, and in his embarrassment could only murmur, " But your Highness—— But your Highness—— "

"Keep to the point," said the big man, gesticulating freely. " I have been assured that some puppy who is staying here provoked this saturnalia ; and I tell you the matter shall not rest there."

"But your Highness—— " stammered the manager, bowing still and in greater distress than ever.

"Well ! What have you to say for yourself ? "

"Why—why—it was not my fault."

The manager evidently wished himself a thousand miles away from his ferocious questioner. He had lost all his self-possession, and could not think of a single excuse. William and Betty had heard every word, and soon guessed in whose presence they were. The young American felt that it was incumbent on him to speak, as the responsibility rested in a great measure on his shoulders, and he also saw that, however unpleasant it might be to enter into the matter, it was a providential opportunity of gaining his purpose.

"Is it not Prince Albrandi to whom I have the honour of speaking?" he said, advancing, hat in hand.

"To Prince Albrandi himself," replied that individual, eyeing William haughtily from head to foot, without taking off his hat.

"In that case," continued the young man, seeming not to notice the Prince's arrogance, "it is for me to make excuses concerning the unfortunate affair to which you have alluded. Moreover, I was just coming to call upon you."

"May I ask to whom I have the honour of speaking?" asked the Prince disdainfully.

"To Mr. William Keniss of New York. If you will be good enough to come into the drawing-room, I shall have the honour of explaining——"

"Then it is of you I must demand the reason of this foolery?"

The Prince, without recalling to mind the fact that it was Mr. Keniss who had sent him the telegram from Paris, put the question with such offensive haughtiness that William could no longer pretend not to notice it, and he returned icily—

"No, sir, of my valet, for whom I thought it my duty to offer myself as substitute, but with whom I will leave you to discuss the matter, since you seem to prefer it."

Nothing confounds insolence like a coldly polite speech, which immediately gives the insolent one an uneasy feeling of inferiority. So great was the Prince's surprise at anyone daring to take such a tone with him that he supposed William must be a personage of great importance, so he took off his hat and replied in a softened tone—

"I am ready to listen to your explanation, sir." And, followed by William and Betty too, he entered the drawing-room

There the young American gave an account of the adventure in a few words, and the reasons which had caused all the echoes of the Villa to resound with Prince Albrandi's name, and ended by again expressing his regret at an inconvenience which must be attributed rather to stupidity than to any wish to annoy an honourable gentleman. When William saw that the Prince, being amused at his recital, had calmed down, and seemed inclined to forget the attitude he had first taken, he told him frankly the object of his journey, letting him know what an important place he himself had therein, and, leading him up to Betty, who had remained apart, he said by way of conclusion—

"This is my rival, Miss Betty Scott, also of New York, whom I am proud to call, in spite of our competition, the best and most faithful of my friends."

Then, densely conceited though he was, the Prince

launched out into politenesses. He prayed to be forgiven for having shown himself at first in so unfavourable a light, and manifested a tardy desire to make himself agreeable to his two fellow-philatelists.

"One thing causes me great concern," he said. "It is that this stamp of mine, which is the object of your keen desire, is not for sale."

"Not even if you fix the price to suit yourself?" asked William insidiously.

THE PRINCE EYED WILLIAM HAUGHTILY

The Prince hesitated before the magnificence of this disguised offer, but pride for the moment triumphing over cupidity, he returned—

"No; do not press the matter. It is the finest thing in my collection, and I cannot part with it."

"Two hundred thousand francs?" insinuated Betty.

"No, no," said Albrandi brusquely, as if he feared to allow himself to be tempted. "But, in any case, I hope you will do my collection the honour of examining it. Many connoisseurs hold it in high esteem, and I should greatly value your opinion."

"With much pleasure," said William and Betty with one voice, delighted at the opportunity thus offered them.

"But wait," said the Prince. "It happens that to-morrow evening I am giving a fête at my Pausilippe

Palace, and I shall be flattered and delighted if you will do me the honour of attending. Forgive the impromptu invitation, seeing it is given with so much goodwill."

Such kind attention could only meet with acceptance, so the two young people promised all he wished, and after he had taken leave of them declared him to be the most charming man in the world. But the thought that they had undertaken a fruitless journey, and that the stamp was found at last, only to escape them, filled them with profound melancholy.

"We shall at least have the satisfaction of looking at it," said Betty philosophically.

"A very small satisfaction," returned William.

They received another visit that same day from the head of the police, who also came to learn all he could concerning the scandal of the previous evening. This amiable man, totally different from the police in the north, did not trouble to put on a dark and sinister air. He was highly amused at the recital which William went through again for his benefit, and seemed delighted that the two Americans were invited to Prince Albrandi's on the morrow.

"We shall meet again there, and I congratulate myself," he said, adding, as he rose to leave—

"By the way, I am on the track of your thief. In addition to the pleasure of seeing you to-morrow evening, I shall have that of telling you of his arrest."

(To be continued.)

SPECIAL CORRESPONDENCE

Our Italian Letter

ROME, 22 *September,* 1905

The New Provisional 15 c.

THE lowering of the postage on inland letters in Italy is an accomplished fact. On 1 September appeared the new stamp with surcharge "C. 15" on the 20 cent. of 1901, as chronicled already by *G. S. W.*, and also a letter card with the same surcharge. But this card is of a special printing, as the figures "20" in the heading have been replaced by "15." It has not been mentioned hitherto that the provisional stamps and letter cards have been ready since 1903, when the project of the postal reform was laid before the Chamber of Deputies for the first time. A supply of 22,140,000 stamps was prepared at that time, and last June there was another printing of 20,000,000, which gave a total of 42,140,000 stamps, a very respectable figure. As to the letter cards : 58,000 were printed in 1903, and 100,000 in 1905. Thus neither the stamp nor the letter card is likely to become rare ; there will be enough for everybody.

The Proposed New Pictorial Issue

The daily political newspapers have announced as "near at hand" the issue of a set of "artistic" stamps of Italy, these stamps being after the designs made by our painter Michetti. There has been some talk thereof for some time,* but the truth of the matter is that nothing has been decided upon so far as to their issue. As a rule people are not satisfied with the present types, and there is a wish to do better, and this is doubtless very praiseworthy. But, in my opinion, it is wrong to wish to compare our surface-printed stamps with those, for example, of the Congo Free State, of the United States, of Crete, etc. In most cases one does not take into account the fact that in surface-printing, no matter however carefully it be done, it is impossible to obtain the sharpness and brilliancy of impression obtained in engraving the stamps from steel plates. Now, our "Officina Governativa delle Carte-Valori," that is, the Government

* See *G. S. W.,* Vol. I, No. 9, page 145.

Postal Printing Office, was founded in 1865 on the model of the firm of De La Rue and Co., of London, which supplied the material, and that only for the production of postage stamps, State fiscal paper values, etc., made by typographical processes. The regulations of the Italian Postal Law now in operation compel the Ministry of Posts and Telegraphs to have the stamps, cards, etc., made by the Government Printing Works. In the present Ministry of Posts there is a desire to get rid of this obligation ; there has been a question of entrusting to a private firm the making of the stamp of 15 c. decided upon. I do not think I am wrong in saying that a start has been made in this respect. This has stirred the staff of the Government Printing Works, and a protest was made, as it was feared that the work would grow less. Moreover, the terms of the law to which I have alluded have not been changed, and it is believed that an alteration is necessary in order to be able to give a private firm the order to supply the stamps. I really do not know how the matter will turn out. Still, we shall have something new before long. Let us hope that it will be a step in the right direction.

A San Marino Provisional

The lowering of the postage on letters has extended itself to the republic of San Marino, which, postally, is a sort of dependency of Italy, and has furnished it with a suitable opportunity for providing us with new surcharged stamps. A "little bird" has told me that that good man Herr Otto Bickel, who was the father of the surcharged stamps of 1892, has betaken himself to San Marino (a walk to Mont Titan is very agreeable in summer), and has instigated the issue of a surcharged stamp, of which, it is needless to say, the stock has been bought up, and thus this provisional is on the rise already. It is really shameful to see a republic, which was proud enough to refuse an offer made by a society which wished to found there a great gambling-house on the lines of Monte Carlo, give way to a petty speculation in postage stamps. But perhaps I am in the wrong, and somebody may think it is all very right.

THE STAMP KING

By G. DE BEAUREGARD AND H. DE GORSSE

Translated from the French by EDITH C. PHILLIPS

WILLIAM AND BETTY ARRIVED

CHAPTER XXIII

The untoward fate of the fête of Prince Albrandi

IT was an event long looked forward to in Naples, this fête of Prince Albrandi.

His magnificent establishment, his love of luxury, and his illustrious family, allied to the Carracciolo, the Carafa, the Sangro, and all the nobility of the two Sicilies, all caused him to be looked up to as a great personality, and invitations to his receptions were universally sought after. He had, as can well be imagined, many friends and many backbiters, who all, but particularly the latter, rejoiced in his magnificence and feasted continually at his table. Beyond the pleasures which he lavished upon them, this often gave them the opportunity of effecting a good stroke of business.

The Prince, in fact, was an omnivorous collector, but not a collector for the sake of the inward joy of obtaining a long-desired specimen by some happy chance, or after weary and patient research. He collected for the purpose of accumulating, that he might have the largest possible display of brilliant and costly things, arranged with more ostentation than taste, more pride than pleasure. Thus the principal rooms in his palace were given up to a permanent exhibition of his numerous acquisitions—pictures, sculpture, antiques, Chinese ornaments, Oriental trinkets, furniture, minerals, shell-work, coins, and, finally, stamps.

But these things, lavishly bought, piled up in profusion and often of doubtful authenticity, showed only a desire to dazzle, to the entire exclusion of either art or science.

In his house there was but one complete and perfect collection—that of the parasites and bloodsuckers who assisted him to squander his fortune royally. So they had no hesitation in spreading, on the quiet, the most

unflattering rumours about him, and the talk of the day was to the effect that he had only organised this fête, which was to surpass all the others by its splendour, to impose upon people concerning his financial position and restore his shaken credit.

However that might be everyone expected a great deal of pleasure from it, and none of the fortunate invited ones felt inclined to refuse the invitation.

When the evening arrived the Pausilippe Palace offered indeed a veritable scene of fairyland. A luminous vault extended from the entrance right over the gardens; and those who have beheld illuminations arranged by Neapolitans will admit them to be masters in the art of this kind of decoration. The smallest shrubs were full of many-coloured lamps, and the lawns and flower-beds had disappeared under a glittering carpet. Brilliant electric lights thrown on to the fountains gave an appearance as of enormous jets of pearls and diamonds. The outlines of the palace, the curbs of the basins, the edges of the walks, and the parapets of the terrace were garlanded with lights, which drove night far into the distance and delighted the eye.

As the evening was enchantingly calm, only just freshened by the lightest breeze, the lights burned brightly and shone from one end of the domain to the other.

A double line of powdered footmen, in the green and gold livery of the Prince, stood on the steps; and in the vast entrance hall, filled with rare plants and glowing lustres, stood the Prince himself, receiving his innumerable guests with a smile of welcome.

William and Betty arrived just before eleven.

"Oh, Prince, we are not living in one evening, but in the thousand and one nights!" the young American exclaimed.

"That is very kind of you," said Albrandi, bowing. Then, turning to Betty, he said—

"As you are newly arrived in Naples, Miss Scott, and do not know anyone, I shall keep you near me, and ask you to let me do the honours of my house myself. And you, too, Mr. Keniss."

The two young people, delighted at so much kindness, bowed their acquiescence, and ranged themselves behind the Prince to allow the newcomers to approach. A multitude of people presented themselves—princes, dukes, marquises, knights, even canons and bishops. All the titles in the world passed by, crushed and mixed together in the utmost confusion. Diplomatists arrived in full uniform, with ribbons, stars, and orders of every description, gold and colour flashing in the light; and ladies in low dresses, covered with precious stones.

The chief of police arrived in his turn, and, seeing William, went up to him with outstretched hand, saying, when the first greetings had passed—

"Good news, monsieur. Your thief is just about to be arrested. His hiding-place has been discovered, all arrangements made, and it was only by the merest chance that he escaped being taken this afternoon."

As Signor Petto was speaking they heard the announcement—

"The Consul-General of Russia and the Count Orsikoff!"

These two personages, one as bedizened as the other with stars and decorations, advanced, and the Consul said—

"My dear Prince, will you allow me to present one of my compatriots, recently arrived from France, and most highly recommended by the ambassador of his Majesty the Czar in Paris! I have taken the liberty of bringing him into the midst of all these wonders——"

"A happy inspiration!" cried Albrandi. "The Count is most welcome."

On leaving the Prince the Count and the Consul passed close by William and Betty. With one impulse the two Americans, who had been looking in the other direction, turned round, and both received a shock. Count Orsikoff, meeting them thus suddenly face to face, could not suppress an expression of horror, grew pallid, and turned quickly away.

"What an extraordinary thing!" murmured William in Betty's ear.

"Nothing could be more extraordinary, and I should be positive that I recognised our thief by those eyes if I had not known that they were just about taking him prisoner."

"We are possessed," concluded William, laughing, "and see that scoundrel everywhere. We must not give way to such weakness."

The rooms were now well filled, and as there were no more guests arriving the Prince offered his arm to Betty and led her through the palace to the terrace overlooking the Bay, where there was a glorious view. Facing them in the distance twinkled the lights of all the towns scattered along the shore—Portici, Resina, Torre del Greco, Torre Annunziata, Castellamara, Vicameta, Sorrento, Mana. It was like another burning girdle of light, continuing the illuminations of the park and encircling all the Bay, above which glowed, like a colossal ruby, the fire of Vesuvius.

At a given signal electric lights were suddenly thrown on the sombre waves below the terrace, where boats were seen passing to and fro, filled with musicians, from whom arose strains of incomparable sweetness.

On every side arose exclamations of delight, and the guests looked on and listened in an ecstasy, which lasted until the host invited them to come and see his various collections, already known to nearly everyone, but which he delighted to show again on the slightest excuse.

They passed through a regular suite of galleries bordered with glass cases, wherein the most diverse objects were arranged, till they reached at length a small study, the walls of which were completely covered with postage stamps, arranged in arabesques and many fanciful designs.

"Behold the temple!" said the Prince to Betty.

Then he opened a costly piece of furniture, standing in the middle of the room, and took out a large album, composed of several hundred loose leaves of smooth parchment. It was the Stamp Collection.

"This collection," said the Prince in a loud voice that could be heard by all—for he deigned to act the showman himself—"this collection is worth about a million and a half. It has cost me at least that. You see," continued he, showing some of the pages, "what a number of stamps there are. I have some of the utmost rarity, with watermarks scarcely visible or reversed or absent altogether; in fact, perfectly unique specimens. But this is the pearl of my collection!"

And he took out one sheet from the number, whereon was fixed, alone, resplendent, the golden Brahmapootra stamp, at which William and Betty gazed with an eagerness which we can well understand, and not without a sharp pang of envy.

"But two copies of this stamp exist," continued the Prince—"this one and one other, which is the property of Mr. Keniss here. But mine, if I may say so without discourtesy to my amiable compeer, is far the more valuable, since it has the undeniable superiority of being unused. Moreover, yesterday I was offered two hundred thousand francs for it."

At the mention of this sum a murmur passed through the crowd, and many envious eyes were turned in the direction of the little square of paper which represented it.

The guests having admired the collection with more politeness than sincerity, the Prince left the study, followed by his little group of courtiers, saying—

"Now you must see this matchless specimen in such proportions as will allow you to appreciate it."

And there, at the end of a long gallery, was stretched a sheet, on which was thrown by a magic lantern a photograph of the famous stamp, enlarged a hundredfold.

"How very interesting!" said William. "I have never seen anything like that. How do you manage it?"

"Oh, nothing could be more simple," returned the Prince; but you must only use photographs or reprints, or else risk the loss of the original, which is not often done. A copy of the stamp, then, is soaked in hot water for two hours; then a pane of glass, just warmed, is covered with a thin layer of turpentine; on this the stamp is carefully stuck, that it may adhere all over, and left to cool for two hours longer. After that time it is rubbed carefully with a wet finger, so as to rub off all the paper and leave on the turpentine only the thin film composing the picture. Then it is covered all over with a coating of transparent varnish, and there you have a positive, ready for use in the first available lantern."

"It is most ingenious," said William.

"Now I am going to show you the Brahmapootra stamp a third time and on a still larger scale," said the Prince.

(To be continued.)

A VERY HANDSOME PRESENT.

Packet No. 69, 2000 varieties. A grand packet, every stamp being different and genuine, and thus forming a choice collection in itself. £3, post-free and registered.

THE STAMP KING

By G. DE BEAUREGARD AND H. DE GORSSE

Translated from the French by EDITH C. PHILLIPS

THE ROCKETS FLASHED TO AN ENORMOUS HEIGHT

CHAPTER XXIII (*continued*)

The untoward fate of the fête of Prince Albrandi

THEY left the gallery and went out once more on to the terrace. On the way Betty saw Count Orsikoff gliding through the crowd as if returning to the stamp room that they had just left; but, as it was not her place to keep an eye on the guests, she passed on and thought no more about it.

The terrace had been thrown into a state of semi-darkness, which at first caused a little wonder; but this was soon explained, for at a fresh signal a number of rockets burst from a pontoon moored in the Bay, opposite the terrace, where a magnificent display of fireworks had been arranged. The rockets flashed to an enormous height and descended in a rain of many-coloured stars, with very fine effect. Then followed a succession of other brilliant fireworks, Roman candles, and Bengal lights, which burned, flashed, and wound upwards in a glittering network, calling forth continually the enthusiastic applause of the spectators.

But the enthusiasm mounted higher still when, in an immense sea of fire, the outline of the Brahma-pootra stamp appeared, traced in jets of light in a frame more than ten yards high. It only lasted a minute, but was sufficient to call forth thunders of applause and clapping.

Finally, a sheaf of four thousand rockets, all let off at once, terminated the wonderful show, when the lamps and electric lights were turned on again as if by enchantment.

Compliments were heaped on the Prince.

"It was marvellous!"

"I have never seen anything so fine!"

"Or so grand!"

"The picture was unrivalled; worthy of being painted and framed!"

"It was beautiful! Brilliant!"

The Russian Consul was particularly impressive in his enthusiasm.

"But what have you done with Count Orsikoff?" asked the Prince. "Has he deserted our fête?"

"He left me after the magic-lantern show," returned the Consul, "and I really do not know what has become of him."

"In any case you will tell him how delighted have been to see him here," said the Prince kindly.

He had scarcely spoken the last word when a footman, breaking through the admiring crowd, cried in a broken voice—

"Your Highness! Your Highness! The gold stamp has been stolen!"

"What nonsense is this?"

"Stolen, sir; stolen this very moment!"

"By whom? How?" cried the Prince, alarmed by the excitement and evident sincerity of his servant.

"By a Russian count, Count Orsikoff, I believe."

"There! I could have sworn it was Tilbury!" murmured Betty.

"It was Spartivento," agreed William.

"What! What!" exclaimed the Russian Consul. But the Prince had turned furiously to the footman. "Careless wretch!" cried he. "Why did you not catch him?"

"I threw myself upon him and caught him by one of his stars, but the star came off and he escaped."

And he piteously showed the great Russian star of Saint Anna, which everyone recognised as having shone, an hour earlier, on Count Orsikoff's breast.

They hastened to the stamp room, where the servant's story could only be verified.

The doors of the cabinet were hanging disjointedly with their hinges broken; the pages of the collection, with the exception of the most important one, were strewn on the floor; and the disorder showed plainly enough what had taken place.

"Well," said the Prince drily to the Consul, "what do you say to this, sir? Is it the custom among your boyars to repay hospitality in this manner?"

"I have been deceived like yourself," stammered the unfortunate diplomatist. "The man must have been an adventurer. I did not know him, and without his letter, which I believed to be from the ambassador——"

"THE GOLD STAMP HAS BEEN STOLEN!"

"You would do well to be more circumspect another time, sir, and not bring to people's houses persons of whom you are not certain."

And the Prince added, turning to the chief of police—

"This matter is in your hands, sir. I rely on your diligence and devotion."

"Be comforted, Prince," said the functionary with an important air, never falling short, as we have seen, in the matter of promises, "the man will be arrested to-morrow."

We can easily picture the chill thrown upon the festival by this unexpected disaster. In spite of all the efforts of the Prince, who, being a great nobleman to the very backbone, exerted himself to the utmost and affected absolute indifference, the charm was broken. The guests felt that, under his calm exterior, he had no longer any heart to enjoy himself or to see others enjoy themselves. So they stood about in corners or in small groups, looking embarrassed and speaking only in whispers, as if there were someone ill in the house.

"Come," said Prince Albrandi, trying to shake off the general torpor; "don't let us allow this accident to spoil our pleasure."

But his words had no effect, for the uneasiness dominating the brilliant assembly had by this time become insurmountable. Little by little the rooms thinned till there remained but just enough guests to join in the cotillion which the Prince had prepared for them. William and Betty left at a somewhat early hour, to the great grief of their host, who wished them to stay longer, and made them promise to come and see him again. And as the landau returned to the Grand Hotel they marvelled over the strange theft, and the audacity of the thief in thus perpetrating it in the midst of so large a gathering.

"It is lucky for us that they saw him," said William, "for otherwise, the object of our voyage being known, they could not have failed to suspect us."

CHAPTER XXIV

Wherein William and Betty, after having been robbed, narrowly escape being taken for the robbers

AS soon as morning came William and Betty, scarcely giving themselves time to snatch a few hours' sleep, went on board a boat with the intention of spending the day at Capri.

"Faith," said the young man, as the steamer glided through the calm waters of the Bay, "we must not think we have lost everything. As we cannot have the stamp, let us explore the country and take back souvenirs."

"All the same," returned Betty, "you may as well confess that it really is vexing, and that our misadventures are enough to make us cross."

"Bah! You are exciting yourself to no purpose, Miss Betty. Do not let us think any more about it, but let us enjoy Nature in her beauty."

The boat, crossing the Bay obliquely, passed in review the enchanted shores whereon gleamed in the sun white houses, dark orange, and grey olive trees, which clothe the sides of the volcano. Sea and sky were so blue, mountains so rosy, and the whole scene so bright that one could scarcely believe it to be a terrestrial landscape. Everything seemed living, palpitating, from the gulls skimming the waves with rapid flight, to the sails of the fishing-boats, whose graceful outlines were dotted like so many topazes on the dark background of sea.

Little by little the two Americans felt the charm of this divine country grow upon them. The Blue Grotto, which they visited, sent them into transports, as did the varied and magnificent views on the island —the imposing ruins of the palace of Tiberius, its dreadful rocks and majestic pinnacles.

On the return journey they saw quite different lights and colours. It was the sea now which had taken a rose tint in the rays of the declining sun, while Vesuvius had clothed himself in a most marvellous shade of violet. The sky had become purple, the distant houses gleamed like gems, and Naples, stretched at the foot of the hills, seemed like a garden of flowers, whose petals were glistening in the fleeting rays of the sun.

Standing silent in the bows William and Betty gazed around, marvelling at the inimitable harmony of the lights, so constantly changing in hue, yet never producing a discordant combination. So great was the influence of the scene that they no longer troubled about anything, and had completely lost sight of the object of their journey.

As William landed on the quay, his thoughts still fixed on all he had so lately seen, he caught sight of John, waiting for him and beckoning him with signs of despair.

"What is the matter?"

"They are perhaps going to arrest you!" returned the valet in a stifled voice.

"Arrest me?" cried William, recalled at once to mundane affairs.

"Yes, sir. The chief of the police came this

morning to search your room and Miss Scott's. He turned everything out and rummaged everywhere without saying a word, and then left this letter for you."

"This is cool!" said the young man in a tone of irritation, breaking the seal of the letter.

It contained only these words :—

"SIR,—Be good enough to present yourself at my office as soon as you return. If you fail to comply with this request I shall be forced to compel your obedience.

" Yours, etc.,

"GIUSEPPE PETTO, Chief of Police."

"This is cool indeed!" repeated William, hastily entering the hotel.

It certainly seemed as if a pitched battle had taken place in the two rooms. Trunks wide open and empty; portmanteaus with their locks picked; dressing-bags flattened out, their contents strewn about in confusion. It was heart-breaking.

"The scoundrel!" said Betty.

"Let us go at once!" cried William, quite beside himself. "I will give him his deserts!"

"For goodness' sake," said Betty in alarm, "don't make things worse than they are. Discuss the matter with him and see what he wants."

But before reporting themselves at the police office they called on the United States Consul, who, unfortunately, was not in. William left his card, on which he added a few words of explanation, and they went on together to the Municipio. Here they had not to wait any time, as the chief's orders were that they should be admitted immediately.

"We are waiting for you to speak, sir," said William frigidly.

The functionary was not quite sure where to begin, for he was a little intimidated by the composed attitude of his auditors, in spite of all his assurance.

"Well," he began at last, "you must have been surprised that I should think it my duty to institute a search in your rooms——"

In vain he awaited some sign of astonishment or blame. William and Betty maintained their icy demeanour, which put him out visibly.

"It was certainly a very painful thing to do," he began again. "But judge for yourselves if I could have acted otherwise——"

The same coldness. The same silence.

"Can't you speak?" cried the chief.

"Your pardon," replied William. "You forget that we are here, not that we may be permitted to appreciate your actions, but simply to receive information concerning some crime—at least, so I suppose."

"Oh, a crime!" said Signor Petto, reddening a little.

"Certainly. For if no grave accusation is lodged against us I shall find myself under the painful necessity, sir, of proceeding against you for trespass and defamation——"

"You would do that!"

"I am quite prepared to do so, as you seem so reluctant to give us any information concerning the pillage of our apartments, and the very strange summons you have sent me."

The chief was not a man to feel uncomfortable in the presence of two "clients" against whom he had instigated proceedings; but this case required more careful handling than usual from the fact that, unable to get possession of Tilbury, or of Spartivento, or,

consequently, of Orsikoff, he had risked, in an access of discomfited rage, a search without warrant, in the rooms of foreigners whom he had but the most superficial reasons for suspecting. Convinced at first that it was a flash of genius which had established a connection in his mind between the movements of the two Americans and the thefts of the false count, he now began to consider the situation in cold blood and to feel he had gone a little too far.

For a moment he had hoped his victims would show signs of fear or attempt to escape. Some of his agents had, therefore, waited for the travellers on their return from Capri and never lost sight of them. But far from seeking to avoid him they had shown themselves more angry than frightened, and quite ready, to judge by appearances, to take up a very ugly position against him.

"This is all very well," he began again, "but after all, what have you come to Naples for?"

"I have already had the honour of enlightening you on that point, sir," returned William. "You will be kind enough, then, to spare me the trouble of repeating my statement."

"Who is to assure me, then, that this pretended Russian is not an agent employed by you to get possession of this stamp, which you, for some reason quite incomprehensible to me, covet so greatly?"

"Really, sir," said Betty with remorseless irony, "you had such a wonderfully good opportunity of coming to an understanding with Count Orsikoff himself on this matter that I wonder you did not summon him also."

William added his word.

"Indeed," said he, "you do seem to be born under a lucky star. To abuse the innocent and so obstinately avoid arresting the guilty shows nothing less than a genius for clear-sightedness."

"But who is to prove you are indeed the people you say you are, and are not usurping a false position?"

"Alas that you did not apprehend Commander Spartivento!" returned William. "All my papers are in his hands."

"Oscar Tilbury holds the same place of Keeper of the Records with regard to me," said Miss Betty, "for he has not left me the smallest proof of my identity."

Signor Petto was now in an absolute rage about this villain, who was so hard to catch, and who had so cruelly taken upon himself three different incarnations, as it were, under his very eyes.

"I shall hold you at my disposal," he snarled.

"I protest against it," said William, rising.

The chief was about to reply when the United States Consul arrived, and very much against his will he was compelled to let him come in.

"What is this I have just learnt?" said the Consul. "Mr. Keniss and Miss Scott troubled by the police?"

"But," said Signor Petto, "who is to prove that these two people are——"

"I am. I tell you so. I formerly knew Mr. Keniss' father, and I remember Miss Scott very well, having seen her in New York, though she was very young at the time. We talked a good deal together yesterday at Prince Albrandi's, and I can assure you that, being in possession, between them, of a hundred million dollars, they have no need to resort to highway robbery."

"A hundred million dollars!" repeated the chief of police, a benevolent expression dawning on his face at the mention of so fabulous a sum.

(To be continued.)

THE BEST STAMP HINGES.

We have just prepared a new stamp hinge, of convenient size, put up in *air-tight tin boxes*, each containing 1000 hinges of good tough paper, doubly gummed, and thus easily peelable. Post-free, 7d. per box.

Stanley Gibbons, Ltd., 391, Strand, London, W.C.

THE STAMP KING

By G. DE BEAUREGARD AND H. DE GORSSE

Translated from the French by EDITH C. PHILLIPS

A POLICEMAN HANDED HIM A TELEGRAM

CHAPTER XXIV (*continued*)

Wherein William and Betty, after having been robbed, narrowly escape being taken for the robbers

IN recognition, no doubt, of the principle that a certain amount of wealth renders virtue an easy matter, Signor Petto, in common with many others, could not possibly believe in the guilt of rich people. He indemnified himself for this weakness on the poor, who had a very bad time when they fell into his hands. What innocence then these happy mortals could boast, possessing between them five hundred million lire! The change in his behaviour was by no means gradual, the ingenuous functionary having no false pride in the matter.

"Forgive me," he said, with his former bland smile, "and pray do not blame me for the way in which I felt obliged to act this morning."

"Oh, certainly!" said William. "But another time do pray put back in their places the things you do not want."

Signor Petto laughed a little constrainedly at this remark, and cringingly conducted his visitors to the foot of the staircase, whence the two Americans, after thanking the Consul for his opportune intervention on their behalf, went to dine at the Café d'Europe, on the Square of St. Ferdinand, delighting in the impromptu repast served on a little table in the midst of the buzzing crowd.

"Well," said William, after contemplating the lively scene before him, and raising his voice that he might be heard above the tumult, "I should not mind betting anything that that idiot of a chief of police will never catch our thief."

"Very likely not," said Betty, shaking her head.

"Then we have nothing to do but to go back."

"Oh, no! As we are here let us wait a few days longer. Some accident may cause his arrest. And then, the stamp being lost, or as good as lost, it would be a shame to leave this lovely country without seeing more of it. Goodness only knows when we shall have another chance."

William agreed to follow this advice, and guidebook and map being at hand, like the precise Americans they were, they began at once to arrange their plans.

This was the evening of Thursday, the 21st of May.

"To-morrow, then," said William, "we will go to the Camaldules, Pozzuoli, Cumae, Baiae, and Procida; the day after, Saturday, we will explore Ischia and return to Naples; Sunday morning we will see Pompeii; at four o'clock we will come back and pay our farewell visit to the Prince, and at 10.45 in the evening start for Rome. Monday, Tuesday, and Wednesday study Rome; Thursday morning at 9.10 depart for Paris, where we shall arrive on Friday, the 29th of May, at ten o'clock in the evening, just in time to catch the *Normandie* at Havre at eleven the next morning."

"Lovely!" cried Betty. "That will be employing our time well, and I haven't the least objection to make."

This plan was carried out in detail.

Being millionaires they had carriages and boats

always at their disposal ; horses waiting for them at difficult passes ; meals, ordered beforehand, served the moment they appeared. So they were enabled to fulfil the whole of their programme without fatigue or weariness.

The first day they rode on horseback to the Camaldules Monastery overlooking Naples, the view from which is certainly the finest in all Italy, and that is saying a great deal. Thence stolid mules carried them down to Pianura, and brought them to Astroni, the royal park planted so curiously in the midst of a vast extinct volcano. A landau took them up from this point and carried them to Pozzuoli, by the dried Lake of Agnano and the Grotto del Cane, celebrated for its carbonic acid vapours.

At Pozzuoli (the ancient Greek town, formerly called Dikearchia) they saw the old Roman mole, the temple of Serapis, by turns plunged into the sea and brought again to the light of day by volcanic action ; the amphitheatre, one of the most perfect known ; and the Solfatara, a miniature volcano, still sending forth sulphurous gases.

Thence, continuing their route, they passed on to the foot of Monte Nuovo, which rose out of the earth during an eruption in 1538 ; round by the Lake of Avernus, whose solitary shores still retain something of the infernal character given them by the ancients ; then to the ruins of Baiae, the seat of elegance and luxury in the time of Cicero and the Emperors ; and to Misenum, whose old harbour, formed by Agrippa, is almost unrecognisable, but whose many antiquities, the Piscina Mirabilis, for example, are sufficiently well preserved to tell of its ancient grandeur. They ended this well-filled day at Procida and Ischia, where a special boat was to meet them, whereon they spent the night.

Saturday was passed on the larger island in visiting the scene of the terrible earthquake of 1883, and in ascending Monte Epomeo, whose summit rises to a height of more than 800 yards.

On Sunday there were the marvels of Pompeii, that town brought once more to the light after being buried for eighteen centuries. They wandered all over the ruins, which are so full of eloquence that the catastrophe seemed to have but just happened, and they could almost hear the convulsive groans of the victims of the eruption of 79—whose bodies, lying about in every direction, were preserved in ghastly completeness by the ashes.

But the third day came to an end, and William and Betty, punctual like all true citizens of the Union, took the train for Pausilippe, that they might take leave of Prince Albrandi.

"What do you want?" was the brutal question of the first domestic to whom they applied.

"To see Prince Albrandi."

"Pooh ! he has other fish to fry."

Astounded at such language and such a reception, William and Betty did not know what to do, or whether to press the matter. But as they were starting that very evening they thought it better to make one last effort to see the Prince and thank him for his gracious reception.

"Your pardon if we are importunate," returned William, his affected politeness contrasting with the rough tone of the valet. "We are leaving Naples to-day and are very desirous of being received by your master. Kindly have this card sent in to him."

The servant cast a disdainful glance on the piece of cardboard, and holding it out to one of his comrades, who was marching along at the end of the entrance hall, said—

"Here, Antonino, take this to the patron and tell him the people are here."

Then he turned his back on them.

Presently the second valet reappeared.

"You can come in," he shouted from the end of the passage.

They advanced and, following their conductor,

were taken into a large room used as a waiting-room, round which several people were seated. These persons were talking together in an excited fashion, and the two Americans, who knew enough Italian to understand it, were not a little surprised at the snatches of conversation which they caught.

"It had to come ; this has lasted for ten years."

"Ah ! no doubt it could be easily foreseen."

"As for me, I won't wait any longer. He shall pay or I'll have him sold up."

"When you think of such a waste ! I'll wait no longer myself. Why, in three years he has bought from me sixteen hundred and thirty-four lire worth of trouser-braces alone ! "

"And he owes me, for the two years that he has paid nothing, a hundred and twenty thousand lire for bread."

"And me, eighteen hundred lire for blotting-paper."

"And me, twenty-five thousand lire for sponges and tooth-brushes.

"It's horrible ! We really can't wait any longer ! "

"No ! and we won't ! "

At this moment a door opened, and the Prince himself appeared showing out a visitor, who was saying in an arrogant tone—

"You quite understand ? You pay for my fireworks in less than a week or I have you sold up."

"You charge me three times their value," said the Prince wearily.

"Not a bit of it. At eighty thousand lire they are given away."

"Given !"

But perceiving William and Betty the Prince blushed, got rid of his creditor, and motioned to them to come in.

"We were here first," cried the others with one voice.

"One instant, just one instant, I pray you," said the Prince almost supplicatingly. "This lady and gentleman will not detain me a minute."

And as they continued their protestations he closed the door of his study, leaving himself alone with the two young people.

"Excuse me for receiving you in the midst of this crowd," said he. "It is settling up day to-day, and I am in the habit of receiving my tradespeople myself."

This was said with a painfully constrained smile, and it was clear that his indifference was a very superficial one. Betty, observing this, was suddenly struck with an idea, which seemed to her a brilliant one, for it had the double advantage of being decidedly profitable to the Prince, and eventually also to herself.

But she would not announce it at once, lest he should think she had come on purpose. She let the conversation pass through its usual banalities, spoke of their recent excursions, and of the wonders of the neighbourhood ; and then, when the subject began to lose its interest, she suddenly asked—

"Well, Prince, and what news have you of the stamp?"

"Alas, Miss Scott ! I am greatly afraid that I shall never find it again."

The Prince spoke with profound melancholy, in which might be traced his bitter regret at not having received for this little scrap of paper the two hundred thousand lire which Betty had offered a few days earlier, and which would have paid off the most pressing of his debts.

"Well, I am less pessimistic than you are," returned the young girl, "and have not lost all hope. In fact, so little have I lost hope that my offer still holds good, if you care to sell it."

The Prince made a sudden movement at these words, and the light of desire appeared in his eyes.

"But how can I sell a thing which is no longer in my possession?" he asked.

"Nothing is easier, Prince, in the way I mean."

"Please explain !" said the Prince quickly, the hope of such a windfall returning in force.

But William had caught at Betty's plot, and it was he who hastened to reply.

"Prince," said he, "it is very true that you have not the stamp, but it may be found again, and all the more probably, because the thief will want to make as much as he can out of it. Now for this he would have to sell it to some big collector, who will hasten to make his find public. People will know, I shall hear of it, and you see what follows. So I will buy of you, not the stamp, as you haven't it, but the proprietorship of the stamp, or, if you prefer it, the right to reclaim it if it is found again, a right which belongs to you, naturally."

"Ah! but permit me," protested Betty, "this is my offer, and I ought to have the priority."

"Let us say that our offers are simultaneous," said William in a conciliating tone. "Neither of us has any wish to wrong the other. So let us conclude the bargain with the Prince, each on our own account, and thus acquire equal rights."

"But to sell the same thing at the same time to two different purchasers is somewhat unusual!" said Albrandi.

"What does it matter if we both consent?" cried Betty, beguiled by the prospect of a fresh contest between herself and her fellow-philatelist.

The discussion was here interrupted by the free and easy entrance of the chief of police, who, annoyed as he was at finding William and Betty there, would not allow himself to show it, but greeted them effusively.

"Well, is the pretended boyard in custody?" asked the Prince.

"No, but very near it. They are shadowing him. He has gone by train to Brindisi this morning to catch the *Orient*, and I shall have a telegram before the evening is over informing me of his arrest."

"But if they are shadowing him, why in the world didn't they catch him before he got into the train?" cried William impatiently.

"Very true," said the Prince.

"And obvious," supported Betty.

Signor Petto shook his head intelligently several times, and said with a mysterious gesture—

"You cannot understand?"

"No, I give it up," said William, shrugging his shoulders imperceptibly.

Then, in a few words, they informed the new-comer of the bargain about to be struck. He could not grasp the idea at first, and begged for further enlightenment.

"So now it is you who cannot understand," said William, laughing. "Well, listen. This stamp, which has disappeared, may be recovered."

"Naturally, since you have been told the thief is to be arrested this evening."

"Let us be prepared for the worst," said the sceptical American, "and suppose the capture put off for a few hours—a few days—a few months."

"That cannot be."

"Well, in a few months—a few years——"

"You are jesting?"

"Not at all. Moreover, if you do arrest the thief, he may not have the stamp in his possession."

"Well, then?"

"Then we will both—Miss Scott and I—buy from Prince Albrandi the right of calling ourselves its legitimate owners if it is found, and if not the right of searching for it by any means in our power."

"But you will both purchase the same right, and that is not possible."

"That is our private business, Miss Betty's and mine, to be arranged between us."

"And what price will you give?" asked the chief curiously.

"A hundred thousand francs each, money down."

"It's perfectly absurd! You must be a couple of fools!"

The Prince threw a crushing glance at Signor Petto, and said drily—

"Sir, you will oblige me by not expressing any opinion upon a matter which does not concern you."

"Fools or not," said Betty, rejoicing in a little innocent revenge on the poor chief, "we conclude the bargain of our own free will, and I assure you it will not give you any cause for searching our portmanteaus a second time."

The officer struck his flag without more words, and William began again.

"You have not told us yet, Prince, whether you accept our proposal."

Albrandi felt he ought to show some reluctance, though he greatly feared it might be taken seriously.

"In point of fact," he said, "I do not know if it would be right for me to——"

"What, Prince!" cried Betty. "Not when we offer it? When we beseech you to take it? You have no responsibility at all in the matter."

"Well, since you really wish it——"

And the Prince immediately drew up two identical receipts for a hundred thousand francs each, by the terms of which he ceded the full and entire proprietorship of the Brahmapootra stamp, in whatever place it might be found, to Mr. William Keniss and to Miss Betty Scott; engaging, in addition, to let them know at once if he heard any news of it, and to forward it on to them if it should be returned to him. In exchange for these two documents William and Betty handed the Prince two cheques for a hundred thousand francs each, on the Neapolitan banker, Meuricoffre, with whom they had, since the previous evening, opened an account, through their New York bank.

This accomplished, the two Americans retired—after mutual thanks, endless polite speeches, and prolonged farewells—in company with the chief of police, who was returning to the Municipio to wait for the despatch announcing the capture of Tilbury-Spartivento-Orsikoff. But he had not the trouble of going so far, for scarcely had he left the palace when a policeman, who had been sent in search of him, handed him a telegram, which he immediately opened.

"Is he arrested?" asked William, slyly.

"No, not exactly," returned Signor Petto, in an embarrassed tone. "He was not to be found in the train when it arrived at Brindisi. But the men tell me they are quite certain of apprehending him to-morrow morning."

The two young people smiled at each other, and the chief saw how little credit, and with reason, they gave to his words.

"Well, good luck!" said they. And with this the three parted. Signor Petto went on his way, and the other two returned to the Grand Hotel to dine.

"We've done a good day's work, in my opinion," said William.

"You think so?"

"Well, don't you? Here we are the legitimate possessors——"

"Of an object which we haven't got——"

"But which we may recover——"

"By Easter!"

"Yes, or Trinity Sunday!"

This reflection highly amused the two philatelists, though it left them a little thoughtful. They could not, in fact, help reflecting on the time they had lost and the trouble of all sorts they had brought upon themselves during a journey so long, so stirring, and —it must be confessed—so fruitless.

such an amount of red tape at headquarters, these little matters are kept as secret as if they were great State secrets; consequently I have not been able to find out what really is going to happen. Perhaps it is to follow the idea of Natal and Orange River Colony, of having the lowest, most-used values printed in single colours, and the others in double colours—although the stamps of the Cape Colony, which uses more than the other colonies, look very pretty in their single colours, and certainly cost less than the bicoloured ones.

A search for 6 p. stamps

Since the cable brought us the news that a Transvaal 6 p. stamp had been sold at £105 at a London auction, everybody is speaking about it, and the chance of finding some in old correspondence, forgetting altogether that Tommy Atkins never left a stamp or a bit of paper resembling one behind when he marched through the country: even six-foot-high safes did not stop him from getting at them.

It is useless to try to remember how often I have been asked if I had any of this class of stamps. Could I just let them have a look at it? Would it not be wiser to turn the stamps into real estate? Why would people pay such prices for bits of paper? etc. etc. People are the same all the world over; what they said at home about the 1 p., Mauritius, they repeat here now that it is a 6 p. Transvaal. It is the money which makes them say anything.   EMIL TAMSEN.

THE STAMP KING

By G. DE BEAUREGARD AND H. DE GORSSE

Translated from the French by EDITH C. PHILLIPS

BETTY SANK UPON THE CUSHIONS OF THE CARRIAGE

CHAPTER XXIV (*continued*)

Wherein William and Betty, after having been robbed, narrowly escape being taken for the robbers

SO William Keniss and Betty Scott walked on for a few minutes without a word. The girl was the first to break the silence.

"It's all very well," said she, "but what shall we do with our equal rights, if by any chance the stamp is found again?"

"Oh, that's a very simple matter," returned William. "We'll toss for it."

Such a solution of the difficulty amused Betty greatly.

"Well done!" she cried. "Mind you don't go back from that."

They dined hastily, and immediately afterwards took their places in the landau which was waiting for them, and drove to the station, followed in another carriage by John and Victoria, whose few days of close intercourse had made them the best friends in the world.

CHAPTER XXV.

William and Betty find themselves face to face with a fresh mystery

"OH, I am worn out!" cried Betty, sinking upon the cushions of the saloon carriage which was to take them back to Paris. "My eyes ache, my limbs tremble——"

"Ah, but we have seen some grand sights!" said William, who was paying her a visit in her compartment.

"Yes, but we lack a Spartivento to give spice to our return journey."

"Well, Miss Betty, you can't have everything, you know."

The two young people often amused themselves with remembrances of the adventurer, for the present lost in the mists of the past. The journey continued without any remarkable incident through Italy, France, and Paris, till on the morning of Saturday, May 30th, they arrived at Havre, and went on board the *Normandie*.

As the vessel steamed out of the dock on her way to New York the two friends paced the deck together.

"You can hardly imagine," said Betty, "how glad I am at heart to be returning home, and how I congratulate myself on having you for a companion."

"Ah, Miss Betty," said William in his gentlest voice, "I feel, indeed, how priceless that assertion is to me, and I am merely uttering a truism in giving you the same assurance."

"Thanks, my good friend, thanks. But really, you have been during the whole journey so perfect a cavalier, a rival so kindly and thoughtful, that I feel compelled to tell you how I have been touched by all your delicate attentions. Not one of them has passed unnoticed, I assure you."

For a minute they walked on slowly without a word, each wrapped in a sweet dream, and then the luncheon bell brought them brusquely back to earth, or, rather, to the sea.

They sat down to table, and for a time there was little animation to be observed among all these people, gathered from the four quarters of the globe, and knowing nothing of each other. But the lovely weather, calm sea, and delicate fare loosened their

THE CAPTAIN OF THE "NORMANDIE"

tongues little by little. The captain talked to one and another, doing his utmost to break the ice and establish a feeling of companionship among his passengers, who were to live together for a whole week. Noticing that a place near him was vacant, he presently said—

"The Admiral cannot have heard the bell."

"Have we an admiral on board?" asked Betty, who was seated at the captain's right hand.

"Yes, Miss Scott."

"Of what country?"

"The High Admiral Campanas y Banastero, in supreme command of the navy of the Honduras Republic."

"Oh, a personage of distinction, then?"

"Yes, of very high distinction."

And the captain requested a steward to go to the High Admiral's cabin and inform him they were at table. The steward returned to say that the High Admiral was not well and would not appear.

"Not well?" said the captain in surprise. "It cannot be sea-sickness, for we have never had such calm weather."

"And then," remarked Betty, "an admiral is the last person in whom such a thing would be permissible."

"Just so, Miss Scott, and no doubt we shall see the illustrious sailor this evening."

Lunch was finished, the afternoon passed, and they

met again at dinner without anyone being able to boast of having even seen the High Admiral.

"It is very curious," said the captain, turning to Betty. "I received him myself when he arrived on board, and he seemed perfectly well and in the best of spirits. Then suddenly, at the very moment you were crossing the footbridge, he took a regular leap backwards, shut himself up in his cabin, and has not been seen since."

"Was it the sight of me that frightened him so?" asked the girl, laughing.

"I should not think so, Miss Scott. Such an aspect would rather attract than repel."

Very soon little was talked about but the High Admiral. Everyone was asking what could be the matter with him. The captain had sent the ship's doctor to see him, but the strange invalid had not let him even come into his cabin. Even the steward who took him his meals had received orders to put the dishes down in a corner and go away immediately without turning back. But his malady was evidently not a serious one, as the voluntary recluse ate with a good appetite.

Some of the passengers thought that his exalted position making something of a personage of him, the High Admiral wished to avoid impertinent curiosity. But then, why had he himself chosen his place at table if he never meant to occupy it? It was certainly a mystery. Everyone was interested, but particularly the ladies; and when at the end of two days it became certain that this enigmatical person meant to live in his cabin the desire to see him grew beyond all limit.

"Do you know, I have actually seen him!" said one gentleman confidently, as they sat at luncheon the second day.

There was no need to be more precise, for everyone knew of whom he spoke. So in the midst of such a dearth of news a great interest was manifested.

"Impossible!" "You are favoured!" "Where?" "What did you do?"

"Oh, it was very simple. I could not sleep last night, and growing weary of lying awake I dressed and went up on deck. I had been there a few minutes breathing the fresh air when the door of the mysterious cabin opened and a man came out, after looking round carefully to see that there was no one about. I saw him take a few steps, stretch himself, yawn. Then he passed close by me, looked at me well without seeming to mind me at all, and after a few turns he retired tranquilly to his cabin and shut himself in again. And I went back to bed."

"Well, what is he like?" asked William.

"He is tall, of imposing presence, and with long grey whiskers."

The lucky passenger who had had the good fortune to see the High Admiral became an object of envy, and the general curiosity was only excited the more.

As they left the table a group formed, composed of William and Betty and a few other Americans, who had soon become friends.

"I declare I really will see this extraordinary Admiral," said the young girl suddenly. Adding, with a laughing little grimace, "I am so interested in him that I can no longer sleep; I am losing my appetite, and shall fall ill if I do not make the acquaintance of this intrepid seaman with the least possible delay."

There was a general laugh, showing how little credit was given to this melancholy prediction.

"But it's a very serious thing," said she, "and, moreover, it's unworthy of good Americans to allow themselves to be mystified, and I propose that we try a bold stroke."

"Yes, but what?" said a big Chicago manufacturer, who formed one of the little group.

"I have an idea."

And signing to her auditors to form a closer circle round her, Miss Betty continued in a mysterious voice—

"Since one of the passengers saw the Admiral at

THE PRINCE AT ONCE GAVE THEM TWO RECEIPTS

three o'clock in the morning, it is evident that he chooses this ridiculous hour for his promenade. Now we might meet at a quarter to three, form an ambush in the shade not far from his cabin door, and profit by the moonlight to catch a glimpse at least of his whiskers. What do you say?"

A chorus of approbation followed this speech, for there were young people in the party who loved a bit of fun, and to whom the idea was altogether congenial.

"That's it!" "Just the thing!" "Bravo!" were the laughing murmurs.

It was arranged that with the exception of those then present no one was to be told of the project, not even the ship's officers. The secret was wonderfully well kept, and the only thing remarked on was the fact that the young Americans retired for the night at about nine o'clock, which was much earlier than usual.

"You are very rational to-day," said the captain, when William wished him good night.

"What can you expect? The sea air makes one so sleepy."

No more was said, and quiet soon reigned over the steamer.

It was a lovely night, all silvered by the moon, whose light was reflected from the shimmering waves. Only the lightest breeze was blowing, and in the bluish shade no sound was heard but the groaning of the screw and the ripple of the foam left by the steamer in her wake. At about half-past two in the morning a door opened cautiously, then another, then a third, and ten minutes later the last of the little company had stealthily gained the deck, to the great surprise of the night-watch, who knew nothing of this strange expedition.

By common consent Betty had been appointed general. She entered heart and soul into the campaign, and arranged her army in two divisions, one on each side of the mysterious cabin, in order to blockade the High Admiral if necessary.

Then they waited.

Unfortunately dark clouds soon appeared, blotting out the moon. The deck was now only lighted by the electric lamps, placed at distant intervals, and left there to facilitate the working of the ship. At last the clock struck three.

"Behold the fateful moment!" whispered William.

A few minutes later one of the conspirators who was on guard signalled that the High Admiral's door had just turned on its hinges, and that His Excellency was now on deck. Then they saw what appeared like a tall, moving mass emerge from the shade, advancing slowly, and seeming to glance carefully in every direction.

"There he is! There he is!" was whispered round with stifled bursts of laughter.

It was, indeed, a most grotesque sight. The High Admiral, for it was evidently he, advanced with short, hesitating steps; and as he passed under one of the lighted lamps they saw he was rolled up in a number of rugs, and wore a hat with a turned-down brim that quite hid his face. He had scarcely taken two strides before those of the two groups who were behind him followed with noiseless tread, so as to cut off his retreat, while the others advanced to meet him, that they might get a nearer view.

Turning a corner suddenly Campanas y Banastero found himself surrounded by five or six intruders, who were emulating one another in trying to see his face under the protecting hat. Stupefied, he turned to retrace his steps, only to fall into another ambush, to wheel round again, and absolutely fly to escape his persecutors, who laughingly gave up all attempt at concealment and chased him mercilessly. The unfortunate sailor was the more troubled because he had no wish to appear to flee, and endeavoured to keep up to the end an air of decorum.

It might have been noticed that a meeting with Betty or William appeared specially distasteful to him; for whenever he caught sight of them, even at

a distance, he lowered his head, pulled up the collar of his coat, and immediately started in another direction. Once William, who had hidden in company with Betty behind a mast, struck a match under his very nose; but it was only a flash, for the High Admiral, with one vigorous breath, blew it out. At last, just as the unfortunate night-walker had escaped back into his cabin, after the most exciting chase, the captain, awakened by the shouts of laughter and furious stampede, appeared on the scene and demanded the cause of the tumult. Though he would much have liked to enjoy the fun himself, he pretended to be a little vexed.

"You put me in a very awkward position with regard to this great personage," he said. "I beg you to go back to your cabins and leave the High Admiral to please himself. An incognito, no less than sickness, is a thing to be respected."

The guilty parties, like so many schoolboys in disgrace, listened meekly to the lecture, and at once went to bed. The next day the very sight of each other made them laugh.

"Well, have you seen him now?"

"Oh, don't talk to me about it. It was a foolish thing to do!"

"Which doesn't alter the fact that it was great fun!"

"Yes, but Senor Campanas y Banastero cannot have found it so."

"He has a fine head!"

But a new idea had occurred to William and Betty.

"You will laugh at me," said the girl to her friend, "but the Admiral's eyes, though I only caught a glimpse of them by the light of a match, reminded me——"

"Why, that's just what I thought," said the young man, with perfect comprehension.

"But it would be the most extraordinary thing in the world, since the Naples police were certain our man went to Brindisi."

"All the more reason he should be here, Miss Betty, when you think what Signor Petto is. But even so, I dare not believe it. Such a coincidence is beyond all probability."

"We really are becoming monomaniacs on this subject. Everywhere we go we see Tilbury—Spartivento—Orsikoff!"

"Well, our sight has not been in fault so far."

"No, I tell you, it is madness."

John and Victoria were questioned as to what they had heard about the High Admiral, but they were both so absorbed in their future prospects—especially Victoria, who was overflowing with joy at the idea of returning to her native country and taking back her restive *fiancé* with her—that they could give no information of any interest, except that it was all the same to them!

THE STAMP KING

By G. DE BEAUREGARD AND H. DE GORSSE

Translated from the French by EDITH C. PHILLIPS

THE SEA WAS LET LOOSE IN ITS FURY

CHAPTER XXVI

Wherein William and Betty, arriving at the winning post, nearly run a "dead-heat"

DURING the final days of their crossing the wind suddenly began to rise, upsetting the equilibrium of the *Normandie*, and the digestion of most of the passengers. Several, however, were not at all inconvenienced by it—among them Betty and William, who seemed to have received a dispensation from this unpleasant tribute to the stormy ocean.

The very evening before their arrival in port, the sea being let loose in its fury, they were passing the door of the High Admiral's cabin in company with a few other intrepid souls. This part of the deck had become the favourite promenade of those who had not given up all hope of gaining a closer view of the illustrious personage, and who were always seeking, but in vain, to get a glimpse into the carefully closed apartment.

They were just passing then, when some vague sounds issued from the interior.

"Do you hear that?" said one. "One would say that Admiral Campanas is not altogether comfortable!"

And they all drew nearer and listened through the chinks of the door. The High Admiral appeared to be as much tried by the element over which he exercised command as any man could be, and as unable to appreciate its more playful moods as any landsman. He was violently sea-sick, of that there could be no doubt. In the intervals of less acute suffering he would give other relief to his feelings—

"*Ah! sacrebleu de nom d'un chien! Ah! sapristi!*" Then a fresh access of sickness, followed by more language. "*Ah! d——n the sea! Ach! Ich armer Mann! Teufel! Mein Gott!*" More sickness, finishing with a fresh imprecation, "*Che cattivo mare! Diavolo di maledetto viaggio!*"

"This is very learned sea-sickness!" cried William. "Sea-sickness in every known tongue!"

There was a general laugh, and as the state of the sea rendered their position somewhat fatiguing, they retired to the saloon.

But even when, on the morning of the seventh day, the steamer reached the smooth waters of the Hudson, and was in sight of New York, the High Admiral did not put in an appearance.

"Well, at any rate, we shall see him as we go on shore," said Betty, during the course of their last meal on board the steamer. "I have quite made up my mind to get a close view of him in full daylight."

"You will soon have that satisfaction," said the captain, "for we arrive in less than two hours."

"Very good," said Betty. "At one o'clock in the afternoon, in the month of June, one ought to be able to see clearly. So I propose that we all arrange ourselves in a row on the landing-stage, and that when the High Admiral deigns at length to appear in our midst, we receive him with a respectful ovation, to make amends to him for his seclusion, and to ourselves for our long period of waiting."

"Bravo! Agreed!" was the cry all round the table. "To Miss Betty Scott's health! To the health of Mr. Keniss! To the health of our excellent captain!"

Which was drunk enthusiastically in the best champagne, provided by William as a stirrup-cup.

The *Normandie* once moored, and the visit of the customs officers over, the confusion of disembarkation commenced. A few passengers, followed by their servants, and others alone, carrying their smaller baggage in their hands, carefully crossed the moving bridge thrown from the wharf to the boat, to be received with welcomes and embraces from the friends and relations assembled to meet them. These latter wished to carry off the new arrivals at once, but they, instead of proceeding to their carriages, omnibuses, and trains, formed up obstinately into a double line, between which the rest of the people had to pass as they came off the steamer.

"What is it? What are you looking for?" asked the New York friends.

"For the High Admiral Campanas y Banastero, who will have to show himself at last."

And the double line grew longer and longer, being composed now of passengers, customs officers, porters,

were dragging him towards the foot-bridge with the intention of making him land.

"But really, sir, you must leave this boat," said the captain, tired of the scandalous scene.

"Why couldn't you leave me alone? I should have gone when I was ready!"

"But, sir, why did you not receive the customs officers? Say what it is that you want, and give your reasons."

Though he thought the behaviour of the famous seaman most suspicious, the captain was determined to show him to the last the greatest deference. So he followed the group, in the midst of which Admiral Campanas was still struggling, more exasperated than ever now that he found himself upon the foot-bridge and close to his numerous admirers. But suddenly, perceiving William and Betty in the front rank facing him, he made a superhuman effort to get free and escape. His four conductors had to use all their

HE MADE AN EFFORT TO FREE HIMSELF

drivers, sailors, and a continually increasing number of people of all grades. But the High Admiral, who from the port-hole had taken note of the reception prepared for him, absolutely refused to come out or to let anyone whatever enter his cabin.

The captain of the boat, the customs inspector, and the captain of the port assembled in front of his door, discussing the question as to what they should do, not daring to use violence in the case of so high a dignitary, who might, by his complaints, bring about diplomatic trouble. However, they felt they must put an end to the situation somehow. From entreaties, shouted through the door, the captain passed to a summons; then, receiving no answer, he thought himself secure from responsibility and gave the order for the door to be broken in.

The crowd on the landing-stage followed these formalities with great impatience, and a huge uproar arose when they saw four sailors of the *Normandie* drag from the broken-in cabin the High Admiral himself, furious and fighting like a madman.

"Let me go! Let me go!" he cried, seeing they

strength to hold him, and had the greatest difficulty in avoiding falling with him into the sea. One of them, in the confusion of the struggle, seized him by one of his luxuriant whiskers—and to his horror and surprise the whisker came off in his hand!

Roars of laughter and cries of all sorts arose on every side, in the midst of which William and Betty were hardly heard to cry, as they rushed upon the Admiral—

"Spartivento!"

"Sir Oscar Tilbury!"

In the face, so suddenly become smooth, they had recognised, beyond the shadow of a doubt, their cosmopolitan thief, the false Count Orsikoff, who had stolen the Brahmapootra stamp, and whom the Naples police believed to be at Brindisi.

"I've got you, you scoundrel!" cried William, shaking him as if he had been a plum tree.

But Betty had called a constable, and, without any loss of time, summoned him to arrest the pickpocket.

"What is the charge against him?" asked the police officer coldly.

"The charge!" said the girl, "why, it would take me all the rest of the day to tell you. Suffice it that I have been most impudently robbed by him, and many others besides me."

At sight of the police Tilbury-Spartivento-Orsikoff-Campanas rose to a supreme height of audacity.

"Don't dare to touch me or you will hear of it!" said he haughtily.

So in spite of the protestations and assurances of William and Betty the constable hesitated to compromise himself by a manifestation of authority, always dangerous towards people of position. However, he soon reflected that there was some reason for doubting the authenticity of a High Admiral with false whiskers; and as the accusers were well-known New York millionaires, he concluded that their side of the scale at least balanced the other, and, laying his big hand on the Admiral's shoulder, he pronounced the time-honoured phrase—

"I arrest you in the name of the law."

Some more constables immediately threw themselves upon the thief and dragged him away to a carriage, in the midst of maledictions from the crowd, who showed the keenest desire to lynch him, though without in the least knowing why.

"Well," said Betty, as the rabble ran shouting behind the captive's carriage, "I don't think Providence has managed this business at all badly."

"It is almost time for us to toss up," said William, producing from his pocket a bright new dollar, "and this will serve our purpose before long!"

.   .   .   .   .   .

William Keniss and Betty Scott, who had now begun to hope again after believing the game irretrievably lost, drove off to their respective homes, pondering over the curious chance which had brought the thief who had stolen the Brahmapootra stamp over to New York in the very same steamer as themselves. To think they had gone so far in search of this stamp, and all in vain, when they need have done nothing but just wait, since it had arrived at their very point of departure of its own accord, or, rather, thanks to a thief!

But, let us hasten to add, neither William nor Betty regretted their long and picturesque wanderings, for during the journey, in the course of which they had passed several days in most pleasant intimacy, they had learnt not only to know each other, for they had been almost strangers at the beginning of it, but to hold one another in the highest esteem. Our two young philatelists, if they could not bring back from Europe the rarest of all rare stamps, brought something of much greater value—a close friendship, which must soon develop into ardent affection.

But for the moment philately absorbed them, and they could think of nothing but the closing incidents of their voyage, and the unexpected arrest of the sharper who had so infamously and obstinately cheated them during the course of their adventures. So after dinner, moved no doubt by the same feeling that they must have news at any price, William Keniss and Betty Scott each sent out one of their servants to buy all the evening papers. From these they learnt that "An individual of more than doubtful character, after passing for the High Admiral Campanas y Banastero during the whole voyage, had been arrested on landing from the *Normandie* and straightway shut up in the Central Prison."

"That's splendid!" said both the Stamp King and his rival. "I shall be at the Central Prison at the earliest possible hour to-morrow morning."

And so it came about that as the hour of six was sounding from all the clocks in the vicinity Mr.

William Keniss and Miss Betty Scott were laughingly shaking hands before the heavily-barred door, behind which the unfortunate Campanas must be sadly reflecting on the inconveniences that a man has to endure who is not just a common scoundrel, but a gentleman, an Italian Commander, a rich boyard, or a High Admiral.

"Come, come!" cried Betty brightly. "We mean to run it close to the very end, and it would be hard to say at the present moment which of us is going to get the victory."

"But the time has come to decide," returned William, "as we arrive at a dead-heat, and in a few minutes, at our request, the stamp is to be extracted from the rather too deep pockets of our illustrious travelling companion. So, according to our agreement, one of us two, chosen by chance, must abandon the strife and, tearing up the paper signed by Prince Albrandi, must give up all right to the stamp."

"We have plenty of time," pretty little Miss Betty hastened to interpose, not being at all anxious to stake her last chance on a toss.

But while they were exchanging these few words William Keniss had twice knocked loudly at the door with the heavy bronze knocker, and slow steps were now heard approaching from the interior, succeeded by a terrifying rattle of chains.

"Ugh! it makes one's blood run cold!" cried Miss Betty.

"Especially if one were going in for good! I can just imagine the face our dear High Admiral would make on hearing such a grinding of bolts!"

"I expect it cost him his second whisker!" At this moment a little shutter, arranged in one of the door panels, opened, and the crabbed face of a gaoler appeared behind the grating.

"What do you want?" he demanded in a surly tone, showing plainly his dislike of being disturbed at such an early hour.

"We wish to speak to the governor."

"The governor? He isn't here."

"What!"

"I tell you he isn't here!" And without another word the sinister fellow slammed the wicket, and William Keniss and Miss Scott heard the renewed sound of steps dying away this time into the depths of the prison.

"This is a queer sort of customer!" cried William furiously.

"You can hardly expect gaolers to be amiable," laughed Betty.

"Well, he might at least have given us some information—told us at what hour and what part of this terribly imposing building we might apply to see the governor. Suppose I knock again?"

"What good will that be? They wouldn't come a second time. And besides, you never know what may happen. They might shut us up for having made a noise at the prison door."

"That would be the last straw!"

"But what are we going to do now?"

"I really don't know."

As they were debating this knotty point a carriage stopped in front of them, and from it issued a man of about fifty years of age, in a big hat with an absurdly broad brim and a long overcoat down to his heels, with a rosette of many colours for a buttonhole. He crossed the pavement to the prison door, and knocked nine times in a peculiar and evidently prearranged manner. Hasty steps were instantly heard in the interior of this American Bastille, and the door was thrown wide open.

"This must be the governor!" murmured William to Betty.

"No doubt," returned the girl. "Speak to him."

THE STAMP KING

By G. DE BEAUREGARD AND H. DE GORSSE

Translated from the French by EDITH C. PHILLIPS

CHAPTER XXVI (*continued*)

Wherein William and Betty, arriving at the winning post, nearly run a "dead-heat"

WILLIAM advanced towards the unknown just as he was disappearing into the mysterious passage.

"I beg your pardon," said he. "The governor of the prison, I believe?"

"Yes, sir, at your service."

"Well, Mr.——?"

"Halifax," returned the governor.

"Mr. Halifax—but first let us introduce ourselves. Miss Betty Scott—William Keniss."

"Oh, I know! I know your names. You must be the famous stamp collectors about whom we hear so much."

"Just so, and it is on the subject of a stamp that we wished to speak to you."

"A stamp!" cried Mr. Halifax, in great astonishment, wondering if perchance they could be trying to hoax him. "About a stamp? Pray explain."

"You have among your prisoners," continued William, "one who was arrested yesterday on landing from the *Normandie* on account of a little public manifestation caused by us, who have been shamefully robbed by him on more than one occasion."

"Yes, yes, I know of whom you speak. That ingenious rascal who passed himself off as a high dignitary of Honduras—Admiral Campanas y Banastero."

"That is the name he took during his last passage from Havre to New York, but as a matter of fact he changes his name almost as often as his shirt, and has appeared to us—for we have had the ill-fortune of meeting with him several times—now as Sir Oscar Tilbury, then as Commander Luigi Spartivento, and again as Count Orsikoff."

"Clearly none of these names belong to him," said Mr. Halifax, "and from the inquiry I had begun yesterday evening immediately after his arrest it seems pretty certain he belongs to a gang of cosmopolitan thieves for whom we have been looking a long time, and who, as everything tends to show, have their working and social centre here in New York. Our High Admiral must certainly be one of the most distinguished members of this interesting association, possibly even the president. In any case we must hold him fast, and, no doubt, through him we shall get to know all his accomplices. But I suppose you have come to lodge your complaint against him, so will you kindly follow me to my study?"

Whereupon Mr. Halifax conducted the two young people to his office, leading them through a perfect labyrinth of long, dark passages, from the pavement of which their steps aroused lugubrious echoes. .

"We came to see you, not so much for the purpose of lodging a complaint against our thief and making a deposition, which will not be greatly in his favour, as to try to regain possession of a very rare stamp in which Miss Scott and I have equal rights," said William. "This pickpocket of ours took possession of the stamp a few days ago, during a reception at Prince Albrandi's palace at Naples, to which we all—or, at any rate, we two—had been invited. No doubt this man of so few scruples still has the precious little scrap of paper about him, and as it belongs to us we have come to reclaim it."

"But, pardon me," interrupted Mr. Halifax, "to whom does this stamp belong? To you or to Miss Scott?"

"To both of us!" returned William Keniss and Betty Scott in the same breath, as each produced the receipt for a hundred thousand francs, drawn up by Prince Albrandi, in which he recognised the right of each of the young people to claim the Brahmapootra stamp on the day when it should be found again.

"To both of you?" said the governor. "But I don't understand. How can the same thing belong at the same time to two different people?"

"It is a fact, however, in the case of the Brahmapootra stamp," said William laughingly. "And in addition to that, you see, it has already found a third proprietor in the person of the High Admiral, Campanas y Banastero."

"But that does not explain how it comes about that——"

"That we both claim possession of the same object? It is a very simple matter though."

And William Keniss explained the nature of the transaction between Prince Albrandi on the one hand, and Miss Betty Scott and himself on the other.

"Very ingenious!" cried Mr. Halifax. "But you place me in a most embarrassing position, for how am I to know to which of you to restore the stamp? Unless we carry out Solomon's idea——"

"Oh no, no!" cried the rival philatelists with touching unanimity.

"Well, then?"

"Well, Miss Scott and I had better adhere to our original intention and toss for it."

And taking a dollar from his pocket and turning to the little American, he cried—

"Heads or tails, Miss Betty?"

"Heads!" said the girl.

William shook the little piece of gold in his hands for a few seconds, and then tossed it up to the ceiling, which it struck and fell sharply to the floor. The two opponents dashed after it as it rolled into a corner of the room.

"Heads! Heads! I have won!" cried Miss Betty joyfully.

"True!" said William, forcing a smile, though vexed enough at heart at this stroke of fate. And taking from the pocket to which he had restored it Prince Albrandi's agreement bearing his name, he unhesitatingly and with something of an air tore it to pieces before the smiling eyes of his pretty rival.

"It is done," said he. "The Brahmapootra stamp has now but one owner."

In the meantime Mr. Halifax had rung for one of the warders, and given the order for number twenty-three to be brought from his cell. This was now the title by which, for want of a more legal cognomen, the noble and distinguished Sir Oscar Tilbury, Commander Spartivento, Count Orsikoff, and High Admiral Campanas y Banastero was known. He entered the office of Mr. Halifax between two gaolers. He had lost most of the assurance of former days, and hung his head sheepishly. As soon as he recognised William Keniss and Betty Scott, partly from shame at being seen in such a miserable condition after all his splendour, and still more from fear that his victims had spoken out and given a detailed list of all his doings, he turned very pale and sank like a log into one of the chairs placed near the table.

"You see, my friend, you are caught," said the governor, "and it's no use putting on airs, or trying to escape justice. We know, if not who you are, at least what you are worth. What is your name?"

The thief hesitated before replying. What name should he give? It was evidently not the moment for clothing himself in some fresh high-sounding title. So, after a few seconds of reflection, he decided on giving his name, which he let fall from his lips in a piteous, stifled voice.

"James Mamby!"

"Is that your real name?" demanded Mr. Halifax.

"Yes, sir, it is."

"Then stand up, James Mamby, and deliver up the Brahmapootra stamp which, it appears, you stole from Prince Albrandi at Naples, and which you have, no doubt, hidden in the lining of your clothes, since it was not found on you when you were searched yesterday evening. Come along! Give me the stamp!"

"I haven't got it now," muttered the thief.

William Keniss and Betty Scott stared stupidly at each other. Had the stamp escaped them again, at the very moment when they felt so certain of securing it?

"If you haven't it still, will you have the kindness to tell us where it is?" continued Mr. Halifax.

The prisoner was silent.

"Do you mean to answer me?" said the governor. "Consider, my friend, confession lessens a fault, and we shall be more indulgent to you if you do not persist in an obstinate silence, which can do you no good at all."

This little speech decided the ex-High Admiral.

"I disposed of the stamp as soon as it came into my possession," he said.

"Did you sell it?" demanded Mr. Halifax.

"No, but not wishing to keep it about me, on account of its great value, I sent it out of Europe to one of my friends the very day after I took it from Prince Albrandi."

"To one of your friends? One of your accomplices, you mean."

The rogue shook his head.

"No, one of my friends," said he.

"It is no use denying it any longer," said Mr. Halifax. "I know everything."

"Everything!"

"You belong to an American gang of thieves whose speciality it is to rob passengers on the main lines of trains and steamers. You were returning from one of your tours in Europe when you were arrested. Is not this a fact, James Mamby?"

"It is."

"You see I am well informed. But if you don't wish us to be too hard on you, you must give up the names and addresses of your accomplices."

"Never!" cried the thief heroically.

"As you will. Your silence will cost you half a dozen years longer in prison."

"Half a dozen years longer!" murmured the poor wretch, trembling in every joint. "I shall be imprisoned, as I have been since yesterday, for half a dozen years longer if I do not speak?"

"Undoubtedly!"

"Then I prefer to speak. The head of the gang, who is also the receiver of our stolen goods, is called Thomas Simpson, and he lives at No. 45, Jefferson Street."

"Very good," said Mr. Halifax. And, turning to the two warders, he continued, "Conduct the prisoner back to his cell."

The two gaolers took the aristocratic pickpocket by the shoulders and hustled him out of the room without the slightest regard for his former nobility.

"Now you know as much as I do," said the governor to our two friends. "I am about to send three or four of my picked men to try and arrest Master Thomas Simpson. Do you care to go with them? You may possibly be in time to catch him, and to take possession of your famous Brahmapootra stamp."

"Yes, yes!" cried Miss Betty and William together. "We should most decidedly wish to accompany them."

So Mr. Halifax wrote the name, Thomas Simpson, on one of the numerous warrants he had by him, ready signed by a police magistrate, and gave it to one of his cleverest detectives, whom he had summoned for the purpose, saying—

"Here is a chance for you to distinguish yourself, and if you succeed there will be an ample reward. This lady and gentleman will go with you."

"Very good, sir."

"Go at once."

A few minutes later William and Betty started in a carriage for Jefferson Street, in company with four detectives, two on the front seat and two on the box. The carriage stopped at the address given by the thief.

"Mr. Thomas Simpson?" inquired one of the detectives of a tradesman, who was taking a little fresh air in front of his shop, which occupied the ground-floor of the establishment.

"Mr. Simpson? He cleared off this very morning, taking a pile of luggage with him. The landlord is in a furious state, for he has gone without paying his rent, and has not left a single thing behind."

"Nothing whatever?"

"Absolutely nothing but the four walls."

"And he has left no word of his future address!"

"None."

The detective turned to William Keniss and his companion.

"We are done!" said he. "The accomplices of Admiral Campanas y Banastero were, no doubt, waiting for him at the landing-stage; and, having received information as to the disguise he would assume on crossing from Havre to New York, they would have no difficulty in recognising him at the moment of his arrest. Hence their haste to make themselves scarce."

So William Keniss and Betty Scott took leave of the detectives, and, recognising that at the last moment all hope of regaining the stamp had vanished for ever, they returned in a melancholy mood to their respective homes, after arranging to meet again at the grand dinner of the Philatelic Society which was to be given that very evening—in spite of the fruitless results of so long a journey—to celebrate their return, and render homage to their perseverance and the way in which they had carried through the Old World the glorious flag of Philately.

THE STAMP KING

By G. DE BEAUREGARD AND H. DE GORSSE

Translated from the French by EDITH C. PHILLIPS

SHE PRESENTED THE ENGAGED COUPLE

CHAPTER XXVII

Showing how one may always leave something to chance

WHEN evening came, William, who, without saying anything about it to Miss Betty, had spent his day in fruitless efforts to recover the lost traces of Mr. Thomas Simpson, at length determined on wending his way to Montgomery Street, where, as we know, the rooms of the Philatelic Club were situated.

Since that morning the Stamp King had been indulging in what is generally known as "a fit of the blues." He could not forgive himself for having burnt Prince Albrandi's receipt, that receipt which would have given him the right of claiming the Brahmapootra stamp, if he could but discover where it was. Was there not at least a chance that he, William Keniss, might be the first to find it and not Miss Betty Scott, who, certain now of victory sooner or later, would most likely rest in fancied security?

So William Keniss was walking sadly towards the Philatelic Club, when, passing through a narrow street, but dimly lighted by the fading day, he noticed, stuck on the inside of the window of a little *bric-à-brac* shop, a sheet of about a hundred stamps of various colours arranged in rows. Like a true philatelist William Keniss stopped to examine this sheet, to make quite sure that no rarity had by accident found its way there. And we can well imagine his stupefaction when he recognised among those common specimens the one stamp for which he had

been searching so long in the charming companionship of Miss Betty—the celebrated Brahmapootra!

"Impossible!" he cried, starting forwards and peering anxiously into the window. "I must be mad or dreaming! I must assuredly be the victim of some strange and wild hallucination!"

The young American pinched his arm till it was black and blue in order, through any sensation whatever, to bring himself back to commonplace realities. The pain it caused him forced a cry from his lips.

"No, I am certainly not dreaming!" he murmured. And, in fact, he was not. It was indeed the Brahmapootra stamp at which he was gazing, and, as he easily recognised, the same wonderfully fine copy which Prince Albrandi had allowed him to admire at his leisure at Naples, the very evening that Count Orsikoff, taking advantage of the solitude in which the rooms of the villa were left, had with such incomparable audacity made off with it. It was the very same stamp, there was no doubt of it, and in the company of the common stamps that surrounded it on the sheet, it produced, as you might say, with its beautiful golden lustre, the effect which would be produced by a real diamond in a necklace, all the other stones of which were paste.

But how, and by what concatenation of circumstances could the stamp have got there? William Keniss wasted no more time looking at it, but precipitately entered the shop, to discover by what mysterious chance a small dealer like that came to possess an article of so great value.

"You have a stamp in your window which is not priced," he said, pointing out the famous little scrap of paper, "and I should like to buy it. What do you want for it?"

"Ah, yes! Well, I hardly know. I bought it this morning with a number of other little things from a man who came in and seemed in a great hurry to dispose of them."

"Our receiver of stolen goods," thought William.

"They won't bring me in much, when all's said and done. Here, you can have it for five cents if you like."

"Five cents!" cried William, in a tone that would have convinced the dealer, if he had only been a little more wide awake, that he was making, to say the least of it, a bad bargain. "Five cents! Certainly, I will take it without hesitation."

"There you are then." And the dealer took the Brahmapootra stamp from the sheet and handed it to William Keniss, who gave him in exchange the required five cents.

The Stamp King certainly felt some compunction at paying so ridiculous a price for such a rarity, but he had no wish to give more for it just at this moment because he wanted to astound his friends at the Philatelic Club, and particularly pretty Miss Betty, with the intelligence that he had just given five cents for a stamp that, to an enthusiast like himself, was absolutely priceless, or, at any rate, worth hundreds and thousands of dollars.

"I will make up for it by bringing a nice little sum to the good dealer to-morrow," thought William, as he hastened towards the Philatelic Club.

But this little adventure had made him somewhat late, and when he at length arrived he found they were only waiting for him to sit down to dinner. Every one was there, even to Mr. Hartlepool, who, as we remember, was not always to be relied upon for punctuality.

"Come, come, now we can begin!" cried the fat Dr. Buxon, seeing his young colleague enter and start round the room, shaking hands with every one he met.

"Are you so hungry as all that?" asked little Mrs. Tilmarnock.

"As all that! On my word, my heart's in my boots!"

"Has it indeed sunk so far below your waist, do you think?" interrogated Mrs. Evans-Bradford, who, since the last club dinner, had not overcome the habit of enlivening the conversation with a little spirited repartee.

"High or low, what does it matter?" grumbled Buxon, slightly piqued. "It is nearly half-past seven, and so high time for dinner! I like stamps very well, but not enough to make me lose my appetite for good food and drink!"

This unexpected outburst on the part of the fat doctor provoked a general chorus of protestations from the assembled philatelists.

"Wretch!" "Traitor!" sounded from all parts of the room. But luckily for Buxon a waiter appeared at this very moment to announce that dinner was ready.

So William Keniss offered his arm to his friend Miss Betty, and the various couples filed off to the dining-room, Mrs. Tilmarnock on Mr. Hartlepool's arm, Mrs. Evans-Bradford escorted by old Pearding, and so on. As for the enormous Buxon, gallantry was not in his line, and he was quite content to march off to his seat alone, after which his first speech, as he noticed the radiant faces of the Stamp King and his companion, was—

"Well, considering their ill-success, they look pretty triumphant!"

"It is not success which brings happiness, but the sense of a duty accomplished," retorted the Hon. Tilmarnock frigidly.

It is unnecessary to state that from the very commencement of dinner the only topic of conversation was the journey to Europe of William Keniss and Betty Scott. The little American had, before this, commenced an account of her exploits, which she now finished. Then it was William's turn for his, and he gave it, we need hardly say, with a sufficiently good grace. No detail of their stirring adventures in London, Paris, or Naples was forgotten. The interview with the Maharajah, the numerous incarnations of Mr. Mamby, Miss Betty's plunge into the ocean, Prince Albrandi's fete, etc. etc., every detail, in fact, of this extraordinary journey was supplied by one or other of the travellers.

"And to think that after such efforts and the display of so much courage you should have to return to us with empty hands!" cried Mr. Hartlepool.

"Yes, it is enough to discourage the boldest among us," said Mr. Whitby.

"Those who pride themselves on their courage need never be daunted," said Miss Betty vivaciously.

"But——"

"Don't speak of 'but.' Whatever you may say, I do not consider myself the least bit beaten, in spite of the ill-success of my first attempts, and no later than to-morrow morning I intend to begin again!"

"Bravo! Bravo! Hurrah for Miss Betty!" sounded on all sides.

"Hurrah for the Stamp Queen!" added William Keniss.

The name was taken up at once, and every member of the Philatelic Club, with the exception of the great Buxon, who was just absorbed in an enormous help of *foie gras*, rose to his feet with one accord and shouted enthusiastically—

"Hurrah for the Stamp Queen!"

Miss Betty coloured deeply with emotion.

"Ladies and gentlemen," she said modestly, "I do not know how to thank you for having so spontaneously conferred upon me a title to which I have really no right."

A significant and protesting "Oh! oh!" showed how deep and general was the admiration which the dauntless young girl had aroused.

"It seems to me," she continued, "that it is not at all my health that you ought to drink this evening, but that of Mr. William Keniss, who is in truth the Stamp King, and whose collection, in spite of all my efforts, remains to-day the one only complete collection in all the world. So here's to Mr. William Keniss, the Stamp King!"

"The Stamp King!" was the universal cry as the glasses clinked again.

But William Keniss had risen, and in the midst of a silence which would have been profound but for the regular movement of Buxon's heavy jaws, he began—

"Miss Betty has just made a statement to the effect that mine is the one only complete stamp collection in the world. Now in this Miss Betty is mistaken."

The philatelists all stared at one another in astonishment.

"There are, in fact, two complete collections!" continued William.

"Two complete collections?" cried Betty sharply.

"Yes, Miss Betty."

"Two!"

"Mine—excuse me for mentioning it first—and yours!"

"Mine?"

THE STAMP KING

By G. DE BEAUREGARD AND H. DE GORSSE

Translated from the French by EDITH C. PHILLIPS

CHAPTER XXVII (*continued*)

Showing how one may always leave something to chance.

WILLIAM KENISS took from his pocket the stamp he had bought a short time before for five cents and handed it to Miss Betty.

"This belongs to you by virtue of our agreement," he said.

"The Brahmapootra stamp!" she cried.

"Yes, Miss Betty. Now confess that you did not expect to get it this evening."

"No, indeed I didn't; but where did you find it?"

"Oh, there is a little story attached to it, which I will tell you after dinner."

"No, no! At once, at once!" cried with touching unanimity all the members of the Philatelic Club, who, hardly able to believe their eyes, had risen to their feet to gain a closer view of the rarity. So the Stamp King was forced to comply, and to recount how he had found the Brahmapootra stamp in New York after having sought it so long and so far. And there was a general feeling of stupefaction when he announced the price he had paid for it—*five cents.*

They now left the table to return to the drawing-room, and Miss Betty took advantage of the occasion to thank her rival, and having expressed her gratitude, she added—

"But all the same, you must deeply regret the fact of having burned Prince Albrandi's receipt."

"Oh, Miss Betty, how can you think of such a thing!"

"Your collection is now no longer unique!"

"What does that matter, so long as you are pleased?"

"Now, don't pretend to be better than you are, but just confess that at the bottom of your heart you are a little bit disappointed; just a little tiny bit?"

"Right away at the very bottom, then!"

"There, you see!" Then with downcast eyes and in the lowest of whispers she added—

"There might perhaps be one way out of the difficulty."

"A way out?"

"Yes, if our two collections were for the future to form—but one?"

William Keniss understood, and seizing Betty's little hand he rapturously pressed it to his lips.

"Ah, what happiness!" he murmured. "You are the most charming of friends, and will make the most delightful of wives!"

"Excuse me, but I haven't given you the right to

woo me yet," she said. "Wait, at least, till our engagement is announced."

"But must I wait long?"

For all reply Miss Betty took her friend William Keniss by the hand, and led him to that part of the room where the philatelists had assembled for coffee.

As they drew near all eyes were turned upon them.

"Mr. William Keniss," she said, "just now conferred upon me, with more gallantry than justice, the title of Stamp Queen. I intend to earn my right

MISS SCOTT STOOD UP

to the title by bestowing upon him my hand, since he himself is the Stamp King."

It would be impossible to express the outburst of enthusiasm provoked by these words. Frantic cheers alternated with frequent bursts of clapping, while their healths were enthusiastically drunk in the punch which had just begun to circulate. A dozen times William, who still retained in his the hand of his charming *fiancée*, demanded silence, but the cheering only grew louder, and at length became so frantic that John and Victoria, attracted by the uproar, appeared at one of the doors to see what it was all about.

"You are just in time to hear the announcement of my approaching marriage with Mr. Keniss," said Betty to her maid.

"And you of mine with John!" returned Victoria triumphantly. "The wretch has made up his mind to marry me at last."

"Then you are happy?"

"As happy as you are, Miss Betty!"

Betty then signed to them both to advance to the middle of the room, and turning to her friends—

"Allow me," she said, "to present to you another engaged couple, the pair who have been our most valuable helpers, and, I am happy to say, our most faithful friends during the course of our long and perilous journey."

The new-comers had now to respond to the toast of their healths in the punch which the noblest there did not disdain to present to them, after which they retired, a little bashful though immeasurably happy.

"What a splendid opportunity for having the Maharajah's diamond mounted in an engagement ring!" said Mr. Hartlepool.

"You have not the merit of invention there," said William, "for I had already thought of that."

At this moment a growling, deep and prolonged, made itself heard in one corner of the room. It was the fat Buxon, who, true to his character, drew a practical conclusion from all these adventures by grumbling—

"There's only one thing Miss Betty has forgotten, and that's the unfurnished flat in Broadway that she promised the Philatelic Club."

"Unfurnished, but which I intend to have the pleasure of furnishing," said William.

The two young people then handed the doctor two little oblong strips of paper.

"Behold the proof that we have a better memory than you give us credit for!" said Betty.

Buxon cast his eyes on the papers, and with a sudden start of surprise he cried—

"Why, this is truly worthy of the Stamp King and Queen!"

The members of the Philatelic Club all pressed forward to obtain a closer view, and a general clamour arose.

Each cheque was for five hundred thousand dollars!

The cheering was taken up again in so prolonged and so infectious a style that even the enormous hands of Doctor Buxon were brought into requisition, and with tumultuous energy led the applause.

NOTE.—The translator of this story, and it must not be forgotten that in its present form it is a translation, not an original work, feels that it is impossible to make the concluding scene, in which the two great American philatelists decide to unite their collections and their fortunes into one unsevered pair, appear quite natural to the British reader. The publishers cannot but recognize that this is a subject upon which, in their corporate capacity, they are quite incompetent to offer an opinion, but they venture to suggest that in the description by a French author of the *dénouement* of an American courtship some little incongruities are only to be expected.

THE IMPERIAL ALBUM.

Tenth Edition. Size of pages, 8¾ × 11½ inches. The present edition is arranged in *three* volumes. Two causes have acted to bring about this result. First, the ever-increasing number of new issues, for which accommodation must be provided; and secondly, the demand by collectors that space shall be found for varieties of perforation and shade, errors, etc., to conform as closely as possible to the lists given in the Publishers' Catalogue. Vol. I. The Stamps of the British Empire; post-free, 10s. 9d. Vol. II. The Stamps of Europe, and the Colonies and Possessions of European States; post-free, 12s. 9d. Vol. III. Foreign Countries, except Europe and Possessions; post-free, 10s. 9d.

Stanley Gibbons, Ltd., 391 Strand, London, W.C.